The Story of a Life

Volume I: Liberty Lost

To Mr. Sal Nuzzo with the author's appreciation

Simone M. Kleckner

November 25, 2015

SIMONE M. KLECKNER

Translation by Theodor Massim

PAGE PUBLISHING, INC.
New York, NY

First originally published by Page Publishing, Inc. 2015

ISBN 978-1-68213-393-4 (pbk)
ISBN 978-1-68213-394-1 (digital)

Printed in the United States of America

To my families and friends in two beloved countries—
Romania, where I was born, and the USA, where I
experienced liberty, rights, and a happy life.

Acknowledgments

First and foremost, I have to thank my many friends for their encouragement to write my memoirs based on the idea that there are things and former happenings that have to be brought to light for the benefit of future generations. I wrote the first volume about the heartbreaking events that almost crushed my life under the communist system in Romania from memory with the help of my father's saved archives and with the suggestions pointed out by my friend Maria Lungu, for which I am thankful.

I am grateful to Iren and Grigore Arsene, the Romanian publishers of *Curtea Veche* ("The Old Yard") for accepting my story as well as to the praiseworthy editing of Mrs. Doina Jela, and the respective staff, for the publishing of the two volumes in 2013 and 2014.

As for the English version, my gratitude is wholeheartedly extended to my great friend Theodor Massim who was very kind to translate these volumes from the Romanian original. His work was a labor of love and patience enriching the original with educated and comprehensive footnotes that are instrumental for the English-speaking public to understand certain references in this book, as well as for his valuable suggestions. Also, I am very grateful to Mr. Edward Claflin for his editorial suggestions.

The writing and publishing of a book is impossible without the help of friends and family. Therefore, I want to mention with gratefulness Joshua Kandel (George's son), Viorica Belcic, and especially Andrei Ungureanu for their interest shown to the procedure to publish the English version of my memoirs in the USA.

Of course, special thanks go to my husband, Rudi Kleckner, my first reader, the one who created the right ambiance at home without which my story would not have seen the daylight.

At last, but not least, I want to acknowledge the Page Publishing Agency and its editorial board for accepting the story of my life imposed and directed by communism for the American public. Indeed, not many books cover the subject of communism.

Contents

Foreword

Simone Marie Kleckner's memoir *The Story of a Life, Volume 1: Liberty Lost* covers personal events over almost forty years, from 1927 to 1966. The memoir is written by a very sensitive and knowledgeable witness, gifted with an extraordinary memory. Together with extremely minute details of her personal life, the author evokes important social and historical moments in the prewar Romania and Europe, the instauration of communism and the life under oppression. These are all firsthand accounts, for she, her family, and friends have been subjected to expropriation, social discrimination, and jail. Practically, the wealthiest and most educated Romanian families had to live in poverty and socially emarginated when not in the terrible communist prisons. Simone writes with skill and emotion about all this unfortunate period of time, in clear contrast with her happy childhood and adolescence spent at the wonderful estates of her family in Oltenia.

The major merit of this passionate memoir is the fact that the author sees always her life in context, furnishing invaluable information filtered through her own personal experience and feelings.

This is a true story that would highly benefit the American reader, especially the younger echelon sometimes not very familiar with what communism meant for the people and countries in Eastern Europe.

Written in the first person, Kleckner's memoir makes an excellent reading that captivates at a very high level, for it is full of substance, action, remarkable characters, and unique in its kind.

Radu D. Popa

Lecturer in Law
Assistant Dean
Director of the Law Library
NYU School of Law

What Made Me Write My Memoirs

My urge to write my memoirs stemmed from the strong desire to give an honest assessment of the heartbreaking events that almost crushed my life under the communist system in Romania and from an equally strong desire to show the blessings that I discovered in America. Those contrasting experiences were a dividing point in my life.

As one who experienced the crimes of the communist regime, I thought it was my duty to share with others the tragic aspects of the communist holocaust, since very little has been written about that historic anomaly compared to the tons of volumes written and the movies made about Nazism. As it turns out, the Russian created crisis of 2014–2015 in Eastern Ukraine is proof that exposing its expansion is still a topical subject.

The first volume starts with an account of the period prior to WWII when the Romanian Monarchy modernized the nation—known at the time as Great Romania—turning it into one of the richest countries in Europe. During that time, my family was part of privileged intellectuals and land owners. Then, after 1939, the Nazi period came, depleting the country economically and after 1945, Romania was plagued by Soviet-imposed atrocities.

During the communist times, I bore witness to the ways in which that system destroyed the Romanian economy through forced collectivization of agricultural land, through currency devaluations and the nationalization of private property. All of us, with the exception of those in power, were reduced to poverty.

I also witnessed how the regime marginalized competent people with solid educations and suppressed individual liberty, initiative, and hope.

I lived through times when there were horrifying, massive, periodic arrests that were meant to instill fear in the population and keep us under control. Thousands died or were killed in the communist political prisons. Four family members endured prison terms of various lengths in the inhuman conditions of the communist political prisons or gulags. And indeed, we all lived in a permanent state of terror. Even in our private lives, we avoided speaking openly as we were suspicious of each other, fearing that many of us might be collaborators with the secret police, the feared "Securitate." Most of us were even fearful of attending religious services.

When the "Iron Curtain" fell, I was forever separated from my first husband. The communists also prevented me from pursuing my juridical career. My personal file was a constant threat which made me feel that I was a pariah in my own country where in fact I was stigmatized as an "enemy of the people."

How did I manage to survive under communism? I prayed. And my prayers were always answered. They helped me make the right choices or put me in touch with the right people. Prayers were my weapons against evil. If it hadn't been for my governess who since early childhood had taught me to believe and pray, I wouldn't have had the strength to face everything that came my way. I remain forever grateful to her for making me a stronger and better person.

Communism not only opened my eyes to its true nature but also helped shape my political opinions. Therefore, I used my life story as a thread that connected the dots between the international events of the time as well as the internal upheavals in my country— upheavals that were no different from those experienced by all the other Central and East European countries.

In this first volume most of the documentation regarding various personal data came from my memory and from my father's saved archives.

Finally, in my second volume I write about my American experience after 1966. There, I had the luxury to make my choices freely and fulfill whatever I set my mind to. I love my adopted country, where I regained my liberty.

Prologue

The railway station presented a scene of utter chaos. Under the soaring, vaulted arches of Bucharest's immense North Rail Station, the clamor of voices rose in a continuous wave, only to be broken now and then by the rumble of trains arriving and leaving. Everywhere—stretching as far the eye could see—was a mass of people who seemed uniformly tattered and despairing. They were all cramped, lying on the pavement with small bundles of personal belongings next to them. They formed a solid mass of people, like a field of greenhouse mushrooms stretching as far as the eye could see. Most of them appeared as if they had no place to go.

As I searched for the familiar face of my mother, it seemed impossible that I could possibly find her here. The forlorn figures crowding the platforms resembled a scene from Dante's *Inferno*—and I knew the hell that these stoic men and women had been through. Imprisoned for the most trivial of offenses by agents of an utterly corrupt political system, they had somehow endured the vast, complex, and inhuman prison system designed to break their will and destroy all hope. Each one of these hunched figures had lived through unimaginable horrors. Now, some unseen officials deep in the heart of a demented deliberated policy had decided they would be released, to be spewed out on this platform where they waited, forlorn and desolate, for the arrival of friends or relatives who would take them in.

And somewhere in this mass of humanity was my mother.

Now, looking around that station, I found it hard to believe she was really there. It had been nearly nine years since I had seen her. In all that time, I had not been able to visit her, nor had I heard from her. How could I find her in this mass of decrepit humanity? Would I even recognize her?

I stepped into a phone booth, planning to call home and talk to Aneta, the cleaning woman who told me that my mother had called. Perhaps she could give me additional details. Maybe my mother had told her something more—anything that would give me a clue to help find her in this crowd.

As I picked up the phone, a figure in the distance, rising from the floor, caught my attention. Could it be? There was almost nothing to distinguish her from any of the others, yet something seemed familiar. I put down the phone, left the booth, and began walking toward her—with difficulty, since I had to make my way among the cramped people lying on the pavement next to their bundles.

The woman I was approaching bore only the faintest resemblance to my mother. She was painfully thin, and her face had the pallor of someone long deprived of sunlight. Disheveled strands of grey, unwashed hair fell to waist height, bound up with a discolored string. There was a gaping hole in her front row of teeth. Her swollen feet were scarcely confined in her shoes, toes protruding where the leather had been cut away. As she lifted her hands to her cheeks, I saw that her brown nails were long and untrimmed. But the clothes that hung on her shrunken body were familiar. Yes, this is the very dress my mother had been wearing when she was arrested in Craiova, nine years before. For an instant, I felt as if I was staring at a ghost.

A moment later, all doubt vanished. Her pale face was illuminated with a joyful expression. The voice I heard was unmistakably my mother's.

"Moni, how glad I am that you came!"

The next moment she was in my arms. As we embraced, I was keenly aware of her frailness. Through the thin fabric of her dress, I could touch every rib. She felt so fragile, I was afraid to give her more than a slight hug, fearing that a stronger embrace might crush her.

I took her hand.

"Let's try to move."

She nodded, without asking where we were going. It was as if she was not even interested. As long as I was with her now, she was safe.

There was so much we had to say to each other. But first we had to escape from the crowded, noisy station where so many people, like her, awaited rescue. She leaned down to pick up her two ragged bundles. The way she cradled them, I assumed they must hold something precious. What could that be? I could not even imagine. She looked terrified when I offered to take them from her, then relieved when she saw I was not going to throw them away. Firmly grasping the bundles in one hand, I offered her the other. Her fleshless fingers slipped into my palm, and we shuffled ahead, making our way through the despondent crowd.

Few looked up as we passed, and those who did quickly averted their gaze. But I could see the disappointment in their faces. How they must envy my mother. She, at least, had been rescued. Resuming their hopeless waiting, the others seemed to shrink into themselves. How many clung to faith that they would be rescued?

"Moni," my mother said softly, "Please walk more slowly. I'm feeling dizzy."

I realized I had been pushing ahead too rapidly, eager to escape the throng. My mother could not keep up. I slowed my pace, checking her expression to see that she was all right.

When we came alongside the phone booth, I handed the bundles to my mother and asked her to wait a moment while I called Aneta. I wanted to tell her that she needn't worry. I had found my mother. And we were on our way home.

* * *

Not until many years later would I learn the full extent of what my mother had endured during those long years before I found her in the North Rail Station.

It had been the fifth of December 1955, a bitterly cold day in the middle of winter when Mancy had been arrested. She was not allowed to bring any clothes other than the light dress she wore. Thuggish guards from the security force, the "Securitate," took her to a former mansion that had been turned into secret police headquarters. It was a transit prison, a center where torture was used for interrogation. The guards grilled her with questions. She was stripped, body searched, and escorted down to a tiny basement cell. The floor was wet concrete strewn with broken glass, and a horrible stench permeated the cells. Outside the cell door was the dumping ground for the bodies of convicts who had been tortured and executed.

Someone tossed her a thin blanket. For the next two days, my mother lay curled up on the concrete floor, covered by nothing more than the threadbare covering. When the guards finally came for her, she was paralyzed.

She remained inside the Craiova prison from April to August 1956. Every morning, two sergeants dragged her up to the medical section on the second floor, where a young doctor treated her with unknown medicine for an undiagnosed illness. She did recover, but in the meantime endured daily interrogations. She was forced to stand for hours, wracked by illness, the sweat pouring from her damaged body as an officer barraged her with questions, sometimes shouting in her face or shoving her around like a stubborn animal. He wanted a confession. But what did she have to confess? What had she done? Her interrogators found some notebooks she had kept, and threatened to punish her. She was certain they intended to exterminate her.

That ordeal came to an end after a mock trial on April 10, 1956. An officer read out her sentence, ten years in prison. Four months later, she was moved to Miercurea Ciuc, the most feared prison in Romania, a stone fortress with shutters nailed to the windows to block out all sunlight. Prisoners were housed together—political prisoners among common-law convicts including thieves and criminals. Each cell was illuminated with one small, dim light bulb. There were iron beds. The inmates knew there was an informer among them, someone who watched over the borrowing of soap, paper, pencils, and reported anyone who complained about their treatment or plotted to escape. My mother, along with all the other prisoners, was subjected to repeated body searches

The overcrowded, unheated cells were like tombs. Inmates risked suffocation from the stagnant air. Rats scurried across the floor. Between six and ten women occupied each cell, all sharing a single chamber pot, a bucket placed in the middle of the cell. The stench was beyond imagining.

Often, convicts were forced to share a bed, chilled to the bone, with only a torn blanket to cover them. In each door was a "visor," the opening where guards peered in, keeping constant surveillance, primarily to prevent suicides. Prisoners slept from 10:00 p.m. until 5:00 a.m. Roll call was twice a day, morning and evening, with names read out from a register. Barefoot, dressed in rags, prisoners were assigned chores. As part of the daily regimen, they did forced labor in workshops—tailoring, fabricating carpets with bone needles, spinning and weaving combed hemp.

Meanwhile, investigators carried out their ruthless orders with brutal methods dictated by the Ministry of Internal Affairs. For exercise, prisoners were blindfolded and led out for mandatory walks that could last anywhere from a few minutes to many hours. During one twenty-minute walk in a temperature of minus twenty degrees, Mancy's feet got badly frostbitten. (She would carry the scars for the rest of her life.)

For breakfast, prisoners got a coffee substitute made of chickpeas, a cube of marmalade, and a ration of bread. During the rest of the day, their meals came in tins, without spoons. The diet included bean soup, sour barley-grains soup, potato skin soup, rotten cabbage, and occasionally a piece of moldy corn cake.

In disgust, Mancy would sometimes refuse to eat, even if it meant lying awake at night suffering from hunger or thirst.

By March of 1959 my mother had been transferred to Arad prison. Conditions were no better. The mattresses were bags filled with wet straw that could only be dried by the warmth of bodies. Half of the four hundred women incarcerated in Arad got tuberculosis, including Mancy. An infection flared up in her right arm—but it was only when pus began dripping from her arm that she received treatment from a convicted nun working as a nurse.

Over the next three years, conditions continued to deteriorate to the point where many prisoners were on the "dystrophic" list, exhibiting symptoms of severe nutritional deficiency. Mancy had, by then, become a shadow of her former self. Eventually, even the authorities became alarmed. On October 30, 1962, many prisoners, including Mancy, were moved to Oradea Mare, a modernized prison where prisoners slept four to room in heated rooms furnished with four beds. They were given access to a club room, books, and journals. Reasons for the improved living conditions soon became apparent. Rumors circulated that some prisoners were going to be released. Obviously, some officials had begun to worry that the released prisoners would make a bad impression. An "educator" began making visits, introducing the inmates to TV so they would appear to be familiar with all they had missed during their extended incarceration. The educator also gave them "lessons," attempting to instill appreciation for communism among the captives of that system.

Late in 1963, officials started release procedures. Those departing first left behind whatever they could spare for those who stayed. In the toilet room—where these goods were transferred—Mancy had found a pair of leather shoes that had belonged to an Ethnic German woman from Sibiu. She cut holes in the toes to accommodate her swollen feet. Without those shoes, she would have walked of the prison barefoot

On July 28, 1964, a guard began unlocking the cell doors.

When the time came to read out the names of those who were to be released, Mancy was not on the list. The communist "educator" informed Mancy that she should return to her cell. My mother assumed she would be kept for at least another year. But the following day, July 29, an officer came by to announce that Mancy had to bundle up her scant belongings. A train was leaving for Bucharest. She was to be one of the passengers.

* * *

20

I knew none of this at the time. As we left the station and found a taxi, I only felt immense joy that this frail woman in a thin dress—my mother—had survived. Seated in the taxi, she still clung to her bundles with quiet desperation A quick examination had told me there was nothing of value in them—just some ragged patching material and an improvised sewing needle, a small bone with a hole. But I did not try to separate Mancy from those bundles. Along with what she wore, this was all she had in the world. The rags and needle might appear worthless to me, but to her those bundles were precious. In time, I would try to separate her from them. There was no need to do so immediately.

Despite her frailty, Mancy's mind was as sharp as ever. We had only been in the taxi a moments before she began asking questions about friends and relatives. As I answered her questions, my mind was racing. So much had happened in my life since I had last seen her. There had been no way to communicate. Now, she was about to be introduced to life in my new home—to my husband, Rudi, whom she had never heard of, and to my mother-in-law, who had just arrived the night before for a visit. How would she absorb all this? How would she readjust to life outside prison?

I knew her resilience. It had been previously tested. She had been in and out of prison once before. Somehow, after her first incarceration, she had managed to resume a somewhat normal life—to the extent that was possible. Could she do it again?

Her "crime," this time, had been something so small that it would have laughable—in any other non-communist country, that is a fortune-teller had visited the house, and someone had informed the fact, and for this which represent proof—an unpardonable offense under the communist regime—she had endured years of untold suffering.

Now she was "free." Yet we knew that none of us were free. In our homes, in our schools, at work, in our streets, the darkest of clouds hung over our lives. The communists who had imprisoned my mother had also driven my entire family from our ancestral home. They had stolen our possessions—prevented me from using my law degree and making a career for myself. What had happened to my mother could happen to any of us, at any time, without cause and without warning. We in Romania, doing our best to go about our normal lives, knew that our fate was not in our hands. Those who ruled would dictate who could work and who was barred from the workplace; who would suffer and die in their prisons and who would be allowed to go free.

I was overjoyed that my mother had finally been released, that she could come home. But I also knew that we could not continue to live in constant fear under the thumb of communist rule. Such a life was unendurable.

I had been born in Romania. I had always considered it home. However, after twenty years of communism, I knew for certain that I would like to feel free, to live normal life. But how that would be achieved—or when—was unknown. Nothing was certain except the one certainty in my own mind.

CHAPTER 1

70 Vasile Lascăr St.

I was born between the two World Wars. At that time, among families of our social status, the prevailing wisdom was that women should give birth at home with a midwife or nurse, under the supervision of a doctor. As a rule, the business of raising children was initially entrusted to a nurse and then to a governess.[1] From stories told by my father, George Vrăbiescu, I understand that my family had hired a nurse to make all necessary preparations in anticipation of my birth On the date I was due to arrive into this world, my father and his brother Nicolae, were anxiously waiting in a room adjacent to the bedroom where my mother was in labor. Both hoped, secretly, that they would soon be congratulated for the birth of a little baby boy. And indeed, I did not let them wait too long. But, when the nurse emerged with a broad smile, it was to announce emphatically that "it's a girl!"

My nervous father rushed in to see his new-born daughter. He would later admit to me his initial disappointment that I was a girl.

---

1. Especially formerly, a woman employed to care for the children and teach then a foreign language in their own homes.

But what alarmed him most was the first sight of me. I was very tiny, red like a lobster and had a bush of dark wiry hair on my head. With a really concerned voice but in a fake joking tone he asked the obstetrician, "Well, Doctor, what you think about this chunk of meat?"

Without saying a word, the doctor held me up by the ankles and took me to the window, head down and arms dangling, resembling a little St. Peter crucified head-down in Rome. After giving me a little shake, he finally replied, "Mr. Vrăbiescu, there is no reason to be worried. She is well built and will be OK. Just make sure that she will be nourished properly! You will see that I am right, and she will be fine!" Quite relieved, my father thanked the doctor and rushed back to share the news with his brother, "Hey Nicu,[2] the baby girl is quite small, but the doctor assured me that she will be no trouble." To that my uncle's only reply was, "God bless, dear Gică!"[3] He then embraced my father, muttering in a barely audible voice, "Too bad she is not a boy!"

Like my father, my uncle too would have preferred to see a son who would carry down the Vrăbiescu name carried to the next generation. Certainly at the back of both of their minds was concern about the inheritance of our properties which—in keeping with our family's tradition—was preferably to be handed down to the male line of the family. Had they known what the future had in store for us, the idea of who is inheriting the family properties would not have bothered them at all. (By grabbing all private property, the communists would see to it that people no longer had such worries. The distinction between boys or girls would make no difference.)

I was brought into this world when Romania had become an independent state under King Carol I.[4] The country had become united in 1918 under the stewardship of King Ferdinand and Queen Maria,[5] helped in part by the zealous diplomatic undertakings of the

---

2.   An informal appellative in Romanian for Nicolae, like Nick is for Nicholas in English.
3.   An informal appellative in Romanian for George.
4.   Romanian for Charles
5.   Romanian for Mary

Brătianus.[6] I was born during a period of prosperity enjoyed by the majority of the population following the land appropriation reform of 1922. During that time, Romania's citizens were free and property was protected and guaranteed both in rural and urban areas. The Romanian currency, the *leu*, was so strong it was often compared to the Swiss *franc*. Bucharest was such an attractive city it had been dubbed "The Little Paris." All indications were that I had stepped, with my best foot forward, into a beautiful, flourishing country that could boast a strong middle class of industrialists and entrepreneurs as well as an intellectual and political elite (many educated in prestigious West European universities) who were true patriots. Many had outstanding oratorical talents demonstrated either in politics or in university halls. This political and intellectual elite had shaped a modern country under the leadership of a Monarchy that, in conformity with the Constitution of 1923, observed the principle of the separation of powers in the state. It was a government in which monarch played the role of an arbitrator among governing parties. Under such auspicious circumstances Romania seemed destined to become an equal partner with her sister West European countries, among whom she had earned a certain degree of respect. This stature was due, in great part to the living and intellectual standards of a substantial part of its population, including my family.

But, only four short months after I was born, signs of Romania's long downward path were already apparent. After the death of King Ferdinand in July 1927, the successor designated to take over the throne was his underage nephew Mihai,[7] who was only six years old at the time. (The boy King Mihai was only appointed successor because the legitimate heir to the throne, King Ferdinand's son, Prince Carol, had forsaken his rights to the crown.) Mihai's accession to the throne was not a problem in itself because the affairs of the state were handled in his behalf by a Regency made up of respectable and able

---

6.   Brătianu was a prestigious Romanian family of politicians, founders of the National Liberal Party (PNL).

7.   Romanian for Michael

men of state. The problem was that Carol Caraiman,[8] who apparently realized that he was better off living in the Royal Palace than in self-imposed exile, changed his mind and decided to return, which generated dissension among the politicians of the time. Eventually Carol managed to return to Romania and dethroned King Mihai, dissolving the Regency, and on June 8, 1930, was proclaimed king under the name of Carol II.

But let me put politics aside for the moment and continue with my narration of events that occurred after I was born on Vasile Lascăr[9] Str. My oldest recollections are from the time when my upbringing was passed over to a governess with whom I shared the same bedroom. There were two entrances to the bedroom, and one of its two doors was declared off limits for us. I was sleeping in a baby crib with sliding sides. One morning I woke up when one of the sides was already down and took the opportunity to climb out of bed and, in my white sleeping gown, make my way to the "forbidden door." As it turned out, that door led to my parents' bedroom. Proceeding on tiptoes, I managed to turn the door knob, open that door and get into the forbidden room when, bad luck, I stumbled on a low coffee table. A Turkish brass tray fell to the floor with a bang. My mother, awakened by the noise, was startled to see me. "What are you doing here?" she demanded as she rose from her bed. In a very stern tone she ordered me never again to do that. As punishment, she took me by the hand to a corner of the room and ordered me to stand there for five minutes facing the wall. I obeyed her without saying a word, my nose was pressed against a wood armoire with a light orange veneer and darker nervures. I could not understand what was happening to me: it was my first experience with that kind of punishment. When

---

8. The future Carol II of Romania and elder son of King Ferdinand and Queen Maria, who used the name Carol Caraiman while he renounced his succession rights to the throne.

9. As prime minister of Romania at the end of the nineteenth century, Vasile Lascăr managed to pass a law concerning the improvement of life in rural areas; he promoted the law following his own research in rural areas by the Danube and in part following lengthy consultations with my uncle Iulian Vrăbiescu, who was a county prefect.

the five minutes were up, my mother took me back to my room, not through the "forbidden door" by a roundabout route. Once back in my room, the governess—relieved that I was safe and sound—took me in her arms. It was only then, that I burst out crying. In any case, I had learned my lesson and since that incident I never again ventured through that "forbidden door." To this day the nervures of that light orange veneer are fresh in my memory

Another early childhood recollection is related to a meal. One day at supper I refused to eat a plate of spinach that was a side dish to a meat roast. My governess, who was of Finish origin, urged me to finish up everything. As I stubbornly insisted that I did not want any spinach, she went to ask my mother what to do, then returned and took the spinach away. But the spinach had been returned as the only dish for supper. I was hungry but again did not touch it and, again, off it went. But even though I was going hungry, my mother did not flinch in her determination to give me a stern education, the same as she had received from her mother. She wanted me to know that children were supposed to unconditionally obey the grownups. No ifs, ands, or buts. So the following day, I got the same plate with spinach for lunch. By then I was so hungry that I caved in and ate it, and—you know what?—It was not bad at all. The first time I refused to eat the spinach, I had probably been turned off by its color. To this day, spinach remains for me a symbol of the discipline and obedience that was expected of me during my childhood.

Back to my years in Vasile Lascăr Street, my mother hired my second governess, Fraulein Betty Haager, called Haagerchen by my parents and Haagi by me. Coming to Romania from Austria, Haagi had been forced to seek a governess job due to the financial crisis of 1929, when her family had sold their house. (The sum of money her family had deposited into a bank account was later worth just about four pairs of shoes.) Her first employers in Romania were the Costinescu family, and when she stopped working for them, they gave her a very good letter of recommendation, on the basis of which my mom decided to hire her. Haagi filled my life for thirteen years.

It had become a routine for Haagi and I to go for a walk. Our final destination was one of the two nice parks not far from our house. On Sundays we stopped over at a Roman Catholic Church on Pitar Moș Street to attend part of the mass. The priest conducted the service in Latin. Though I could not understand the language, nevertheless I was fascinated by the choir of the nuns with their angelic voices. All parishioners were lining up to take communion and I could not understand why I could not do the same, despite the fact, as Haagi had explained to me, that I was baptized in the Christian Orthodox religion while that was a Christian Catholic church. I was too young to understand the difference, and deep in my soul, that bothered me. Nevertheless, Haagi would explain to me that God Almighty and Jesus Christ were the same in both religions, and as such, I could pray to them to keep my parents and my loved ones in good health and rest assured that those prayers would certainly be answered. There I sat next to "Tante"[10] Grete Benesch and her daughter Helga, who was two years older than me and one foot taller. Those two would remain my best friends for as long as fate allowed.

When my mother had hired Haagi, she did not make my governess aware that she was going to divorce my father. She only broke the news to Haagi shortly before she decided to move out. Haagi, being the only person who witnessed the separation of my parents, later told me how it happened.

One evening, when my father had returned home from a trip to the town of Craiova he asked Haagi, "Where is the mistress?" In reply, Haagi handed him the letter that mother had left on the dining room table. With the letter in hand he immediately asked Haagi where I was. Told that I was sleeping in my room, he rushed in, made sure that I was OK, kissed me and left the room without waking me up. After a while Haagi overheard him relating the contents of the letter to Uncle Nicu. In my father's archives I found that letter in which mother explained to him the decision to seek a divorce, saying she had chosen to leave home while he was out of town to avoid useless discussions. From Haagi's stories I understood that my father was deeply affected by mother's decision to move out. In an effort to cut

---

10. German for aunt

himself off from painful memories he decided to move us to another house at 26 Negustori Street

In that house I lived with uncle Nicu, my father's brother, and grand ma Ecaterina Vrăbiescu, born Brănețu. Grandma, whom throughout this book I'll refer to as *Maman Titi,* became a widow in 1904 at age thirty-seven when Grandfather Iorgu Vrăbiescu died (he was fifty-one). My Grandma never remarried. At that time my father was twelve and his younger brother Nicu was eleven.

After my mother moved out, she went to the town of Craiova[11] to live with her mother, Grandma Lucreția, born Mirică. She too was a widow. Her husband had died in 1906, when Lucreția was just twenty-four. Her two daughters, Clemența and Constanța—called Mancy and Tancy, for short—were aged only three and four. She and her daughters lived in Switzerland for a while before she returned to Romania. She settled in Craiova in 1921 and married Nicolae Defleury. (Throughout this book I'll refer to Lucreția as *Manini* and to Grandfather Defleury, *Tata-Lae.*)

The two grandmothers were not very much alike but did have a few things in common: both, widowed at a young age, took care of their children with the help of governesses, and both were dedicated mothers who brought up their children with lots of love but with strict discipline

The only father figure for my father and his brother was their Uncle Nicolae Vrăbiescu, *Nea Nae,*[12] the younger brother of Grandfather Iorgu while for my mother and her sister the father fig- ure was their Uncle Marinică Mirică—*Nenea Marinică.* I'll mention other relatives with whom my life intersected, and about whom I have fond memories.

---

11. Craiova—Romania's 6th largest city and capital of Dolj County, is situated in the central of the historic region of Oltenia in Southern Romania

12. *Nenea* of the abbreviated *Nea* are familiar ways address an older member of the family, usually an uncle.

CHAPTER 2

26 Negustori Street

In 1926 my father was offered a professorship in the Civil and Criminal Procedure Department of the Bucharest University School of Law. The year before, my father had sold our house in the town of Craiova and bought the house at Twenty-Six Negustori Street in Bucharest. Initially only my paternal grandmother, Maman Titi, and my father's younger brother, Uncle Nicu, moved to that house. Then all of us who had moved out from the house on Vasile Lascăr Street joined them. The house on Negustori Street had two floors and an interior staircase connecting them. Haagi and I occupied a large room with a terrace overlooking a backyard.

As a child, I had a lot of fun hanging around the backyard where we kept all kinds of farm fowl brought from Genune. And of course, there was Joc, Uncle Nicu's hunting hound and his insepara-ble friend.

Haagi was the only member of our household who was not very happy about the move. For one thing, she was now far from the Pitar Moş church and from the Icoanei and Ioanid parks where she would meet with other governesses that she had befriended. In addition, there were more people in this house to boss her around. The stern

Maman Titi had become the *old mistress*, replacing my mother. Then there were my father, Uncle Nicu, Uncle Nae, and Cici, who was a frequent guest for dinner. In addition, the household included our live-in housekeeping staff, the old-timer Leana, Justine the cook, and the junior housemaid, Marie

Waking up very early in the morning, Haagi would help with my morning toilette, combing my hair to make it shiny. When I felt sick she would come to my bed and run her hand through my hair to determine whether I was running a temperature. When I was well, however, she made me adhere to a daily routine. She always made me line up my slippers neatly close to the bed, which was meant to teach me orderly habits. Often she taught me songs or read me stories. At bedtime, after I said my prayer, she would pull up a blanket to cover me. Gazing down at me with her serene blue eyes, she would give me a tender kiss and wish me, "Good night, my love." I feel asleep feeling surrounded by the balmy warmth of her loving care.

Haagi was a short, slightly plump woman with blond hair and rosy cheeks and a friendly and sociable nature. She loved light music, but the song that she particularly liked to sing had lyrics that went like this: "Happy is the one who can forget what is unchangeable." To this day, when I hear some of her favorite songs, I get very emotional. There was almost a mother-child bondage between us, and I was terrified by the idea that one day I might lose her. To this day I remember the address of her folks in Austria: Keiser Joseph Plaz 46, Wels, Austria.

Before I reached elementary-school age, we used to take short walks in the neighborhood or, occasionally, board a tram for longer trips to downtown areas such as on Calea Victoriei.[13] Despite being dubbed "the Little Paris" at that time, Bucharest was really a South-Eastern European capital in transition to maturity. Its reputation was due in part to a boom in such fields as education, law, letters, and philosophy.

Even after we moved to the new address, Haagi and I kept returning to the Pitar Moş Catholic Church every single Sunday,

---

13. *Victory Way* in English

even though it was now a greater distance from our home. As before, Helga and Tante Grete were always in church. On our way home, most of the time, we were really in a hurry. Nearly always, I had to almost run alongside Haagi for fear that we might be late for lunch. We knew that would piss off Maman Titi, who would severely reprimand us.

One day, I overheard a vivid conversation that my father had in Romanian. He frequently repeated the word *Nachtigal,* which is the German for nightingale.

Haagi and I found out that *Nachtigal* was in fact the name of the attorney who was defending the nineteen communist activists who were to be tried in Craiova on June 5, 1936, by the Army War Council. They were accused of cooperating with the Communist International or Comintern.[14] That group of defendants, thirteen men and six women, were all destined to become prominent leaders nine years later when the communists seized power in Romania.

Every year on May 10,[15] there was a military parade on Calea Victoriei marking Romania's National Holiday, also known as "The King's Day." As a child, I was strongly impressed by the pageantry and the colorful military uniforms. Another childhood attraction for me was to go to the traditional Thursday Festivals,[16] which were commercial and food fairs combined with circuslike entertainment.

Since I had no brothers or sisters, my playmates were often the children in care of other governesses that Haagi had befriended. One of them was the daughter of Willy Filderman, who served as presi-

14.   The International Association of Communist parties, established in 1919 by Lenin and dissolved in 1943.

15.   May 10 marks three major events in Romania's history: one in 1866 when prince Carol I of Hohenzollern-Sigmaringen swore the oath of office in Romania's Parliament, then in 1877 when Romania declared its independence from the Ottoman Turks, and finally in 1881 when Romania was proclaimed kingdom and Carol I was crowned as the first Romanian King. The date was celebrated as Romania's National Holiday until 1947 when the communist government forced king Michael I to abdicate.

16.   *Joia Moșilor* in Romanian

dent of the Romanian Jewish' Federation during WW II. Filderman, in collaboration with Dr. Sabin Manoilă, a former director of the Bucharest Institute of Statistics, issued a Report on the Jewish Population of Romania during WWII that was published by the Romanian Cultural Foundation of the town of Jassy.[17]

Haagi had remained in touch with her former employers, the Costinescus, whom we would visit occasionally. We visited Princess Marie Costinescu, one of the three daughters of prince Barbu Ştirbey, and her three sons. Before one of these visits, Haagi warned me to be on my best behavior as we were to be received by Princess Marie herself. Just as we entered the big entrance hall, the tall and majestic Princess Marie appeared. She stood at the top of a spiral staircase whose wide steps were covered with a thick carpet. Haagi greeted her as Princess Marie descended the stairs to welcome us. I could not take my eyes off her. What I could not understand was why she did not wear any crown or tiara as did all fairy tale princesses that Haagi had been reading to me about. Disappointed, I exclaimed out loud in German, *"Haagi sie is keine Prinzessin, weil sie keine Krone am Kopf hat,"* which meant "Haagi, she is no princess as she wears no crown on her head." Overhearing that, Marie Costinescu smiled. Haagi, though, was very embarrassed and tried to apologize by explaining how I got that idea.

My playmates were Gheorghe and Alexandru who were close to my age. (Peţu was still a toddler.) Gheorghe became a musician, and years later I would meet him again in New York when he gave a concert at Alice Tully Hall. Through another governess and friend of Haagi, I met four cousins: Adina Koslinski, Lisbeth Hagi-Moscu and the sisters Ileana and Mitzis Carp, with whom I have remained friends forever

Part of our afternoon routine was to visit friends or family, frequently on the same day each week. Tuesdays we visited Helga and Tante Grete. On Wednesdays we would see Istrătel Micescu, whose

---

17.　*Iaşi* (pronounced yashi) is the second largest city of Romania, after Bucharest, both in terms of its population and also in terms of its importance as a cultural, historical and academic centre.

father was the famous Romanian lawyer and law professor Istrate Micescu, at the family's vast countryside estate and mansion—the same estate where Professor Micescu often invited my father and Uncle Nicu to come for hunting sessions.

Other friends were Dinu and Sandu Missirliu whose mother, Tante Cellica, was a descendent of big landowners from the town of Târgu Jiu. (This was in the historic region where the sculptor Constantin Brâncuşi has three of his most-famous works.) The boys' father, Dr. Vladimir or Valodi Misirliu, had been a student at the Sorbonne in Paris at the same time as my father and Uncle Nicu

On Negustori Street, the mistress of the house was without doubt my paternal grandmother, Maman Titi. This was where she was living when she married my Grandfather Gheorghe (Iorgu) Vrăbiescu and raised their two boys before being widowed at the age of thirty-seven. From what I can tell from old family pictures, she was beautiful as a young woman. She had a slender frame, black wavy hair, and deep blue eyes that mirrored her energetic nature. And indeed, she conducted all family affairs with an iron fist. She had administered our estate in the village of Genune, and was a loving mother. But she became quite a stern disciplinarian, especially after the premature and unexpected death of my grandfather. That was when she suddenly found herself solely in charge with two boys to care for, one eleven and one twelve.

Helping Maman Titi raise her children was the governess, Emma Wavreczka, a protective mother figure who looked after everybody in the house and took charge of all the household tasks. After presiding over the lunch[18] table, my grandmother would take a one hour rest and then she would have guests or just play solitaire and listen to political news. She was very well informed, and also opinionated, on all issues concerning Romania and the rest of Europe. After supper, she would withdraw to read a book before going to bed. It was apparent that her mind needed to be at peace, with the assurance that everyone in the house was okay, before she retired for the night.

---

18.   In Romania of those times, lunch was the main meal of the day.

From the moment I landed in that house, Grandmother took it upon herself to see that I was properly taken care of. She bestowed lots of love on me, not just as any other grandmother would do but even more so. To her way of thinking, I had been abandoned by my mother which, going by her moral standards, she deemed reprehensible.

The busiest person in our household was, without doubt, my father who was dividing his time between his busy academic schedules and his activities as a member of the Legislative Council. Born March 9, 1892, my father attended all school grades in the town of Craiova, the capital of the historic region of Oltenia where our family had its roots. Then in 1911, he was accepted as a law student at the prestigious Paris University, the Sorbonne, from where, after some interruptions because of the WWI and his military service, he graduated in 1922 with a JD (Juridical Doctor) degree. His brother Nicu studied at the same university. That put a mark of French refinement on their personalities, overshadowing the influences of the Greek culture that prevailed in Romania at the time.

After graduation, my father George Vrăbiescu worked as an attorney until 1925. He was thirty-four when he married my mother Clementa Cionea who was twenty-three. On January 1, 1926, my father was appointed a full member of the Legislative Council where he would work for the next twenty-two years. In the same year he was offered a professorship at the Civil and Criminal Procedure department of the Bucharest School of Law and Juridical Studies. He declined to participate in politics because it would constitute a conflict of interest with his membership in the Legislative Council—a post in which he was not supposed to have a political affiliation. But he was a conservative patriot by nature. I am sure his love for his country would have set him up as a role model for future generations, had the country not been fated to change so dramatically in the years to come.

Because my father's daily schedule was so full, my chances to spend time with him were limited. At the end of the lunch meal, I was allowed to get off my chair and sit on his lap when he would kiss me and caress me. But one day I noticed my father was a little edgy for some reason. He may have had some work-related problems, or perhaps he received bad news from our estate in the countryside. Who knew! But it was on that day, of all days, that I started to argue with Haagi over some meal that I refused to eat. All of a sudden raising his voice, my father ordered me to leave the room. As I stood up and headed to my room upstairs, I retorted loudly, saying, "I'll leave [this house]!" That touched a nerve in my father. He was still acutely sensitive about my mother's split with the family. He came rushing upstairs, caught up with me, and slapped me a few times on my tushy, yelling, "You too!" That was the first and last time my father spanked me. To this day that incident remains vivid in my memory. It taught me that my father might occasionally have a short fuse, but he never bore a grudge. (Now that I reflect on that, I am sure I am his carbon copy.)

During most afternoons my father would confine himself to this study either to prepare his lectures or to work on the project to codify the Romanian Penal Code. Together with his mentor Ioan Ionescu Dolj, he worked for fifteen long years on the monumental codification project. He did a lot of research, participated in the works of the Parliamentary Commissions, and gave lectures on the subject. Most evenings he would have long conversations on the phone with other academics. I felt deprived of what little time I had to spend with him.

Uncle Nicu was born in 1983 and graduated with a JD degree from the Paris University of Sorbonne in 1921. He practiced law only as an attorney, and for a while he served as an MP for a local district. To him I was the daughter he never had, and he was very affectionate with me. Because his schedule was more flexible than my father's, he could afford to spend more time with me. On December 6, St. Nicholas Day, Onkel Nicu would always invite friends over to celebrate his name day. I was not invited, probably because at my age I was not supposed to mingle with grownups and listen to their conversations. So Haagi would put me to bed precisely at 8:00 p.m. But as I lay in my bed, I was all ears. I remained awake before I heard the final congratulations, and only after that could I eventually fall asleep.

Before Christmas Eve I was happy to welcome groups of Christmas Carol singing children. Uncle Nicu would select the Christmas Tree. Christmas Eve was the most anticipated and happiest holiday of the year. I was, of course, always eagerly waiting to see what presents Santa will bring. Most years, I received all kinds of books. But the gift that made the strongest impression on me was a little drawer cabinet of white wood from Tante Tancy, my mother's sister. Finally I had a place to put my dolls' clothes. To this day I remember how fascinated I was by that present.

Once I managed to get "Onkel Nicu" pretty upset. This occurred during one of the piano lessons that Haagi was giving me. It was an unfortunate fact that I did not inherit the musical talents from my mother's side. My talents, in fact, were then and are now just about zero, just like all the Vrăbiescus on my father's side. So one day, during one of these piano lessons, I was struggling to play a little piece and I got so frustrated that I just refused to practice any longer. Haagi tried her best to persuade me to carry on. I climbed down from my tall piano stool, went to the middle of the room and sat down on the carpet, legs crossed in a kind of lotus position, my chin resting on my arms. I just stared at Haagi defiantly as if telling her to "leave me alone." In a voice of increasing annoyance, she urged me to resume practicing but I stubbornly refused to move from the floor. Hearing us, Uncle Nicu came to see what the commotion was all about. When he realized what was happening, he frowned. His bushy eyebrows drew together in anger and—with a harsh voice that he had never before used with me—he ordered me back to the piano. With that, I got to my feet. But instead of going back to the piano, I rushed into my room. Later on I felt sorry for behaving like that with my beloved Uncle Nicu, and I apologized.

Afterward there were no more piano lessons for me. How did that come about? Well, later that day when my father came home, Uncle Nicu told him and my grandmother about that morning's incident. My father observed, "Well, Nicu, you probably forgot how miserable we felt when Fraulein Emma, on our mother's insistence, was struggling to teach us play the piano. Just leave the little girl alone if the piano lessons make her miserable. It turns out that she is made of the same stock as we are."

And that was it! I was off the hook with my piano lessons.

Another character from my childhood universe was Miss Cici Apostoleanu, who had a clerical job at the Marmorosch Blank Bank She was my mother's frequent guest when we lived in Vasile Lascăr Str. Because she was very fond of me, she continued to visit us after my parents' divorce. Maman Titi had also befriended her, and Cici remained a frequent guest for dinner. In winter time, on Haagi's day off, Cici was the one who took me to the Oteteleşeanu skating rink.

Our most senior housekeeper was Leana followed by Justina the cook who came to Bucharest from Bessarabia,[19] the Easternmost historical region of Romania that borders USSR. Leana was definitely a central figure, a status that was reinforced by the fact that Maman Titi had recruited her when she was coming as a temp worker to help with seasonal chores at our Genune estate. She often took advantage of her advantaged position, feeling at liberty to put her two cents during our conversations or giving Maman Titi all kinds of unsolicited advice. I did not care about all that, but I certainly objected whenever she was trying to undermine Haagi. I have to admit, though, that she has always been very loyal to us.

Haagi felt sorry for me because my mother did not stay in touch in any way, and she knew I was missing her. I expressed my feelings indirectly by consoling my dolls, telling them not to be upset, that my mother would soon return. On my behalf, Haagi took it upon herself to write my mother a letter making her aware of the situation and urging her, at the very least, to keep in closer touch with me. Years later, I found in my father's archives that my mother did reply to Haagi with a letter written in French, quoting (in German) from Haagi's letter. In the archived letter I learned my mother resented

---

19.   In 1940, Bessarabia was occupied by the USSR in accordance with the Molotov-Ribbentrop Pact with Nazi Germany. Subsequently, Romania joined the Axis Powers and recaptured it in 1941 and lost again in 1944 when Bessarabia became the Soviet Republic of Moldavia.

Haagi's suggestion that I was visibly affected by her remoteness. My mother claimed she did not keep in touch because she was busy with administrative work in Craiova. It was our responsibility, not hers, to stay in touch. Her letter indicated further that, at the time, she was really worried about me because she had not received any news from us "in over fifteen days."

Well, that reply was not exactly what Haagi had been hoping to accomplish. But soon became clear that Haagi's letter had, nevertheless, yielded some results. Soon after, Uncle Liky came to visit us and broke the news that mother was planning to visit Bucharest. He mentioned that Haagi and I could visit her, then gave us the date, time, and address where we could meet. Since mother's departure from home, Uncle Liky had acted as liaison: he was always the one to bring us news about her.

Though I just mention Uncle Liky here, I will refer to him often from now on. At that time he was still a young man, very energetic and very much into sports. He was really fond of riding his motorcycle, his favorite means of transportation whenever he traveled between Craiova and Bucharest. With Elene born Gabroveanu, Uncle Liky had a daughter Ioana (who also will be often mentioned) and a son Matei, children born seven years apart.

Following Uncle Liky's instruction, on the indicated date and time, Haagi and I went to the Stănescu Hotel in downtown Bucharest where my mother stayed for many weeks on end during her Bucharest visits. With a huge flower bouquet in hand, Haagi and I took the elevator to my mother's room. When my mother opened the door, she was dressed in a light pink dressing gown. I presented the flowers to her, and she took them with a luminous smile that showed off her pearl white teeth. She bent to kiss me, then hugged Haagi. It was an image that would long remain in my memory. Though my mother was of medium height, her silhouette was majestic. She had shiny black hair, big brown eyes, and very white skin. Years later, I learned she had been the second runner up at a Miss Romania pageant.

While mother and Haagi were talking, I was given permission to play with soap bubbles in the bathroom. The door was ajar, and I could observe Mother making meticulous preparations to go out.

She started by applying a tinted cream makeup to her face, then adding some powder. After putting on lipstick, she applied a blusher to her cheekbones, finishing with touch of eyeliner and mascara brushed onto her eyelids. After her makeup was complete, she pulled on a dress over her head, fixed her hair, put a pearl string on her neck, and fastened her earrings. Finally she checked her appearance in the mirror to assure herself everything was perfect. At that point, Haagi sensed that it was time for us to leave, too. She came to the bathroom to help me put on my coat, only to find me blowing soap bubbles.

Another time when we went visiting, mother asked us to wait for her in the hotel lobby. Her room was on the second floor, but she did not bother to call the elevator, preferring instead to take the stairs. I preserve such a strong image of her coming down the stairs that, to this day, I can still see her in my mind's eye, almost if it were yesterday. She had a smile on her face and the confidence of someone who was used to being admired, well aware that people were watching her. In that later image I have, she was wearing a brown straw hat in striking contrast with her white gown with small brown blobs and a leather belt that contrasted with the loose-fitting folds of the skirt and pulled in at the waist, making her look even slimmer that she was. It was a classical elegant look seen only in movies.

When she came down, Haagi and I went to greet her. I was waiting for her to bend and kiss me, but at just that moment a cab arrived in front of the hotel to whisk us away to a dentist's appointment. When the dental procedure was over, I got compliments from Dr. Kaplan on how quiet and patient I had been as I waited for my mother to come out. Once back on the street after the appointment, we said our good-byes and went our separate ways, Haagi and I headed home, my mother in the opposite direction, God only knew where.

Looking back, I think I can understand the reasons behind my mother's decision to seek a divorce from my father. Her mother, Manini, had become a widow when she was only twenty-four after her husband Anastase Cionea died of a liver ailment, facing the prospect of raising two little daughters all by herself. She thought that being a disciplinarian was the safest way to ensure a good upbringing for the girls. Also, since she lost a little daughter to tuberculosis in 1904, after her husband's death she took Tancy and Mancy to Lausanne, Switzerland, where they lived for a few good years. Over there, she thought, the girls could breathe the dry mountain air free from the humid climate that clung to the banks of the Danube. She also thought the girls could get a good education in Lausanne, where they attended and graduated from high school. Some years they would return to spend the summer in Craiova, mostly with my grandmother's sister in the Calafat Palace. When the girls were in their teens, Manini took them for vacations to Paris and Vienna, also in an attempt to help them develop real ladylike manners.

When the girls reached marriageable age, Manini thought the time was right for them to move back to Craiova. That was a tough adjustment for the girls, who were then forced to plunge into a dramatically different environment. So to follow through with her intentions, Manini started to search for suitable sons-in-law.

For my mother, Mancy, she found George Vrăbiescu. Certainly he was a desirable young man as he had studied law in Paris and was a descendent of a long line of boyars[20] who had a reputation of respectability and solid financial stature. At first glance, there appeared to be nothing wrong with such a marriage of convenience. From the perspective of my future father, George certainly could not go wrong marrying my mother. She was beautiful, well educated, and smart. In addition, prior to meeting her, he had not been seeing anybody of any significance because he had been so focused on building his career. But from my mother's perspective, as I came to understand, the situation was quite different.

Manini totally ignored the fact that her daughter Mancy was in love with a handsome Swiss man, Ernst von Rene. He was a Scandinavian type, tall and slim, with blonde hair and blue eyes—in a word totally different from my father. Significantly, my mother

---

20.   Boyard (Romanian: *boier*)designates the higher ranks of land-owners most of whom had been allocated lands from the princely domains in recognition of distinguished service in the military or civilian administration.

preserved a nicely framed picture of him, and at some point I became aware of who he was. Years later she confessed to me what Manini had said when told that her daughter felt no attraction for George Vrăbiescu because her heart and soul had remained in Switzerland. Her mother's reply was, "I do not think that love should be a factor. You just need to marry him and make children who will inherit the family's fortune."

Manini would not take no for an answer simply because that was the way she herself had been brought up. Her father, Vasile Mirică, had decided it was in her best interest to marry Anastase Cionea, a man many years her senior who had good credentials, coming from a respectable and pretty well-off family of land owners. Personally, I consider myself very lucky that I have lived in more emancipated times.

Anyway, my parents got married in the Danube port town of Calafat[21] on June 6, 1925. After the civil ceremony at the Calafat townhall there was a religious service at the St. Nicholas Church followed by a reception in the Marincu Mansion (or Marincu Palace, as locals call it). Following the reception, the newlyweds spent their honeymoon in Venice, Italy, where they stayed at the elegant Hotel Danielli. Upon their return from Italy, my parents set up residence in the apartment on Vasile Lascăr Street.

I later asked why they chose to celebrate the wedding in the small town of Calafat rather than the more urbane town of Craiova, the capital of the historic region of Oltenia where both families had their roots. The reason, I was told, was that my grandmother's older sister Maria had been married in Calafat. Maria's groom was Ştefan Marincu, a gifted businessman with a very sharp mind who played an important part in the management of the Marincu and Sons Trust, which extended over some 150,000 hectares (roughly 300,000 acres). Ştefan also went into politics, becoming an influential member of the Liberal Party, and in 1911 he was elected the mayor of

---

21. *Calafat* is a town on the river Danube, in the Southern part of the Romanian historic region of Dolj, opposite the Bulgarian city of Vidin to which it is linked by ferryboat.

Calafat. And he was a good husband. Ştefan treated his wife Miţulică like a princess, showering her with expensive cloths and jewels, some coming all the way from the most reputable stores in Paris. They had a daughter who died when she was just thirteen. After a prolonged period of mourning, Ştefan decided to build a big mansion in Calafat in his daughter's memory. The mansion had scores of rooms and was even visited by Romania's king Carol[22] I and queen Elisabeta when their party passed through Calafat in 1913.

As Ştefan's health deteriorated, he decided to write his last will and testament. The Palace, he said, was to be bequeathed to the Calafat municipality with the stipulation that it should be turned into a boarding school for girls in memory of his deceased daughter Marioara. Ştefan died of tuberculosis on June 16, 1914. Later, the communists turned the Palace into the Art Museum of the municipality. All of this family history entered into the Mirica and Marincu families deciding, in 1925, that the palace was the best place to host, in style, a reception for the newlyweds.

Mentioning these families, I would like to share a few details about my great grandfather on my mother's side, Vasile Mirică. He married Maria, born Băloiu and had four children: Maria, Petre, Marin and Lucreţia (my grandmother, the one I called Manini). A man of many talents who had a keen intelligence and sense of humor, Vasile loved music. But, above all, Vasile was a very industrious man who managed to build a pretty hefty fortune for himself solely by dint of hard work, courage, and entrepreneurial talents. The profits he made from this trade allowed him to buy two thousand hectares of land in the village of Bârca from Athanasie Baici de Varadia, a descendent of the wealthy Obrenovici family.[23] Vasile accumulated substantial wealth during his long life which allowed him to make hefty philanthropic donations, travel extensively throughout Europe, and bequeath considerable land estates to all his four children. He

---

22. Romanian for Charles
23. Another descendent of this family Milan Obrenovici, the son of a Serbian general and a Romanian aristocrat Maria Catargiu, became king Milan of Servbia between 1868 and 1869.

died at the age of ninety on May 19, 1905. My mother held him in great respect and often talked about his industriousness and about his highly affectionate relationship with his wife, children, and grandchildren. She always mentioned his distinguished manners and physical appearance.

Petre Mirică was Vasile's elder son who, in his old age, sold his estate in Oieşti and moved to Grand Ma Manini's estate in the village of Bârca. (I have already mentioned Vasile Mirică's younger son, Marin, or Uncle Marinică, who had studied economics in Anvers, France, and worked as an auditor at the Commercial Bank of Craiova.)

The reason my parents eventually separated and divorced was that she was much more interested in arts, fashion, period furniture, travel, and socializing. For example, when I was one year old, she and my father traveled to Karlsbad, the fashionable spa in Czechoslovakia where my father had been invited to attend a penal law conference. To satisfy my mother's taste for luxury, my father chose the posh Hotel Pupp.

Shortly after my mother traveled with her mother to Vienna, I was basically taken care of by my nurse because my father was really busy with his academic duties. As I have mentioned, he really spread himself thin by teaching courses at the Bucharest School of Law, the Military Academy, and the Police Academy while taking on duties as a founding member of the Higher Institute of Criminal Law Sciences or pursuing his pet project of codifying the Penal Code. Not only did these activities take a lot of his time, they also took a toll on their marriage. I am sure that my mother was brooding over the idea of divorce during long, lonely evenings when she was doing needle embroidery to kill time. Their interests were as different as the sun and the moon, and they gradually but surely grew apart to the point where divorce was imminent.

The divorce proceedings lasted for about two years, concluding in October 1935. During the procedures, my mother lived with Manini in Craiova. I find a blend of their character traits in me: I certainly inherited their dedication to work, law, and order as well as their patriotism.

On October 2, 1939, Mancy remarried and moved to Bucharest with her husband Alexandru Radian. I did not feel any resentment on hearing the news. Her absence from my life meant that such a decision, on her part, held little meaning for me.

When the time came for me to go to school, my father and Uncle Nicu decided that it was in my best interest to be schooled in private at home. I started school training when I was just five and a half years of age, which was early by the standards of those times. My tutor was a teacher from a nearby Boys School. (At the time there were no coed schools.) My new duties as a primary school student had an impact on my daily routines and certainly limited my opportunities to take trips around town with Haagi.

My tutor was Miss Petrescu, who came to our house every afternoon, Monday through Friday. She was a tall woman with prematurely grey hair and an imposing figure. But she was never intimidating. Her tender smile and nice demeanor gave me self-confidence and helped me overcome the age handicap. Miss Petrescu also helped me overcome the language handicap because, at the time, Romanian was kind of a second language for me.

At the completion of each school year, I had to go to Miss Petrescu's school for the graduation exam. In preparation, I attended a few of her classes just to get adjusted to the regular school environment. Every time I went to that school, I had to wear a school uniform consisting of a checkered black and white apron, a blouse with a lace collar and a red ribbon bow.

The exams consisted of oral questions that the teacher asked each student individually. We went in alphabetical order. As my name started with a *V*, I became increasingly nervous until my turn came. When my name was finally called, I walked to the front of the classroom, mounted a podium in front of a big blackboard, and waited for the question with trembling knees. There were about thirty boys in the classroom—an intimidating factor for me. I would quickly deliver the answer, looking straight ahead at the teacher and away from the classroom. As Miss Petrescu began nodding approvingly, my nervousness would miraculously melt. By the time she uttered the words, "Very well, thank you, you can return to your seat," I was walking on cloud nine, proud and relieved that I had gotten through that nightmare.

At the graduation ceremony, when Miss Petrescu was handing over the diplomas, I gave her a big bouquet of flowers. She congratulated and embraced me, then exchanged a few words with my father and Uncle Nicu. Of course, my graduation called for some sort of celebration. That usually meant that I was taken to the Monte Carlo garden restaurant in the Cişmigiu Park in the heart of Bucharest. By then, I was already in a summer recess mood and ready for the usual summer vacations, either to the Black Sea resorts, or to Craiova, or to one of the family countryside estates in the villages of Genune, Bârca, or Mihăiţa.

My home schooling during the primary school years finally came to an end. Being home meant that I had been deprived of any interaction with children of my age. But all the time, I had been surrounded by adults whose love and protection boosted my confidence.

After careful consultations with the family, my father decided that it was in my best interest to matriculate me in the exclusive French Boarding School Lycée[24] *Nôtre Dame de Sion,* which was also close to home. Grand-uncle Nae, in particular, advocated the idea because many of my aunts before me had gone to the same school. Not only that—as he would put it—"only those nuns are qualified to give young girls a top-notch education that conforms to our principles." So in 1937, I had to leave the protective cocoon that had been provided by my home schooling and plunge into a dramatically different, demanding, and austere environment.

At the *Lycée* most members of the didactic staff, with the exception of a few lay teachers, were nuns. Though school was private, it was homologated as a public school because—apart for the fact that teaching was done in French—its curriculum was modeled on that taught in public high schools around the country. The French language, of course, posed an additional problem for me. After the stress of having to perfect my Romanian during primary school years, now I was faced with the challenge of having to build my French speak-

---

24.   French for high school

ing skills. All I had as a meager foundation was a limited vocabulary picked up from conversations in French that I could occasionally overheard in our house.

The school had very strict rules. Non-boarders like me could only enter the school through a designated door on one side of the building. A nun was always standing at that door to supervise us, and we were supposed to greet her in French with "*Bonjour, ma mere.*" The uniform was a navy-blue dress which was tailored to our individual measurements. All dress items were available for purchase in the school store. Also required was a fabric girdle with tassels at each end, which we were supposed to wear on our waist at all times. The girdles were color coded for each of the eight grades. There were also different shoulder-to-waist cordons that were awarded to a select few for good behavior or to honor students for their outstanding academic achievements. The ultimate sign of recognition was a wide girdle, "*le grand cordon,*" awarded for both good behavior and outstanding academic results.

All school activities took place in an atmosphere of perfect discipline and order, always under the watchful eyes of chaperone nuns assigned to each grade. Each day followed a strict schedule. We started off with a morning prayer. After that, and before any other activity, the chaperone nun assigned to our group asked each of us, in alphabetic order, to evaluate our behavior of the prior day. I believe it was a good exercise to develop our consciousness and a sense of responsibility.

School days consisted of seven-hour classes. There were five classes in the morning between 8:00 a.m. and 1:00 p.m., followed by a lunch hour, then half an hour of the so-called main break. Afternoon classes began at two thirty and ended at four thirty.

The school church was quite spacious and well endowed. The mass reminded me of those I had attended in the Pitar Moș Church where I used to go with Haagi, and the choir sounded equally angelic.

For lunch we had to go to the refectory.[25] Each student had preassigned seats. We brought our own cutlery from home, with a matriculation number engraved on each utensil. We were supposed to go to the food table one by one, take a plate and then, to avoid talking, use sign language to communicate. Food was served by nuns wearing gray aprons and white, starched bonnets. During the meal, Mere[26] Concitta would tell us a story presented in installments over a number of days to catch our attention and keep us interested. In spite of the hundreds of students present in the room, there was nearly total silence, interrupted only by the clicking sounds of cutlery touching the plates.

After lunch time we would leave the room the same orderly way we had entered. Weather permitting during the remaining part of the break we usually played volleyball. When the weather was bad, we instead would return to our classroom where the chaperone nun told us a story. The narrative would come o an abrupt stop, sometimes even in the middle of a word, as soon as the bell signaled the end of the break.

Every Friday, one of the nuns assigned to supervise our class reviewed the grades we had earned during the week. She reprimanded those who were under performing. At her own discretion, she could temporarily withdraw the little cross chaplet that each of us wore, a punishment that put us down in front of all students in entire school. Most of the time, such humiliation was inflicted on us only for one week, after which the punishment would be lifted for improved per-formance and the cross chaplet would be returned to us.

At the end of each month each of us went through a more thorough evaluation For good behavior we would get "*un cordon de sagesse*."[27] For good academic performance we would get "*un cordon d'application*."[28] And there was yet another award called "*un cordon*

---

25. Dining hall or cafeteria especially in a monastery, convent, or col-lege
26. French for *mother*
27. French for "a rope girdle for wisdom"
28. French for "a rope girdle for talent"

de sagesse et d'application" for both good behavior and good academic performance. The worst shame was to lose the cross at these monthly evaluations.

At the end of the school year, there was "*l'assamblée generale*"[29] that was organized as a festive event in the big school assembly hall, involving the participation of the entire student, academic, and administrative bodies of the school. All students were assembled in rows arranged in a semi-circular pattern, with the smaller classes in front. The event was presided over by "*Notre Mère*" or "mother superior" who was seated at the center of a rectangular table flanked on both sides by senior academic and administrative staff members. After the award-giving ceremony all students would head to one of the two refectories where we would be served sweets and hot chocolate. At that time—as during the birthday celebration of the Mother Superior—the talking ban was lifted. The result was real mayhem, as if we were trying to make up for a whole school year when keeping quiet was an imposed code of behavior. Now, as a mature person looking back to how crazy we could get in an uncontrolled environment, I can relate to those nuns and understand the rationale behind those their strict discipline.

Later in life I came to the conclusion that stricter discipline and higher academic standards are more conducive to solid education than a lax discipline environment where students are not motivated to reach their full academic potential. From what I have observed, students who can choose instead to just have fun in school end up going nowhere.

From the moment I set foot in that school, or *pension* as it was called, a name copies from similar boarding or prep schools in France, I was fascinated by the way those nuns were dressed. With those starched bonnets and long robes covering their shoes, they moved around almost as if they were gliding on roller skates. Their creed was maintaining order and discipline in a clean environment, and they taught us the values of beauty, charity, generosity, sincerity,

---

29.   French for "general assembly"

friendship, courage, modesty, and, above all, the value of keeping God in our lives with reverence and love.

My initial adjustment to that environment was not easy. The fact that my first year was really difficult I would actually blame on my father. He ignored the fact that my French-language education left a lot to be desired, and he did not put me through the "*année preparatoire*" that most other parents did for their daughters. But there were other factors. Before Notre Dame I had been home schooled and had no experience interacting with other students. In addition, I entered the school at an early age, which meant I was the youngest in my class. So for me, it was an abrupt plunge into a very structured, demanding, and competitive environment.

Eventually, my father realized the many handicaps I was faced with and hired a private tutor, Mademoiselle Bonifaci, who was recommended by the school. In the first year she helped me catch up with the other students. She had an extremely pleasant personality and helped me a lot to understand and get more comfortable studying French. Because of my language handicap, I was spending long hours with my homework, sometimes studying until very late. That meant I was going to bed later than I was used to, which meant that waking up in the morning was a nightmare for me.

Haagi proved to be very supportive in my adjustment to the new strenuous schedule. She took me to school in the morning, then returned later to escort me home at the end of the day. With Mademoiselle Bonafaci's help I managed to catch up and get so well integrated in my new environment that I even started to get the envied *cordon d'application* and *cordon de sagesse* awards, which boosted my ego and my performance in school.

I still remember a great number of my former colleagues. Many of them grew to become important personalities in the political and cultural life of Romania. Our teachers also stand out in my memory. Due to their distinguished academic credentials, many went on to teach at universities both in Romania and abroad.

While most of our classes were taught in French, quite a few— such as the religion and dexterity classes—were taught in Romanian The religion classes taught in Romanian were conducted by Father

Cazacu, a Greek Orthodox priest. Girls who were Jewish, Catholic, and other religions (there was even a Chinese girl in my class) were excused unless they really wanted to attend, and could opt instead for a "general knowledge" class. Occasionally, Father Cazacu would take us on a field trip to attend the service at a neighborhood church where one of us would recite El Credo or the Apostles' Creed prayer.

Our music teacher was Miss Jantea, a petite woman who wore very high heels and piled her hair into a tall coiffure to compensate for her short built. Of all the other teachers, she was the one who wore heaviest makeup. As I have indicated, however, music was not my strength. As Christmas approached, Miss Jantea would put together a choir with the participation of the entire class and start rehearsing Christmas carols with us. As much as I would have liked to be part of that annual choir, she excluded me with the words, "Vrăbiescu, you are excused because you are not in unison with the others." Invariably, that made me miserable, but I couldn't argue with her decision. It was in my genes to have a really deaf ear for music. If only I had inherited my maternal grandmother Manini's genes, on the Mirica side of the family, I feel this would have been a total different story! (Manini was so talented, she had wanted to pursue a musical career and become an opera singer: only the provincial misconceptions of the time prevented her from doing so.)

Besides my memories from the school years, I have many other recollections from our time on Negustori Street. I remember that one day the mailman brought us a rather bulky package that had mailed to us from an address in England that was unknown to us. There was a short debate about whether we could possibly be the right recipients of the package, because none of us knew anybody in England. But finally my father took a clasp knife and opened the package. Inside was a metallic box, and when he impatiently opened the lid he found some granulated stuff resembling coarse sand or garden fertilizer that smelled slightly smoky. My father was adventurous enough to take a few grains and taste them, hoping that he might get a clue about what that stuff was. Uncle Nicu did the same, hoping he could shed some light on the contents of the mysterious package, and of course I aped their actions. There was further discussion and, again, both my father and uncle concluded the package had been delivered to us in error, even though the address was accurate. We finally gave up, called Leana, and asked her to take the mysterious box to the basement where we planned to leave until we could figure out what it was all that about.

That evening, we got a number of phone calls, one from Uncle Costinel Vorvoreanu, who was first cousin to my father and Uncle Nicu. At the time, Uncle Costinel was in the process of moving from the town of Craiova to Bucharest. All of a sudden, I heard my father exclaiming, "Oh my god! I cannot believe that! But my dear Costinel, how come you waited until now to let us know?"

Uncle Nicu and I drew closer, curious to find out the cause of my father's excitement. After hanging up, my father told us in a solemn but kind of amused voice, "You will not believe this! We all had a taste of Memerle!"

I shall never forget Uncle Nicu's face, so clearly indignant at Uncle Costinel's negligent failure to warn us about the package. As for myself, I was not sure whether it was appropriate to laugh under the circumstances. I had met Memerle in Craiova, prior to her departure to her native England. Uncle Costinel's wife, Tante Marqueritte, had hired her as a governess for my cousin Ion. After Memerle left, she had hired Mrs. Moeser, who was also English. (She would only have English governesses for her two sons.) Memerle included instructions in her will that half of her ashes should be sent to Romania, the country where she had spent most of her life and had come to love like her own. Because Uncle Costinel was in the process of moving and did not have a permanent address yet, it was our address that he gave to the executors of Memerle's will for the mailing of her ashes.

Maman Titi and Haagi were totally horrified when they realized what the contents of the metal box were. Leana, our domestic, expressed her concern that we might get sick, but as it turned out we were unaffected by our taste of the ashes. May God rest Memerle's soul in peace.

Other memories from those years include bits and pieces of current events that I would overhear the grownups commenting on. I found out that at the beginning of 1938, following what was later known as a "palace coup," King Carol II of Romania[30] abolished Parliament and banned all political parties together with the Constitution that had been in place since 1923. My family was not very happy with the King's dictatorial actions.

From conversations that I overheard, I also became familiar with the name Hitler, a guy who they thought posed a danger to Romania because of his professed position was that the Versailles and Trianon Treaties of 1919 and 1920[31] had to be revised. I did not understand much of their conversations, and at that time could not have cared less about Hitler's attempts to convince the world about the superiority of the German population. But one thing was clear to me—that the grownups were really concerned about the dangers facing the world and our country, too. Being too immature to share their concerns and fears, I just laughed when I heard Hitler shouting during the speeches that were broadcast by our radio stations.

But I realized the seriousness of the world situation when I witnessed how devastated Haagi was after the *"Anschluss"* when Germany annexed Austria on March 11, 1938. At the time, Hitler had started to make aggressive moves against neighboring countries and figured that it was only natural to annex Austria, considered by him to be a German-speaking country. Haagi was particularly saddened by the arrest of the Austrian chancellor Kurt von Schuschnigg who had struggled to keep Austria independent. She was an Austrian patriot but at the same time very attached to Romania. When Germany annexed Austria, she would express her grief to my father and was very appreciative that he fully shared her views.

Later in life, I learned more about Hitler, how he rose to power after becoming the leader of the German Workers' National Socialist

---

30. Eldest son of Ferdinand, King of Romania, and his wife, Queen Marie, a daughter of Prince Alfred, Duke of Edinburgh, the second eldest son of Queen Victoria, was better known for his amorous misadventures than for his leadership skills.

31. Peace treaties after WWI between the Allied forces on the one hand and Associated Powers and Hungary on the other that gave Romania substantial territorial gains.

Party in 1933 and how he managed to escape the restrictions imposed by the provisions of Article XX of the Covenant of the League of Nations. I came to see that as proof of the inefficiency of the League, which had also encouraged him to withdraw from it. (The League of Nations was subsequently replaced by the United Nations in 1945 in Yalta.) I also learned how later, through militarism, he had gained the trust of his nation.

During those childhood years, though world events were the least of my concerns. At that stage in my life I would rather think ahead with great anticipation to forthcoming vacations. In addition, in 1938, my father and uncle Nicu bought a building plot in a beautiful residential area in the heart of Bucharest called the Armaşului Lane. The house to be built there would be larger and nicer than the house in the Negustori Street. That of course made me very excited, all the more so that I got assurances that the fowl, Rita the turtle and all the other little animals from Negustori Street would accompany us to the backyard of the new residence.

CHAPTER 3

Vacations: The Carmen Sylva Resort and Family Estates

In 1934, at Haagerchen's suggestion and following Tante Grete's insistence, my father agreed to let me join Tante Grete and Helga on their annual July trip to the seaside resort of Carmen Sylva. I was overjoyed at the prospect of spending part of my summer vacation with Helga, all the more so that this escape was to the Black Sea where I had never been before. And to top it all off, we were going to the Voicana family villa where a lot of children would be gathered, including Alice, Dan, and Mircea. What a tremendous joy!

(As it turned out, our vacations for the next six years in a row would be equally well planned and eagerly anticipated. Each vacation seemed to be more beautiful than the last, as we spent weeks each summer floating between the sky and the sea with the smell of sea salt in the air.)

In the morning, all the children headed to the seaside under the supervision of Aunt Grete and Haagi, of course. We, the kids, would always leave the grownups behind as we sped down the path through the weeds and reeds of a steep coastline. Our headlong rush took us directly into the water where we would do somersaults, swim, and open our arms to embrace the sky. We often played with a ball while Aunt Grete and Haagi kept a watchful eye on us from the shore, like mama ducks watch their baby ducklings in the water. For us it was all fun and joy, though for them I am sure it involved a lot of stress as they could not wait to see us return safe and sound back to shore as quickly as possible

After lunch and a one-hour afternoon nap, we children would frequently regroup on the field right next to the villa where we would play soccer, run our guts out. We got back to our rooms all sweaty and full of dust. On occasion, we would go visit the mosque with its tall minaret in the nearby resort of Mangalia, where there was a substantial Tartar ethnic community and where women wore multicolored baggy bloomers called shalvars and had scarves covering their faces. In the evening we would eat out at a restaurant, then take a walk on the beach. I shall never forget those gorgeous nights when a full moon, hung in the black starry sky, its light reflected as a long stretch of silver on a calm sea. That fairytale scenery is still vivid in my mind to this day.

Another memory that will forever be with me was the image of the Carmen Sylva resort in mourning with purple flags waving at half mast throughout the city. The occasion was the passing of Queen Mary of Romania, who died in July1938. She was loved dearly by the Romanian people, especially for her successful efforts to get the best deal for Romania at the end of World War I. Mary had been born in England as the daughter of Alfred Duke of Edinburg, Queen Victoria's younger son, and Mary, the daughter of Tsar Alexander II of Russia. Queen Mary of Romania was buried in the Cathedral of the town of Curtea de Arges,[32] but according to her will, her heart was consigned to an urn and placed in the chapel of her summer palace in the Black Sea resort of Balchik. I revisited this palace in

---

32. King Carol the First of Romania, his wife Queen Elizabeth and King Ferdinand, Queen Mary's husband, are also buried in that cathedral

2008, with its English style terraces and gardens climbing down to the shores of the Black Sea. When Balchik became part of Bulgaria,[33] her heart was brought back to Romania.

Before returning to Bucharest from Carmen Sylva, Haagi and I would usually take a train to Romania's main Black Sea port of Constanța to hook up with my father. In Constanța I was always impressed with the big white ships docked in the port as well as the beautiful rococo style Casino by the sea. From there we would head to Hotel Rex, well-known throughout Eastern Europe for its elegance. During our few days' stay I was very excited to be able to swim with my father either in the sea or in the hotel pool. For lunch or dinner we would eat all kinds of crustaceans and fish at the hotel restaurant while hotel guests were dancing to the tune of a live, cafe concert band.

On our way back from Constanța I was filled with joy knowing that we were going back to our countryside estate of Genune. I looked forward to taking the train to Craiova.

In the Town of Craiova with the Vrăbiescu clan

In Craiova we usually stayed in the house of Uncle Miti Brănețu, Maman Titi's younger brother. He lived in a quiet residential area where the silence of the night was disturbed only by the trample of horseshoes on the pavement. Before heading off to the countryside, Maman Titi took me along on family visits where she proudly paraded me.

While describing these family visits I will also take the opportunity to portray some of the numerous members of the Vrăbiescu and Vorvoreanu families, two pretty large clans. In fact, from what I heard they were among the most prominent families in Craiov.

So my grandfather Constantine Vrăbiescu had married Anghelina or Angela, born Caneciu, who was the daughter of the

---

33. In 1940, just before the outbreak of World War II Balchik was ceded by Romania to Bulgaria in keeping with the terms of the Craiova Treaty.

first architect of Craiova. They had three sons and three daughters. The boys were my Grandfather Gheorghe or Iorgu, Iancu or Iulian, and Nicolae or Uncle Nae. The daughters were Polixenia or Aunt Pauline, Matilda, and Eliza. I know nothing about the last two.

Grandpa Iorgu owned a house on Buzesti Street near his sister Paulina and died suddenly of a heart attack when he was only fifty-one years old. Among the Vrăbiescu brothers, the one I knew best was Uncle Nae, because he lived with us during the winter. After graduating from high school, he first went on to study in Vienna at the Therezianum Gymnasium.[34] He later studied engineering in Charlottenburg, near Berlin, Germany, and at École Centrale in Paris, France. Despite his extensive education, Uncle Nae's lifelong passion was to travel the world. Though never married, he assumed many of the responsibilities of caring for his nephews Gică and Nicu, his older brother Iorgu's orphans.

We would also visit Uncle Iulian. He had graduated from the National College Carol I, then studied in Paris, France, where he received his doctorate degree in law. At some point he was elected Mayor of Craiova, and, during the peasant uprising against land leaseholders[35] he was the Prefect[36] of Dolj County. As a member of the National Liberal Party, he became a senator for Dolj County in Romania's Parliament.

Maman Titi would also take me to visit *Tante Pauline,* my grandfather's eldest daughter. My great grandfather sent her to a boarding school for girls in Vienna, and in 1872 she married George Vorvoreanu. For her help during the War of Independence in 1877–1878, she was awarded the Order of the Knight first grade. I vividly recall her appearance: she wore a lace collar over a dark silk dress and

---

34. In some European countries, particularly in Germany, gymnasium was a secondary school where the emphasis was on academic subjects rather than on technical training

35. Land leaseholders were always perceived as the exploiting rural villains as opposed to the respectable land owners who were detached from day to day operations and often financed various local philanthropic projects

36. The highest ranking official in an administrative county.

what were called *mittens*, actually, crocheted lace fingerless gloves. Those gloves mesmerized me as I had never seen their like before.

Tante Pauline's husband, George Vorvoreanu, educated in Germany, was an industrialist and landowner active in politics who became a prominent member of the National Liberal Party. As a great philanthropist, he contributed funds for the maintenance or building of various Craiova institutions.

The Vorvoreanus had ten children, of whom only seven survived. I met all seven of them as well as their spouses and offspring. The house they built was in fact a mansion, one of the largest in Craiova, an imposing baroque structure decorated with paintings by Francis Tribalsky. Tante Pauline died right after Uncle Gogu in 1944 at the age of ninety, which was fortuitous in the sense that she never had to witness their house being taken over by communists. There are reports that the basement of the house was used by the NKVD[37] as a place where politicians were brought, interrogated, and tortured. Subsequently, the Vorvoreanu house became the Metropolitan Building, the name for the residence of the metropolitan bishop of Oltenia.

(Decades later, in 2007, I was informed by a good friend that a book with the title *A Native of Craiova on the World Meridiens: Travel Impressions at the Turn off the 19th Century* had been published in Craiova. I suspected that the native of Craiova might in fact be my grandfather's brother Uncle Nae. So when I went to Craiova, I spoke with the editor and introduced myself as a possible grandniece of the native of Craiova. As I browsed through the pages of the book, my suspicion were confirmed: the book was in fact a compilation the letters Uncle Nae had addressed to his sister Paulina, with detailed impressions from exotic far-away places that he had visited. The letters were written between 1895 and 1926 and were sent from Europe, North America, Central America, South America, and North Africa. I made this discovery at a time when I believed I was the only one in the Vrăbiescu family who set foot in America. What a surprise! From this book, published quite unexpectedly in 2007, I learned that my

---

37.   Russian secret police

Uncle Nae had seen much more of America than I had. The letters were found in the basement of Vorvoreanu house by the metropolitan bishop, who sent them to the Oltenia Archives)

Apart from the family visits, my father used to take Haagi and me to have lunch at the Minerva restaurant and brasserie on Unirii Avenue, built in Moorish style within a hotel by the same name. Once, when Dad, Haagi and I were having lunch there, Haagi asked the waiter to put a pillow on my chair so that I could reach the table. After I had finished eating, a gentleman from a nearby table came to us and introduced himself. My father stood up and politely shook the gentleman's hand but seemed puzzled when the stranger observed, "I suspect that the little girl is yours because she really resembles you, but I would like to know how old she is." Increasingly curious to find out what was that about, Dad answered, "Yes! She is indeed my daughter. She is five years and four months old. But why do you want to know?" To which that gentleman replied, "Ah! I want to congratulate her for her exquisite table manners. I have never seen a child her age handle her knife and fork so nicely. I was impressed by the way she raised the fork to her mouth instead of leaning over the plate." After my father thanked the man for his remarks, the gentleman said good-bye, but not before he pinched my cheek affectionately and kissing my hand as though I had been a grown woman.

When my father translated the gentleman's comments to Haagi, she looked at me with considerable pride in her own accomplishment as well as mine. "See," said Haagi, "I taught you very well how to use the cutlery properly by making you hold a book under each armpit while eating. I am glad someone noticed the results of what I taught you!"

Of course! It all came back to me—how much I had struggled to get to stick something into my mouth while maintaining an almost impossible position, holding the books so they wouldn't fall. But on that day my efforts and perseverance were rewarded!

My father and Uncle Nicu were not regular churchgoers, but on Easter they respected the Christian tradition. On that day the three of us always attended Holy Thursday and Friday liturgies as well as the Saturday midnight Resurrection mass at St. Demetrios Church, the metropolitan cathedral of Craiova.

When I was a teenager, my dad often took me for a walk on Unirii Avenue, one of Craiova's main boulevards, which was always bustling with throngs of people. I was mesmerized by the opulent shop windows, such as the Mendel jewelry store, the Englishman store displaying fabrics of all kinds, or the "Paris Chic" clothing store. From time to time, in the evening we had dinner in the garden of Minerva restaurant. Here I had the opportunity to see Uncle Angel Chiciu, my father's cousin, a local sculptor who had studied in Paris and was a disciple of Constantin Brâncuși.

In Craiova with members of the Mirică family—the folks on my mother's side

In Craiova, Haagi would often take me on extended visits to the house of my maternal grandmother Manini where I would usually hang around with Ioana Herescu, my first cousin. Manini's house was in a nice residential neighborhood the hallway led to a series of rooms that were all beautifully decorated with furniture inherited from the Calafat Palace. In the dining room there was a piano with a beautiful framed photo on top often or Benjamin Gigli, with a signed dedication to his student Lucreția Cionea.

In my eyes, Manini was a woman of many qualities. She had a generous heart and she was a good wife, mother and grandmother, with a fine spirit and refined tastes. She was also a skilled home-maker, famous for her hospitality. The meals she presented were always wonderfully arranged, with crystal glasses, silver cutlery, and special dishes that were always beautifully presented. She herself was exceedingly beautiful, and even as she aged her delicate features were still striking. Her perfect nose was unmatched by anyone in the family, and her fair complexion contrasted with big green eyes that lit up with every smile. Back in her younger days, she was said to have spent substantial sums of money on "haute couture" in Vienna and Paris. She had been educated at a boarding school and was very cultured for her times, speaking perfect French and German. And she was also pious, always attending church on Sundays, where she lit candles in memory of her deceased loved ones.

Manini had a fortunate start in life. She benefited from a dowry left to her by her father and her husband Anastase Gh. Cionea, also known as Shicu (as she would call him). She had two daughters, but it seems her marriage was not exactly a happy one. Later in her life, she spent a lot of time in Lausanne, Switzerland, because she felt that the fresh air over there was beneficial to the health of her girls. Mother and daughters lived at Hotel Cecile with the governess, making a household of four. Uncle Marinică, her brother—slender, elegant, a heavy smoker—would often come to visit bearing goodies and gifts, to the great joy of the girls who saw in him the father figure they never had.

Manini, being fluent in both French and German, was very much attracted by Western civilization and music. Music, especially, was her lifelong passion which she indulged by striving to deepen and broaden her knowledge and appreciation. Endowed by nature with a beautiful voice, she made an initial attempt to cultivate by taking voice lessons at the Cornetti Conservatory in Craiova. Both her voice and her musical talents she had inherited from her father, yet it was her father who cut off her wings by forcing her to marry, at age sixteen, a man twenty years her senior. But while she was abroad and taking advantage of her newly found independence, she resumed her vocal studies.

At some point Manini even studied with the famous tenor Benjamino Gigli. With an impressive breath capacity and a cultivated voice, it seems she had everything she needed to become an operatic soprano. She once told me that even the great George Enescu,[38] whom she had met in Romania when he was giving concerts at the Peleş Castle,[39] expressed admiration for her voice and predicted that she was destined for an operatic career. But as I mentioned, both

---

38. George Enescu (1881–1955) Romanian composer, violinist, pianist, conductor, and teacher.
39. The summer residence of the Romanian royal family

her father Vasile Mirica and her brother Marinică were vehemently against her pursuing such a career which they probably viewed as demeaning for a respectable person.

Unfortunately, Manini's only public appearance on stage was at the Great Theatre of Lausanne. As soon as she got to New York in 1972, my mother—who was a very energetic woman—wrote to the Archives of Lausanne and asked for documents about that performance. Soon after, my mother received the requested documents including the performance poster and several reviews from local newspapers. Typical was an announcement in *Feuilled'Avis de Lausanne* saying, "A Romanian charity event to raise funds for the victims of the Romanian army during the First World War took place on Wednesday, the fifth of June 1918 at 8:30 p.m. with the gracious contribution of Mrs. Lucretia Cionea and actress Lucia Sturdza-Bulandra."[40] In another newspaper, *La Tribune de Lausanne,* the reviewer wrote, "Miss Cionea's interpretation of Romanian folk songs and other songs by composer Constantin Brăiloiu was absolutely remarkable. Miss Sturdza-Bulandra recited poems by Romanian and French poets with admirable emotion. The success of the show was so significant that its proceeds were used to benefit war veterans." From this evidence I can only conclude with regret that Lucreția Mirica-Cionea remained the victim of the provincial Craiovan mentality of the times when women were subject to the will of the men of the family. A career that could have been remarkable was destroyed by their disapproval.

Later in her life, Manini returned to Craiova where she was remarried, in 1921, to Nicolae Defleury, a forty-five year old lawyer whom we called Tata Lae.[41] Tata Lae had no estates, but was a handsome man always smartly dressed. His grandfather was Count De Fleury, who came to Romania as a French Consul General in the time of King Carol I.

---

40.   A venerated Romanian drama actress who, together with her husband, owned a prestigious theatre company
41.   Romanian for *father*

Manini was always happy to have my cousin Ioana Herescu and me visit her home for a few weeks. Each of us had our own room with our own governess—those who had formerly been the rooms of Tancy and Mancy. Ioana, resembling her extremely tall parents, was then the same height as me even though she was four years younger. Manini would spoil us by inviting all the friends who were our age into her spacious home.

One day, when I was about four years old, I opened the living-room door and found myself face-to-face with my mother. Standing there in the doorway, she looked to me like a framed picture—tall, beautiful, and imposing! It was a shock for both of us. She had not expected to see me, nor did I ever expect to suddenly bump into her. Though she seemed to be in a hurry, and appeared confused, she managed to ask, "Was machst Du hier?" (What are you doing here?) Not only was I taken aback, I noticed immediately that she wasn't much impressed to see me there. I started to cry. Mother could not quite understand my reaction and asked Haagi why I was crying, to which Haagi responded, "Veil Moni hat sich erwartet das sie werden sich freuen sie zu sehen und kussen." " (Perhaps Moni was expecting you would be glad to see her and kiss her.) At that moment Manini showed up coming from the kitchen corridor. She too apparently had no idea that mother had come into the house through the front door, but Manini noticed me crying, came next to me, kindly put her hand on my head, and called me, "My little one!" as she usually did when she caressed me. She then grabbed mother swiftly by the shoulders, and off they went into her bedroom. I do not know what she told my mother, but I do remember mother's voice answering "*Mais, maman…Mais, maman*"[42] as if to apologize. I'm sure Manini understood my interior drama caused by the shock of seeing my mother again. Such encounters happened rarely, and on that day it had been completely unexpected.

---

42.   "But mother…but mother…"

Manini belonged to one of Oltenia's high class families,[43] so it was only fitting that she would invite her friends over for tea in the Biedermayer lounge where she set out the Sevres porcelain cups on lace tablecloths. Occasionally their conversations were in French as many of the ladies had been educated in French schools. Some were well-known local philanthropists and one, as I heard, helped the famous Romanian sculptor Brancusi assemble his monumental sculptures in the central park of the town of Târgu Jiu. Manini was always our guide to better taste, saying that beauty starts with what you wear and it distinguishes you from others. Further, she declared "beauty" always depends on the love you express and the interest you show in others. She was never strict with us, which was very unlike the way she had raised her daughters, but on the other hand, we always behaved nicely as Manini was the last person we ever wanted to disappoint.

I still have fresh memories of the mornings when Manini, after busying herself in the pantry and kitchen, would (as a general rule) vocalize for at least half an hour before the meal, which she did to "maintain her voice." After 1941, Tata Lae's son Dǎnel was frequently eating with us, and he would often invite me to dance to radio music before Manini and grandfather came home from the Club. Those were tender moments that I cherish to this day—remembering those times when I was a teenager fast becoming a young lady.

When I grew older, Tata Lae and I used to go for walks that took us all the way to the Youth Club, our final destination.

Each Christmas, Grandfather Lae and Manini would go out of their way to please us. On Christmas Eve the tree was decorated beautifully in the Biedermayer salon, and we would find our gifts beneath its branches. On the first day of Christmas, the whole family would have a festive lunch, and the next day our friends were invited over. Manini and Tancy—always present for the holidays—arranged the table with various goodies for the young ones. There were all

---

43.   Oltenia is a historical province and geographical region of Romania, in western Wallachia.

kinds of sandwiches, along with the customary *Linzertorte*[44] or other chocolate cakes and—of course—the traditional *cozonac*, a pound cake similar to the Italian *panettone* or the Polish *babka*.

Once I had a great surprise. While sitting with my friends at the table, I heard the sound of bells jingling outside in the yard. Ioana and I leapt to the windows just in time to see two horse-drawn sledges pull into our yard. Manini told us to get dressed as the sledges were a present for us. We went outside all muffled up with warm cloths and hats, jumped onto those sledges, covered ourselves with thick blankets, and off we went, riding all the way to the Bibescu-Romanescu Park. Then we walked in the park, immersing ourselves in that enchanting, fairy-tale scenery. Everything in the entire park was covered by sparkling fresh snow. It was simply wonderful! Arranging that sleigh ride for us was entirely Grandfather Lae's idea.

Before Easter, everybody strictly observe Lent, fasting at least during the Holy Week, until after the midnight Resurrection mass that we would all attend at a nearby neighborhood church. Manini explained to us that fasting was the way to both physical and spiritual renewal in preparation for celebrating the Resurrection. On Easter Sunday, Manini and Tancy would hide presents for us in the green garden.

The series of joyful holiday seasons that we enjoyed for many years in Craiova were brutally interrupted in September 1939 by the outbreak of World War II after the Germans occupied Poland. A wave of Polish refugees appeared in Craiova; they were well received and well treated by the locals. Among them were many respectable people such as the Polish countess whom Manini invited to live in her house. She offered the countess her grandfather's former law office and treated her like family. Our guest often ate with us and was invited to the ladies' afternoon tea gatherings or card games. I had a lot of compassion for her though of course it never occurred to me that in a few short years I would find myself in her situation.

---

44. Linzertorte is a cake named after the city of Linz, Austria, where it originated.

In 1940, after the Soviet occupation of Basarabia and Northern Bucovina,[45] the Ion Naiculescu family received in their home a refugee, Ladis Kristof born in Bucovina, whom I befriended. It was he who told us about the horrors of communism brought in the region by the Russians. (I was to meet him again in 1988 at the Congress of Romanian-American Academy held in Portland, Oregon, where Ladis was a professor at the University of Oregon and the organizer of that year's congress.)

During the summers, I was a visitor at the family estates— either Vrăbiescu's Genune, Neamțu's Curtișoara, Mirica's Bârca, Defleury's Mihăița, or Cionea's Radomir (which was administered by my mother).

The Genune Estate

Each of these visits made a great impression on me. Among my favorites was the Genune estate, which had its own history. After the death of my grandfather George (Iorgu) Vrăbiescu in 1904, my grandmother together with her two sons took care of it. Because of my parents' divorce, my dad further split his portion of arable land into two equal areas, bequeathing one to me.

We usually went to Genune by carriage, reaching the Genune mansion after a three-hour trip. My greatest joy was to sit next to the coachman and help drive the horses. My emotions would start going wild with joy at the thought of seeing Genune again. My spirits rose higher and higher as we passed various familiar turnoffs, one to the left opening on a forest of acacias with fox burrows and vineyards, one to the right leading to an orchard of plum trees. The horses accelerated, rushing to get faster in the barn, and by the time the carriage entered the estate, the wheels were turning furiously. We sped

---

45. Basarabia and Bocovina are historical regions of Eastern and Northern Romania. Nowadays the bulk of Basarabia is part of the former Soviet Republic of Moldova while its northern and southern areas as well as Northern Bocovia became part of the Ukraine following the Molotov-Ribbentrop pact of 1940.

through the gates that were opened especially for us and entered an allee lined with big, lofty poplars.

Halting in front of the main stairs of the house, we heard the disturbing screaming of the twenty-two pairs of peacocks that had been alarmed by the tramp of horses. I would jump off the boxwood, thrilled to have arrived. A life all mine! We would be welcomed by the administrator, by those in the yard, and by the dogs which would showed us a real demonstration of happiness and love as only dogs know how to do it. All the dogs came from herding and hunting breeds. The hunting dogs—Joc, Hep, and Tom—were allowed to enter the main hall of the house. Joc had white hair with bricky spots; Hep and Tom were also white but with dark brown spots. All were equally spoiled, cared for, and caressed.

The estate (whose house is shone on the cover of the volume) had been located on a hill to ensure good water drainage. There it stood just like a small citadel, with a high wall surrounding the buildings, flanked by trees, greenery, flowers, birds, and other animals. The big house was white with a tin roof painted red, which was dome-shaped above the main entrance.

Since winters were cold, all the bedrooms had stoves. The long, wide hallway also served as a dining room where a pendulum clock surrounded by many plates in the Oltenia style, was a dominant feature. There was also a fox, preserved by taxidermy and mounted on a board, that was a hunting prize of Uncle Nicu. Right next to the pantry was a ladder leading to the attic where they kept honey, ropes of onions or garlic, nuts, and other food that would be sent on to Bucharest during the winter. The large cellar was a woodworking room, where there was a table surrounded by saws and with tools hanging on the walls. Here were made all kinds of supplies for the estate, including kites for me. I liked to watch the working process and would be amused by the sight of golden wood curls coming of the jointer like furious springs that jumped to the floor.

In front of the house was a large, beautiful garden with flowers and apple trees, plum trees, and big apricot trees. It was separated from the rest of the yard by a fence to protect the garden from dogs and marauding birds. A few pairs of peacocks from the existing flock were allowed to settle in the garden. (Another pair of peacocks roamed freely around other parts of the estate.) In the back of the garden there were white beehives managed by the one and only Uncle Nicu. It was he who oversaw the honey gathering, when the filled honeycombs were placed in cheesecloth and hung over enameled bowls in from which honey as pure as clear amber seeped slowly. Whenever he would manage the beehives, he was dressed in a suit of white cotton, wearing a wire cloth shaped like a balloon over his head to protect him from the bees he troubled while working the hives. At dawn I could hear the chuckle of dozens of fowls when old Dina was feeding them by sprinkling a straight line of corn or wheat to tempt the chickens and roosters of all colors, geese, plain ducks or Muscovy ducks, black, white or beige turkeys, guinea hens, peacocks, pigeons and sparrows. From the back of the yard I could hear the bellow of the cows ready to be milked, the squeal of pigs, the neigh of horses. I also heard the creaking of the chains at the two wells, where clear cool water was hoisted up in wooden buckets,

During the day I moved freely around the estate, always in search of some activity. I would go to the big warehouse where the young female landholders[46] sifted the wheat with shovels to get some air. Among the girls, the most talkative and cheerful one was nicknamed Curca ('turkey hen'). She liked to cover me in wheat all the way up to my neck, so only my head remained visible. A long time later, in 1995, when I returned to visit the country, I also went to Lazu village, and when Curca heard that I was there she came running at full pelt, took me in her arms. We both cried, not only because of the excitement of our meeting again but also because we both knew how difficult the years had been since our separation.

---

46. The Manorial System, a method of landholding by the peasants. The fundamental characteristic of the manorial system was economic—the peasants held land from the lord (Fr. *seigneur*) of an estate in return for fixed dues in kind, money, and services. The manorial system prevailed in France, England, Germany, Spain, and Italy and far into Eastern Europe.

Sometimes, before dinner I would stop at the basement kitchen occupied by the mansion staff where I would have a bowl of bean soup or sheep soup, both incredibly tasty, served with a slice of polenta (rom. *mămăligă*). As for the days when the bread was being baked in the large oven, I remember I always made a point of being there when the loaves were slid out from the heated oven on a wide wooden shovel. Baring my teeth, I bit off the crustiest heel while it was still hot, sniffing its divine smell. Ever since then, whenever I catch a sniff of hot black bread, the scent of newly baked wheat, if I close my eyes—no matter where I am—I associate the bread making with the one in Genune, giving me the genuine feeling that I am suddenly right there, at that place that remained like an adamantine stone in my heart.

We usually had lunch inside the house or in the yard under the big old chestnut where we were surrounded by the hunting dogs. The conversation revolved around the meals, especially if we were having *gibier*,[47] rabbit or quail, and around the latest hunting adventures After lunch, as the climbing turned the afternoon to blazing heat, we retired to the cool house where time seemed to pass slowly and quietly, accompanied by the rhythm of the pendulum clock on the wall. Every now and then the quiet would be interrupted by the hour and half-hour strikes, but the buzzing of a fly, or by sounds from the snoring dogs, Joc, Hep or Tom. Around four o'clock, it was time to entertain myself, which I did by learning how to play back gammon with Uncle Nicu. After that I had my reading time either with Haagi in German or with Maman Titi in French. Since French was the language I had not quite mastered at the time, Maman Titi would force me to read aloud certain translations of the books of Walter Scott's *Ivanhoe*, or Charles Dickens's *David Copperfield, Oliver Twist, Nicholas Nickleby*, and others. But I think these readings were also a pretext for keeping me close to her so she could give me all sorts of advice, demonstrating how much she loved me.

I would often take walks with Haagi through the garden or in the woods. She had always been by my side, but in 1938 when

---

47.   (Fr.) Wild fowl; game.

I became a student at Notre Dame de Sion, my father hired for the summer Mademoiselle Pellee, a French woman, so that I could speak more French. Sometimes when Mlle Pellee called me to start the lessons, I would hide up in the apple tree at the entrance to the garden and pretend not to hear her. At other times I would go together with Uncle Nicu to fly a kite on Tomei hill, where the arable-land hectares of the estate were, and almost constantly, the wind howled and screamed. My uncle would study the direction of the wind before we decided how to elevate the kite on the breeze.

When I turned nine or ten, together with Mitică the administrator or Uncle Nicu I would ride the horses to go see the harvest or the tillage. Sometimes I would go by myself to meet with my girlfriends, the daughters of Mitiță, the priest who baptized me. Our relationship with the locals was based on a sense of mutual respect: the villagers respected the boyar from the mansion that helped whenever necessary, and we would respect their work and friendship. I have the warmest feelings toward those who remain in my memory of those days, and I think that those feelings were mutual.

Whenever my father and Uncle Nicu went to grab their hunting rifles, Joc, Hep and Tom started goofing around like mad dogs, barking, yelping, jumping, running back and forth across the yard to see if we were coming. Once we set out, they would run way ahead of us on the field, sniffing the trails in the stubble or in the corn field. When I grew a bit older, I used to go along with the men, armed with a *flaubert*, and Uncle Nicu taught me how to aim using that small rifle. From my uncle Nicu I learned how to recharge rifle cartridges and also how to skin rabbits myself.

Daddy spent less time with us, as he was held back in Bucharest. When he was expected to go, the empty carriage would be sent to Craiova to pick him up. On his return to the country, I would always be waiting in front of the vineyard to welcome him. When the coachman saw me, he stopped the horses, and I climbed into the carriage directly into my father's arms, at the same time enjoying the welcoming words of Uncle Iancu Hagi-Preda or cousin Mitsu Chiciu who always accompanied him.

I was attached to Uncle Iancu Hagi-Preda, who was not a relative but who treated us as if we were related; in fact, he was like part of the family. Long time in advance of his demise, he had prudently ordered a cross of white marble together with a marble slab on which was marked, all in black letters, the names George, Nicolae, Ecaterina, Mona Vrăbiescu. This monument was placed at the spring well not far from the hill with the vineyard.

(Back then, I had no clue that this cross and plaque would remain the only witnesses to the presence of the manor of the Vrăbiesti family that would survive the year 1949 when everything was looted. It is obvious to me, however, that the locals were afraid and didn't defile the cross, as the atheistic communism failed to completely break the people's faith. When I was there in 2010, the cross and the plaque were gone. Theft had replaced faith.)

When my father arrived, all the people were thrilled to be around him. They wanted to consult with him about their problems—a child in college, a patient in Craiova, a financial problem, and so on and so forth. My father and Uncle Nicu treated all visitors to shots of brandy as they shared their troubles. The Vrâbiescu family had always taken good care of those who shared with them a part of the agricultural land. They respected us and were attached to us, out of consideration for the fair and friendly manner in which they were treated.

Spending Easter at Genune meant living the joy of revived senses, awakened to the spring of life. I can still see the yellow rape field stretching as far as the eye can see, the poplars along the allee, their branches covered with tens of talkative, chirping sparrows that would descend to bathe in little ponds after every rain. Before me was the big white house with red roof, its façade covered in purple wisteria flowers, the abundant colors of roses in the garden. I can still remember the smell of those roses; I can still hear the call of the cuckoo echoing up from the bottom of the valley or the long and frequent cries of the fluffed peacocks that welcomed the coming of spring. These are feelings I still keep intact, to myself, untouched by anyone or anything.

In the summer before the threshing, you could see the wheat fields with the tall grain almost the height of a man rippling in the breeze. Around the threshing floor there was a deafening noise, and in the heat of late afternoon I would get a lot of dust in my hair, on my eyelashes, on my clothes. Always present at the threshing floor were Mitică and Uncle Nicu, surrounded by Joc, Hep, and Tom. Whenever Uncle Nicu was talking with the sharecroppers about the harvest, he would winnow a handful of grain from one hand to another in order to see the size and the quality of the wheat, barley, or oats.

The estate's primary income was derived from selling cereals produced there, or from tithes. The grains were sold in Craiova. Our exporter was Mr. Klein, who enjoyed a high level of respect among the landowners-customers. On many occasions, I heard Nicu or my father talking on the phone with him, to find out the sale price that was established in Amsterdam. The Romanian *leu* was at that time, it seems, on a par with the French franc.

In the autumn Mitică was among those who dealt with harvesting the plums in the great orchard. He then oversaw the distillation of the brandy which was made by fermenting plums in large boilers, an operation that was performed at the mansion. And around the same time, when the Riesling grapes ripened, Mitică dealt with harvesting the grapes and the wine-making operation, which was also performed at the mansion.

Sometimes I would join Dad and Uncle Nicu for Christmas. As we went down to Lazu's coast, we could see the white smoke from the chimneys of the houses rising high into the sky like a wool-spinning demonstration. The moment we entered the house, we were greeted with the warm smell of the wood burning in the white-hot stoves as preparations began for hearty meals with various pork dishes.[48] The golden roasted skin in particular will always be part of my memory of winters spent at Genune.

As a matter of fact, when I was past the age of ten years old, I asked my Uncle Nicu all sorts of questions about my family and about him and my father. When he was willing to talk, it was often while he was smoking. He always carried in his pocket a small polished black box with tobacco and cigarette paper. As I watched, he would go through the ritual of twisting his own cigarette, then insert it in a cigarette holder. After lighting up, he avidly inhaled the smoke while seeming to contemplate what he wanted to tell me. For example, I recall his explanation of why he and my father dropped their law studies in Paris, when Romania declared war on Austria-Hungary on the twenty-seventh of August 1916, to join the Romanian army in the war.

One time, when we were at Genune and Uncle Nicu was telling me about my great-grandfather, Constantine (ex-Brabeţeanu, now Vrăbiescu), I learned that he was born in Craiova, in 1817 and lived seventy-five years until the fourteenth of December 1892. He had a lifetime full of satisfaction, having been elected representative on the country's Divan Ad-Hoc (and later he became a liberal representative of Dolj in the Parliament of Romania). Uncle Nicu also told me about the Church of Brabeţi, belonging to Brabeţeni family, which still exists today. (I visited it in 1998.)

At another time he told me about how landowners managed to be granted land titles. I learned that some of them were rewarded with high offices and lands by the rulers for the services they had

---

48. According to the Romanian tradition on the twentieth of December (on St. Ignatius" Day) a pig is sacrificed by every rural family. A variety of foods for Christmas are prepared from the slaughtered pig such as sausages, sausages made with liver, inferior parts of the pig served in a form of gelatin, etc. The Christmas meal is sweetened with the traditional cozonac, a sweet bread with nuts and rahat for dessert.

rendered. Along with these rewards they were able to assume the rank and title of *boyar*.

Another topic that interested me was related to his memories of the First World War, after the period of neutrality of Romania between 1914–1916. I was all ears, and much impressed, when he told me his views about the suffering endured by Romanian soldiers who fought the Germans. My uncle kept careful track of what he saw and experienced, finally publishing his account in the book *Bune și rele: în război cu Reg. 9 Artilerie, 1916–1918*.

The all-knowing Uncle Nicu presented my source of information about the family members through his stories told with the full weight of respect and without exaggeration. For me, the story of the Genune estate remains at the foundation of what I regard as my paternal family origins. That is what my imagination invokes whenever I have to face troubles or I have a hard time making decisions: its memory is what gives me the necessary strength to cope during difficult times. Genune was the place where I dreamed about the future, a future that would prove to be much different from anything I could possibly have imagined.

The Curtisoara mansion

Although Genune was the most significant—and frequently visited—of all our vacation spots, I remember all the others where we paid visits. A few times I went with my father and Uncle Nicu to Curtişoara, estate near town of Tg. Jiu in Gorj county, which belonged to Cellica Neamțu (named Missirliu after marriage), the mother of my two friends Dinu and Sandu. Their father, Valodi, had been an inseparable friend of the Vrăbiescu brothers ever since their college days in Paris. Curtişoara was located in a semi mountainous region and remains a special place where Sandu, Dinu and myself used to play with deer.

(I revisited it when I returned to the country after 1995. The belfry was there, just as I had expected, but it had been turned into a state museum.)

The Bârca estate

I would also go on many occasions with Haagi to Bârca which belonged to great grandfather Vasile Mirica. We visited at Manini's invitation a mansion on four hectares of well maintained and beautiful land, well suited to appeal to Manini's refined sense of beauty. As you passed by the entrance, a lawn like a green carpet, rich in thick grass, stretched away as far as the eye could see, the vista only interrupted by layers of seasonal flowers—roses, geraniums, and zinnias—guarded by some grafted seedlings of fruit trees (such as the imperial pear trees). There was also a vineyard on the grounds surrounded by a high fence.

The big L-shaped house had more than enough bedrooms Manini and Tancy lived in another, smaller domicile with five bedrooms. In the second courtyard was the house inhabited by the administrator, Mister Gigea, and there was a third courtyard, separated by a wire fence, designated for a herd of buffalos. On one occasion, I made the mistake of going to see the buffalos wearing a red dress, which incited the animals to charge me. I was thoroughly scared, and narrowly escaped their wrath.

After the death of Uncle Petrache, Ioana and I took his room. I clearly remember the nights when there was a full moon, its rays streaming through the window lattice, entering the room, and reaching to our beds, keeping us awake. From the window, enjoying the dense fragrance that arose from the "Queen of the Night," I would grasp at the moon as it ruled over a black sky pierced by thousands of stars. As the moon shown on her smiling face, it made me scared to think that I would ever lose her.

The time spent at Bârca was typical for my maternal family, the Mirica family. We enjoyed the green grass lawns, strolled through the colorful flowerbeds, entertained guests, dined in the garden, and feasted on the cakes that were served. I remember the songs recorded on gramophone records, Manini's vocalizations, taking rides by carriage to visit the neighbors or to go buy fish—all of these special activities that were so different from the ones at Genune.

The Mihăiţa estate

There is only one summer when I visited the Mihăiţa estate. It was owned by Dănel Defleury and had been left to him by his mother, Lily Guran, daughter of former mayor of Craiova. I went there only one summer with Manini and Grandfather Lae, while Dănel was in the army in Sibiu. Here I met Sanda Budiş's family, whom I will see often later in life.

The Radomir estate

My grandfather Anastase Gh. Cionea, a big horse lover, had purchased the estate from the owner Hagi Ţolea, another horse lover. That explained the presence of a large barn. After the divorce my mother alone took over the administration of the estate, even during her marriage with Alecu Radian. (As the saying goes, "The eye of the master fattens his cattle.") Running the estate was my mother's way of fully expressing herself. She was full of life, and when she took the initiative with the estate, it was as if her nature finally found a goal that would allow her to use all her energy. Having now a great responsibility, she hired a new administrator, a man named Johann Schobel who was a young Saxon from Mediaş city with a degree in agronomy, and a good organizer.

Mancy was soon to become very active, buying the latest models of tractors, combines, and other equipment. Thus, the land got to be well cultivated, yielding good crops. After a while, she got the desired success.

I spent several weeks with my mother at the Radomir Mansion, and we lived together in the belfry. Our relationship, I would say, was one of friendship, but it was self-evident that she assumed her position as a mother. For who? For me, no doubt about it! We would talk about the Mirica family members, and she had a great admiration for her grandfather Vasile Mirica, often mentioning his energy and spirit of initiative. She also liked to reminisce about the time spent at the palace at Calafat, with Miţulica, her aunt whom she was very attached to. But there was little time for daily talks. For the most part, we had a busy schedule that she would organize for us.

If we were staying at the mansion, we would take long walks and visit various buildings, cages of chickens, pig stalls, cattle stalls, and horse stables. All, of course, were equipped with modern facilities, electricity, and running water. Bubi, the Danish hound would always be next to Mancy. With a strong personality, full of energy and courage inherited from her grandfather, my mother ran the farm with the expertise of a professional. She always knew what she wanted. She had an organized mind, she strictly followed the daily agenda of what had been planned, she didn't miss any details, and she had many ideas which she put into practice. She had done an outstanding job managing to obtain the recognition to transform the estate into a model farm, certified as such by the agricultural authorities in official documents. Good for her!

It is a shame that all was later destroyed by the communist government. I had to leave behind all that I loved—the land, houses, dogs, horses, hunts, friends, local people, costumes. But I am getting ahead of my story.

Briefly, Oltenia remained the beloved land of my childhood and adolescent period, the starting point of my being and the place of birth for my soul. When I think of Oltenia, no matter how far I go, I find that it is Craiova—either my father's or my mother's estates—that evoke my memories. These are the places that are evoked by all the senses: I hear the noise of carriages and horses on the pavement of Craiova, I see the mansions belonging to the boyars, estates belonging to Vrăbiescu family, or I see the Bârca estate or the road to Caracal heading to the Radomir. I hear the roosters' *cock-a-doodle-doo,* the noise of the tractors, the threshing machine, the creaking carts or wagons loaded with wheat, corn, hay, or the sound of the fluttering wings of a quail in the wheat field, scared of the approaching steps. I sense the smell of freshly mown alfalfa, the smell of hay, or roses and apples picked right from the garden. I see the poplar alley, the wisteria climbing on the house, the yellow rapeseed fields, the lawn surrounded by roses and zinnias and everyone so dear to me. All those things no longer exist, but my memory of them remains deeply rooted and ingrained in my mind and soul regardless of the number of years that have passed, the historical events that have taken place, or the distances that I have traveled.

I particularly remember the end of vacation just before I began the second year of high school. As the train was approaching Bucharest, my thoughts were focused on the new house in the Armașului Lane no. 11. I anticipated the beginning of the school year at Notre Dame de Sion and the pleasure of meeting again with my colleagues and friends.

CHAPTER 4

II Armaşului Lane 1938-1944

1938

In early September 1938 we left Negustori Street for the new home at No. 11 Armşului Lane, a short dead-end street ending in a cul-de-sac. My father chose this residential area in downtown Bucharest because it was close to the Legislative Council where he used to go daily after teaching his courses at the Bucharest Law School. I was especially impressed by the elegant main-entrance staircase with its oak railings, broad stairs of black marble. Downstairs were the living and dining rooms as well as my father's office with a huge floor-to-ceiling bookcase full of books. Upstairs were the bedrooms with bath rooms. The basement had besides a huge kitchen, a pantry, two-car garage and also a windowless bunker called the black cave that was required as shelter for eventual air raids. Remember: Hitler was already on his way to conquer Europe!

I now had a two-hour walk to Notre Dame de Sion, which meant I had less time for homework. Here I also met new friends, some of whom would become very close to me in the future. And that we were closer to each other, we often had dinner at my mother's sister, Tante Tancy. She was much taller than my mother, with a beautiful figure, blonde hair and elegant, tasteful looks. She was a good daughter, a patient wife and good mother. The two sisters were so different; it was as if they hadn't spent their childhood together or received the same education. Tancy was tied to the family and her household whereas my mother didn't have any of these inclinations.

On some occasions I would meet mother at Tancy's, always appearing unexpectedly. When she showed up at Tancy's place, and it happened that I was there too, she would kiss Ioana and me on the cheeks as if I was Ioana's sister and not her daughter.

I called Tancy's husband, Nicolae Herescu "Uncle Nuca." He was also from Oltenia region, a descendant of a distinguished Romanian family of boyards with roots dating back to the sixteenth century. Uncle Nuca was a great Latinist scholar, a writer, and an academic. At some point he was elected president of the Romanian Writers Union. He was always elegant and distinguished looking— standing a bit taller than Tante Tancy—and I think his appearance was conducive to their marriage.

The school year began on the fifteenth of September. I went to Notre Dame de Sion High School that I would attend until I took the capacity exam.[49] During that time I managed to receive sometime a wide belt *d'application,* or *d'application et sagesse.* But I must acknowledge the help of Uncle Nicu who closely followed my schoolwork was priceless.

Because my grades began to be very good, my father decided that I should learn the English language and hired Mrs. Murphy, an Irish lady who came to my home three times a week. She was older, with white hair peeking out from under her brimless hats. She had small blue eyes, a white face, natural pink cheeks, thin edged lips— exactly the Irish type—and a woman I would spend many years with.

---

49. In Romania, to graduate from the lower Secondary School (Gymnasium) one had to pass a Capacity Examination and the scores obtained at that exam were a determining factor in the selection process to be admitted to secondary education.

I attended English lessons without having a clue that in fact they would prove to be the most important for my future.

We had only settled into the new place one month when, on the thirtieth of September 1938, Hitler occupied Austria and annexed the "Sudetenland." My father, outraged, could not understand how the English and the French could go along with such a disgrace.

At the end of November, Maman Titi celebrated St. Catherine's day and not long after her party, we heard on the radio that the arrested legionnaires[50] had been murdered in prison, when Uncle Nicu concluded that the incident was going to cause another break-out of violent revenge.

1939

I remember my birthday celebration on the seventh of March, just because one short week before Hitler occupied Czechoslovakia on the fifteenth. Again my father told us, "Who knows what this fool is going to do next, even with regard to Romania!" Indeed, he did not occupy us but, in May, Romania had been forced to sign an economic treaty with Germany, which needed our oil for its aggressive plans. King Carol II apparently was against this treaty and he visited London where the King had asked for England's and France's support against Germany.

As we were spending the summer at Genune, Dad kept Haagi informed daily with the latest news. She was surprised to hear that Germany signed in August1939, a nonaggression treaty with the Soviets, knowing that Hitler was a staunch anticommunist. I remember well the news while I was still in Genune when, that on the third of September 1939, the Second World War began, with Hitler and Stalin dividing Poland in two, each taking one half. And then, France and England reacted in turn by declaring war on Germany.

I had to be in Bucharest on the fifteenth of September, when I started third grade. Unforgettable events followed when, at the end

---

50.   "Legionnaires" were members of a far-right organization called the "Legion" or the, Iron Guard."

of September, the Prime Minister Armand Călinescu was killed by a group of Legionnaires, exactly as my Uncle Nicu had predicted ten months earlier.

And something that interested me further: the new prime minister who replaced Călinescu was Constantin Argetoianu, who appointed my step-father Alecu Radian to take over the Propaganda Department. I was pleased that before being appointed, Alecu together with my mother rented an apartment in downtown Bucharest, which she arranged really tastefully with furniture from the Calafat Palace. Seven years after divorcing my father, she had finally got the residence she desired in Bucharest. Haagi and I were invited to her place for dinner, and often we would also bring Ileana Poenaru, Alecu's niece. Not only she had now a husband and an apartment, but around the same time Mancy decided to take over the administration of her father's Radomir estate. That was when her life completely changed as she left embroidery for agronomy. A change that was fitting her personality.

Also Militza Pătrașcu, who was a student of the Romanian avant-garde sculptor Constantin Brâncuși made a life-size bust of my mother in white marble. That bust was first displayed at an exhibition in London and is now part of the permanent exhibit at the Art Museum in Craiova.

1940

Due to the war, at home, we always listened to the nine o'clock news broadcast on Radio London in Romanian language. Then all gathered closely around the radio so as not to miss a word, since Germany was in the process of conquering North Europe and its troops succeeded to enter Paris, followed by the capitulation of France. This was a heart breaking event to my father and uncle, who studied in Paris They were furious!

Their renewed hope was when Churchill became prime minister, expecting he would take a firmer stance against Hitler, but unfortunately, President Roosevelt's main concern then was his re-election in November, preoccupying him far more than getting involved against the Berlin-Rome-Tokyo Axis, formed in September.

The decade of the 1940s was to be a bad one for Romania, one in which the nation was shaken, both figuratively and literally by a huge earthquake.

Unexpectedly, in June 1940, there were three amputations of Romania's territorial body. Besarabia Province was taken imposed by Stalin and assimilated with the Ukrainian Soviet Socialist Republic. Then, in August, imposed by Hitler, the Northern part of Transylvania was lost to the Hungarians. And finally, in September Romania lost the territory called Dobrogea[51] to the Bulgarians. As a result, the 1918 Greater Romania ceased to exist, an event which was followed by a great stream of Romanian refugees coming from these lost territories. As a result King Carol II abdicated beginning of September, but not before he formed a new government with Marshal Ion Antonescu head of state and his son with Queen Mother Elena of Greece, young King Mihai[52] restored to the throne. As if all these events were not enough, Antonescu's government collaborated with the Legionary Movement, luckily that lasted only four months.

I have to mention something about the Jewish situation in Romania, because later in life I found out, on the one hand, that the belief of many Congressmen was far from reality, and, on the other, when I met many Jewish friends they either knew nothing about Romanian Jews or had wrong information.

Thus, during the 1940s, when Jews were persecuted by Hitler, they were better treated in Romania than they had been in most territories under German influence (except for the North-Eastern territory of Transnistria). As I learned from reading Great Rabbi Alexandru Safran's opinion in his book *(Un tison arrache aux flammes; la communaute juive de Roumanie* (1939–1947), Stock Publishing, 1989, page 89)* Jews were forced to do the humiliating work of shoveling snow in Bucharest, but at the same time they were exempt from

---

51. Historical region of Romania between the Danube and the Black Sea.
52. Romanian for Michael

the army service and thus were not subject to the dangers of army service as well as the fact that Antonescu agreed that Jews would be allowed to immigrate to Palestine. Likewise, Dr. Filderman, the then president of the Romanian Jewish Community, declared that some of the Jews who were business owners actually flourished during this time, though they took the precaution of changing their firms' names to those of their Romanian business partners (*see The Romanian Morning Star*, Mai 1993, page 17).

Moreover, it must be noted that King Mihai and Queen-Mother Helen helped the Jewish cause during the Second World War. In recognition of her work on behalf of the Jewish people the Queen was appointed by the Yad Vashem Institute in Israel as "Righteous among nations." (Also by Şafran, Alexandru, page 90, 101, 117–118.)

However, after the break with Germany in August 1944, a large number of Jews saw the Russian army as liberators and became communist sympathizers. They destroyed the former Romanian Jewish Federation and dismissed the president, Dr. Filderman, and forcing out his adjunct, the lawyer Iancu Zissu, whom I will meet later in life. Great Rabbi Alexandru Safran was also expelled by the communist government and replaced with the left-leaning Rabbi Moses Rosen. Over the years, the majority of the four hundred thousand members of the Jewish community immigrated to Israel or to other democracies in the West. Jewish emigration was facilitated by President Nixon's initiative to negotiate in the seventies with the Soviets, when Senator Henry Jackson took the opportunity to attach an amendment to a special agreement, whereby the Soviets had to allow emigration from Russia.

In 1940, as I have mentioned, Romania was not only shaken by the multiple territorial amputations but also literally shaken by a big earthquake that occurred the night of November 9–10. I woke up only when Haagi grabbed me by the hand and dragged me directly under a door frame where we both remained, feeling the floor shaking beneath my feet. The walls were bending, and I could hear the noise of the animals in the yard and the neighbor's dogs barking. All of a sudden, my father came in and grasped my other hand, joining Haagi and me beneath the door frame. That earthquake measured

7.8 degrees on the Richter Scale and lasted two and a half minutes. It scared me for life. Even now when a heavy vehicle passes by and shakes the floor, I instantly get terrified.

Coming with Haagi home from school she told me that the Herescus had moved in with us because their house had been damaged, two large bricks had landed on Ioana's pillow. Thank God she was in Craiova with Manini at the time! My aunt had remained in good terms with my father after the divorce of my parents. In fact, after the earthquake our house gradually turned into a kind of general headquarters for our relatives and friends who came to discuss the upsetting political events of the time or the devastating human and material losses caused by the earthquake.

1941

The unusual events continued in 1941 as well, commencing at the beginning of this year when the Herescu family was still living with us. On the evening of the twenty-first of January, I could not sleep because I was hearing frequent outbursts of weapons coming from downtown. I put on some clothes and went downstairs, where I found everyone gathered in the drawing room listening to the radio transmitting alarming news about the Legionnaires.

The sound of the weapons and machine guns continued. It was a bloody rebellion of the Legionnaires, against Antonescu for three days and three nights. In order to suppress this movement, Antonescu called the army to arrest them, but the fight escalated and furious shooting ensued. During that time, everyone was really fired-up, discussing what was happening, each offering comments or suggestions. I was constantly hearing, "Dear Gică, let me tell you...Dear Nicule, I have an idea...Dear Liky, I don't think you're right...," and so on. Wanting to do an impression, at one point I jokingly addressed my father saying, "Dear Gică, I have also an idea..." He turned his head as if puzzled and laughing as he said, "From now on this is how you shall address me!" And so I did for the rest of my life. And that is what happened with Nicu and Liky too. I stopped using the word *uncle*, though Nicu Herescu always remained *Onkel Nuca*.

For three days, no one left the house. Fortunately, Maman Titi had no problem taking care of daily meals because our basement was full of supplies from Genune. There were two barrels of brandy, another two of wine, and also the birds from the back yard—turkeys, geese, ducks, guinea-fowl, chickens and roosters.

After the Legionnaires were thrown out of the picture, my dad and Nicu followed the progression of Western foreign policy with much interest, as it was the only thing that could free us from the Germans. Later reading Churchill's volumes about WWII, I found out that Roosevelt met with him and was granted an American loan, but then again, Roosevelt the politician, a very secretive man (his left hand did not know what the right hand was doing!) also granted a loan to the Soviets. (*The Second World War*, volume 2, page 605.)

After the Herescu family moved back to their house, our guest room was occupied by Constantin Petrescu Ercea, who was my cousin Cristina's father, a commercial law professor at the University in the city of Cluj. He used to come to visit us on a yearly basis when Cristina came to see me more often. Her parents were divorced like mine, only she lived with her mother—my father's cousin.

And from time to time, I was invited along with Dad and Uncle Nicu to have dinner at the house of Istrare Micescu, my friend Istratel's father. Micescu was a brilliant jurist and a famous orator, known for pleading for clients in countless lawsuits that he won. When lawyers knew that he would be presenting a plea in a lawsuit, his colleagues would postpone the deadlines of their own cases just to be present during his orations. Other frequent guests to Istrate Micescu's house were the Maltezeanu family, who were great landowners and who loved game hunting as much as Micescu himself. Coca Maltezeanu had two sons, Radu the elder and Vlaicu the younger, Istratel's friend, whom I hadn't met before. During dinner, I was startled to hear that on the night during the Legionnaire's Rebellion, the Maltezianu's were attacked in their own home by fanatic Legionnairees, and they had to use their hunting guns to defend themselves. That's how I found out that the legionaries were not only against the Jews but also against rich landowners.

After dinner, the three of us—Istrătel, Vlaicu and I—were talking about the upcoming exams that we would take in June. Rather than participate in those discussions, I was more interested in paying close attention to Vlaicu, noting his black hair and the outstanding, curled lashes that highlighted his big black eyes in a way that would steal your heart away. (I mention all these details since they would all come to have a meaning to me.)

As mentioned, in mid-June I graduated the national requested examination after four high school years, earning high grades that won my family's and my own satisfaction. Fourth grade was the last one I spent at Notre Dame de Sion because my father was already in the process of signing me up to attend the Girls' Central School, both because it had a good reputation and also because it was near the house.

The four years spent with the nuns developed my faith and also my respect for order, discipline, and organization. I will always remain grateful for having been exposed to them in my upbringing. Some teachers, nuns, and colleagues were very dear to me and I felt very sorry to leave them.

A week after the national examination, we suffered another blow when Romania entered the war alongside Germany on the night of June 22–23 against Russia. Everybody who came to visit us was of the opinion that it was not acceptable, since most of the population was on the Allies side and Marshal Antonescu had neither consulted with King Mihai nor with other politicians. I had heard that Antonescu's motive had been to regain the territories taken a year previously by the Russians. Actually this happened in July, when the territories were recovered, together with an additional area called Transnistria, which in fact had never ever belonged to us and which will give trouble in 1991 to the Romanian territories which were assimilated into Ukraine.

As I had ever in previous years, I spent the holidays first with Haagi and Helga at Carmen Sylva, then without her but with Tante Tancy and Ioana at a mountain resort, Predeal and finally with Ioana in Craiova at Manini's house. We considered ourselves more like sisters than cousins.

And while we were keeping ourselves entertained on random nothingness, in August 1941 an important event happened, when Roosevelt and Churchill met in Canada proclaiming the principles of the *Atlantic Charter*, which became the foundation for the future of the NATO Treaty of 1949. Romania had been admitted decades later, in 2004, and is playing an important role even now in 2015, when Russian expansionism flexes its muscles again in Eastern Ukraine.

In September, when I started my school year at the new high school, just to make matters worse, Tante Cellica Missirliu recommended that my father to permanently hire Mlle Noel, so that I would not forget the French I had learned studying at Notre Dame. I vehemently opposed this idea because I didn't want to lose Haagi. In the end, Haagi remained.

Mlle Noel had me read many French books but this new language study at home coincided with an opposite change in school, where the teaching was now in Romanian. All those French expressions I had previously learned about history, geography, physics, and mathematics were now useless to me. The effort involved to speak Romanian resembled what I had experienced when I entered primary school and knew only German, or when I entered the French nuns' school when I didn't know enough French. However, this school had a more relaxed schedule, only five classes a day, compared to seven at the nuns'. Thus, I had more time to study since I saved two hours traveling back and forth.

On top of it all, I continued my English lessons with Mrs. Murphy, though this English study, as I've mentioned, later proved to be the most important item for my future. But, then I did not have a clue why I would need it badly.

On the first day of school, I appeared wearing the new uniform with registration number 693. When I entered, school girls who knew each other from previous years were glad to meet again, and quickly took their seats on the benches they had occupied the year before. I was left with three future colleagues, like me, looking for places to sit. We picked two double benches that were still free by the window in the back of the classroom. Each grabbed her seat quickly, then shook hands and made introductions. Next to me by the window sat a tall colleague, brunette with short hair and eyes with long lashes, a beautiful nose, and a friendly smile. She presented herself as Ioana Crătunescu. The name Ioana, together with her height, shocked me. She was the third girl named Ioana I knew, and she was the same height as Helga and Ioana Herescu!

This third Ioana became my best friend. She was lively, cheerful, laughed often, and was always ready to express opinions. My first favorable impression was accurate and never changed. Another reason we became friends so quickly was because we lived very close to each other. After a short while, we were meeting not only at school but also at our homes, often studying together in the afternoons. Sometimes Ioana would come over, other times I would go to her place, carrying our backpacks filled with books and notebooks to study together. Ioana lived with her mother, Zizela, one of the beautiful women in Bucharest, her stepfather, her grandmother, Zizela's mother, and her governesse, Terpi. I was told she looked more like her father, who had died of a heart attack when she was very little.

So Ioana and I had many things in common: we were both missing a parent from an early age, we lived in the presence of an authoritarian grandmother and a caring governess, and we both had quite an appetite. Also she was opinionated! Often, after having a discussion with somebody she'd hum, *"Vous l'avez voulu, vous l'avez voulu Georges Dandin vous l'avez voulu,"*[53] quoting a particular character of Moliere! Our friendship grew ever stronger, and over the years continued unchanged. She had an open nature, was honest, admirable, humorous, and open-minded. We never had a fight even if we did occasionally disagree.

During this winter, all hell broke loose, when in December, Japan attacked America—in Pearl Harbor, Hawaii, whereupon Roosevelt retaliated, declaring war on Japan. This had been followed by Germany which, declared war on America and England, and at the same time on Romania. Due to Antonescu, Romania was supporting Germany, but that position was contradicted by our politicians, Maniu, Brătianu who desperately tried to keep in touch with

---

53.   "'Tis your own fault, George Dandin"

England, being, like most Romanians, against Hitler's Germany. My family supported Maniu and Brătianu, who were upset that our troops had already suffered over thousands of dead, wounded or taken prisoner (as described by Romalo, Mihnea. *Romania in World War II. 1941–1945*. Bucharest, Vestala, 2001, page 35–40) and was expecting that we are going to be defeated since the German forces were advancing really slowly in the winter campaign against Moscow.

1942

Our poor country was in a desperate situation: at war with England and the United States, used by Hitler for his purposes, obviously threatened by Stalin and Antonescu sent another division in Russia to conquer Stalingrad. The only thing we could do was to listen daily to Radio London. In January Roosevelt met with Churchill to discuss European problems and he was in favor to establish the United Nations.

Despite the events that annoyed my father, he kept himself very busy with the University and the Legislative Council. My dear uncle was also missing from home quite a lot as well. I used to imagine him always running, from the Palace of Justice to various Courts. Perhaps some of the times he actually was there but certainly not always. A few days after my birthday, when I had invited over a bunch of friends including Vlaicu Maltezeanu (whose beautiful eyes I could not forget ever since I first saw them at the Micesscu's), when I came home from school I was welcomed by Marioara, the housemaid. She was dressed in a festive black dress and wore a black cap and white starched apron. I asked her what the occasion was. Guessing that I must know something about what was going on, she said to me, "Well, Miss, Mister Nicu brought his future wife to introduce her to your grandmother and Mr. Gică!"

I cannot even express what I felt, but I didn't want to give myself away, so I went straight to my room to control my emotions. I had to be able to keep my cool when I had to face the new lady who was about to take away part of what represented the foundation of my childhood and youth. When my mother decided to leave from Vasile

Lascar Str. everything went smoothly, as she had intended. But now I felt a shock that was difficult to overcome. I thought since Uncle Nicu brought this woman to meet Maman Titi, it meant he had already come to a firm, unchangeable resolution. It was the fifteenth of March!

Before leaving the room, I wiped away my tears and calmed down, aided in part by Haagi's consolations. (She too was troubled by the news.) I braced myself for the moment I could never have dreamed of when I rose from my bed that morning. As I left the room, Nicu met me at my door. He had heard that I had returned from school and wanted to inform me personally about his intentions. As we were face to face, I kissed him on the cheek and congratulated him quickly so that he couldn't see my eyes, all the while tightly clenching my fists as I tried not to cry. Then I went straight to shake hands with Florica, my future aunt, having red hair, dark skin, piercing brown eyes, and elegantly dressed. While I was devastated on the inside, I managed to hide my emotions. After we exchanged a few words under Maman Titi's inquisitive eye, Florica told me that she had heard a lot about me from Nicu and that she wanted to invite me to a play for children where I could also meet her son, Nicuşor.[54] Hearing this, I had to make a pretense of all the good behavior I had learned from Haagi, the grandmothers, the nuns, Mlle Pelle, Mlle Noel, and even Mrs. Murphy. Exercising great control over myself, I was able to thank her and said that I was looking forward to meeting him. Actually, that part of it was not a lie, but I was in truth still overwhelmed by the novelty of the sudden presence of an aunt and a cousin together with Nicu's departure. I was completely devastated! I had to get used to the idea that Nicu was leaving the house and me. And that would be that!

A few days later, on Florica's invitation, we met at the theater. She appeared holding the hand of Nicuşor, a young boy no more than two or three, who was skinny, dark skinned, lively, and very nicely dressed. He twisted continuously on his two restless legs. During that time we got closer together, he and I, and so we were to remain

---

54.   Diminutive meaning "Young Nicu"

for the years to come. After the theater, Florica invited me to her apartment with stylish furniture. Over time, I became very close to Florica, and Nicu compensated for his absence by making frequent visits to our house. Most often, he came by himself.

Also, I remember that year's Easter when I could only think about Vlaicu's eyes and curly eyelashes that had made such an impression on me a while ago at Istrătel's house and again whenever he was invited to my birthday at home. Now it was the so-called tea parties season when I had e opportunity to see him again. My problem was that Maman Titi was a strict guardian, and she wanted me home no later than 11:00 p.m. Now I couldn't wait for Ioana Crătunescu's birthday celebration, on the eleventh of June. I heard that she was getting, for the occasion, a new dress with stylish new shoes. Hearing that, I hurriedly informed Tante Tancy who bought me a jersey dress made of blue *crêpe de Chine*. Around the same time I bought my first elegant high-heeled antelope shoes to match the dress color. I was so excited I could not sleep at night, thinking about how I would look.

At Ioana's birthday party there was a portable record player and American vinyl records. When Ioanna and I saw each other in the new dresses and high heels, we burst out laughing at the thought of what others would say when they saw us looking so elegant. These were the first feminine dresses we had ever worn. Ioana immediately played the records of American music with songs like "Chattanooga Choo-Choo" and "Begin the Beguine" and other music by trendy singers like Louis Armstrong, Ella Fitzgerald, and Connie Francis. I was invited to dance by each boy, one at a time, but Vlaicu was my favorite partner, with whom I had my first cheek-to-cheek dance and who kissed me on the forehead to the strains of the rhythm of "Begin the Beguine" from the island of Martinique, West Indies. Whenever this bolero was played again, Vlaicu would rush toward me before the others. "Begin" became our song, not only then but also at the many other tea parties we attended together. His image was always in my mind, interfering more and more with my daily activities.

At the end of June, while the Romanian cities of Ploieşti and Constanţa were being bombed by the Americans, I finished fifth grade and left Bucharest to Carmen Sylva with Helga and Haagi while my cousin Ioana Herescu went to Eforie. Being in Carmen Sylva one day, Haagi and I took the train to Eforie seaside where Ioana Herescu and Tante Tancy were staying. I enjoyed being with Ioana, and there was no clue that this would turn out to be such an extraordinary day…(I'll explain in a short while).

In Genune during the summer months, I always anticipated the arrival of the postman with letters from Ioana and Vlaicu.

In September, before leaving for Bucharest from Genune I stopped by to see Manini in Craiova. She welcomed me as usual with open arms, but then she hugged me tightly and with welling eyes—which was very uncharacteristic of her—told me, "My little one, the Herescu family, Nicu, Tancy and Ioana had left the country! They promised to come back when and if the Americans come before the Russians…Ah, dear little one, it hurts my soul to be separated from them. Now you and Mancy are all I have left!"

I felt like I had been stabbed in my heart, just as I had when Nicu got married! I was filled with questions:

"Manini, what do you mean? Are they gone for good? Does that mean that the last time I saw Tancy and Ioana that day in Eforie when nothing seemed to be extraordinary?"

When she nodded, I felt stricken, hurt, anguished! What do you mean? Ioana disappeared from my life? I literally felt as if something inside me was breaking. At least when my Uncle Nicu left the house, I understood that it was, after all, his right to marry the woman he loved. But for the Herescu's to leave was a different thing, because they were forced to do so by Hitler and Stalin!

It was the first direct hit caused by the threat of war, together with the coming of the Russians after the failure of Hitler's campaign. Then Uncle Nuca decided to leave the country. Ioana was like my sister, we were always together either in Bucharest, in Craiova, Eforie, Predeal or at the Bârca estate. I suddenly remembered that one night at Bârca when we had been sitting at the window and she smiled in the moonlight.

Although Manini was a strong woman, she was heartbroken. I had to go back, leaving her with a broken soul as she worried about the fate of the Herescu family who had gone elsewhere abroad. Luckily Grandfather Tata-Lae was next to her.

Not having Ioana Herescu around anymore led me to strengthen my friendship with Ioana Crătunescu. She told me that she met Constantin Alimăneştianu. He was the youngest of four sons Mihai, Şerban, Călin, and Constantin—well known in the Bucharest society for being young, handsome, rich and of good family, as their father, Virgil Alimăneştianu, owned several properties including a forest of 4,500 hectares.

I do not remember where I went for the first "tea party" that autumn, but when I heard the melody and felt the rhythm of "Begin the Beguine," I found myself in Vlaicu's arms. We were young and happy and ready to leave all the world's worries for parents to handle. However, even at that age, the failure of the Russian counter-offensive at Stalingrad in the winter of 1942 made a great impression on me. Indeed, that turned out to be a disaster for the Romanian Army, when eighteen Romanian divisions were destroyed out of the twenty-two sent by Marshal Antonescu. *(Romalo Mihnea. Romania in World War II 1941 to 1945. Bucharest, West, 2001, page 50).*

1943

Bad news for Romania! In January we heard on Radio London that Churchill, Roosevelt and Charles de Gaulle all had met to develop a plan for the unconditional surrender of Germany and its satellites, Romania being one of them. My family was alarmed because Marshal Antonescu continued to help Hitler, despite the disaster of Stalingrad.

I was fully aware that important things were happening, but I had my own concerns, namely, how to organize the best tea party for my birthday, on the seventh of March, on a Sunday. I remember this birthday in particular because, one day before the tea party my mother phoned. By accident, I happened to pick up the phone and she asked for Uncle Ionel Anton's phone number. I gave her the number and added, "Mommy, how come you're interested in General

Anton and you're not asking about my birthday party tomorrow and how I managed?"

After a moment of silence, my mother replied, "I'm sure that your father took care of everything. As for me, I invite you to take together a photo at Julieta's after two days at…o'clock."

Thus the conversation was completed but not settled.

The "disentanglement" of our conversation took place in Easter when I went to Craiova to be with Manini. It just so happened that while I was in the city with Manini, my mother dropped by unexpectedly as usual, and when she heard that I was also there she went to sleep over at Olga's, Uncle Nuca's sister. When Manini heard what mother had done (I told her what had happened), I knew I had to fix it. Next day, I went to Olga's house. The doors were kept unlocked, so when I came in, my mother thought it was Olga and invited me to enter. She was in bed reading the newspaper, with the open pages hiding her face.

I said, "No, Mommy, it's not Olga, it's me."

With that, she crumpled the newspaper in a fraction of a second and put it by her side, sitting up angrily, said, "It would have been better if you didn't show up, because we could have avoided this conversation that I do not wish to have."

There it was, as if a delayed fuse on a bomb had just exploded. It was all because I had dared to express my opinion that she took time for Uncle Ionel but not for me. She added, "Please don't push me into it because I already decided not to come at my mother's for Easter dinner."

I replied, "I do not think it's a good decision, you know how much Manini is grieving over the Herescu's absence, you should be there for her just to fill this emptiness."

Angrily, she replied, "Sure I could, but I do not wish to see you." To which I replied, "Don't bother regarding my presence, this is about your mother. You cannot neglect all around you just because of me."

Then unexpectedly I asked, "Do you love your mother or not?"

She was taken aback because she did not expect such a rude question. Her only reply to that was silence. Before I left, I calmly reminded her, "Manini is expecting you for the Easter dinner." I pulled the door closed behind me without expecting any reaction.

I hurried home. Though completely torn up, I wanted to cheer up Manini for all the love that she has always shown me. When I saw her, I announced with confidence, "I'm sure that she will come!"

At the precise hour, Olga arrived together with my mother, superbly dressed and radiating beauty. It was a victory for me, both because of what I had been able to say over the phone and for convincing this beautiful, independent, willful mother of mine to come.

Soon after Easter, I had a motorcycle accident during one of the Sunday walks on Jianu Blvd. Vlaicu had invited me for a ride, and I was thrilled. I got on with him, and we drove off. I don't know exactly what he did, but at one point his motorcycle *lurched* forward and we fell off. Both of us slammed down the pavement and were dragged for quite a long distance. My dress was torn apart, and my hand and left cheek were bruised and bleeding. All the passers-by stopped and stared while Vlaicu was struggling to pull the bike up with the engine still whirring. My head hurt terribly. When Haagi found out about the accident, she felt guilty that she let me go with him, but the truth is even without her permission I would have gone for the ride. When we got home, I confessed what had happened. By evening I was completely disfigured. Many days would pass before I again looked like my normal self. Luckily I did not lose any teeth.

By June, I had passed all my sixth grade exams. I ended my private lessons with Mrs. Murphy and I attended Ioana's birthday party. What changed, however, was my relationship with Vlaicu, which was not the way it used to be. Either he was sorry for what had happened or he was embarrassed that after the accident he had not come to see me to ask about my condition. I never tried to contact him either. When we bumped into each other at parties, all my special feelings for him had already disappeared.

Meanwhile the political issues of the country really took center stage. All the news seemed to favor the Allies, because General Patton had reached Sicily, and Mussolini had been arrested. As always, Romanians were convinced that the Americans would come to save them.

In this hopeful mood I left for Genune. Here, I was reading, hunting, and horseback riding. One day the mailman dropped by and Mitică, the estate administrator, handed me a letter from Haagi, whom we had left behind in Bucharest. I was happy at first to get news from Haagi, but when I opened and read her letter, I felt like a knife had pierced my heart again! Hitler had ordered all the subjects of Austrian-German origin to return home. I was angry, thinking what right did Hitler have to interfere in my life and take Haagi away—she who had always been there for me for over thirteen years? Because of Hitler's insanity, my lovely Haagi was forced to leave! For a time, I simply refused to believe that life was separating us, that I was about to lose a human being who was like a mother to me. I was extremely saddened. It was my second painful break-up after Ioana Herescu's departure—and all because of Hitler, who created a storm in Europe and now got stuck in Russia!

Haggi really loved me and I loved her. She had never raised her voice at me, never punished or threatened me. She had always given me a feeling of security and alleviated my inherent childhood fears. It was she who had planted the seed of faith in my heart—a faith which was to accompany me throughout the rest of my life. I knew that nothing was possible without the support that my faith in God would give me. Relying on God gave me the strength to be resilient and overcome grief without being scared about the future, because I knew He would find a solution to my problems or solve them in unexpected ways.

Haagi used to teach me that I should work hard and be unself-ish, because only then would I receive the help for which I prayed. Also, I had learned from her to always keep my feet on the ground and to control my emotions, using my mind and intelligence when I had to take action. And if, by chance, I encountered a situation that I could not change—like the divorce of my parents—Haagi taught me not to allow myself to be overwhelmed but to accept reality.

Regarding my education, Haagi inspired me to study diligently, to understand the sweet feeling of *fulfillment* resulting from a *job well done*—which will leave me much more satisfied rather than the pleasure of obtaining things the easy way. Also, she added that I should be organized, prepared to give priority to emergencies and to solve each problem one at a time. In addition, her most important advice—based on her own experience—was to accumulate as many diplomas as possible because she knew they would the only wealth that I could count on, more important than inheritances. It was as if she knew what would happen in the future, when indeed my law diploma was the only wealth I'd take with me when I left the country.

Also I remember her prediction about China, which she called *die Gelbe Gefahr* (the yellow terror) that would threaten and dominate the world economy in the future. It was almost as if she could read tea leaves!

Hearing the news of her departure, everyone in the house was struck with sadness. For my own part, I felt as if in leaving Haagi was taking with her an irreplaceable part of my soul. All the same, I realized that I could not change anything. I remembered the lyrics of "Viennese Waltz" by Johann Strauss that she used to hum, "*Glucklich ist—der vergiest—das nicht mehr zum endern ist!*" (Happy is he who can forget what cannot be anymore changed.)

Following her departure, for a long time I received letters from Austria in which she told me about her friends, her longing for Romania, for us, and for me. I would respond. But after the summer of 1951, the foreign correspondence stopped, and I had no idea what had happened to her until I was able much later to travel to Austria. Her memory and teachings remained deeply ingrained in me and put a mark on my life. I remained grateful for all that she meant to me.

In September when I came to Bucharest at the beginning of the school year, Romania's situation was bad. The Russians were heading in our direction while the Allies bombed the oil wells in the city of Ploești, because they were used by the Germans.

The all-important Conference in Teheran took place in November–December, when Churchill and Roosevelt met for the first time with Stalin. We were all sitting around the radio listening. The outcome of the conference spelled disaster for Eastern Europe. Even Churchill later wrote that "Roosevelt and Stalin opted for a speedy landing across the English Channel," although Churchill was concerned about Europe, favoring a landing in the Balkans, which was supposed to eliminate the Russian influence there to ensure free movement of British ships through the Suez Canal" (*The Second World War*, London, 1948–1954 volume 4, page 332). But Churchill's views were overpowered by Roosevelt and Stalin. Historian Ivor Porter wrote that "England lost any political ground maneuver in Romania, and also the prospect of unloading any Allied troops over the Balkans...because Roosevelt himself didn't see any advantage in unloading American troops in Eastern Europe...The conference was dangerously wrong about that, as Stalin managed to impose his point of view, pushing the Allies away from his area of influence...While in the meantime, Maniu still believed that the US troops will come to back up a possible strike of the Germans against Romanians..." ***(Porter, Ivor *Operaţiunea "Autonomus,"* Bucharest, Humanitas, 1991, page 127–129.[55])

I experienced what truly happened in Tehran. Roosevelt, trusting Stalin as an ally, had condemned millions of innocent souls to Russian totalitarianism, including the citizens of Romania.

1944

After Tehran, Romania had been in a hot spot. Stalin, no longer fearing the presence of Anglo-American forces in the Balkans, immediately undertook an extremely powerful offensive by crossing the river Dniester toward Romania, and all the while American planes were bombing us.

By early spring we had already started to get used to the passive defense exercises, those occasions when we heard the prealarm warning sirens and headed for shelters even though there was no actual bombing. However, Bucharest was under orders to stay camouflaged during the night as a preventive against air strikes. We had our window panes covered with dark paper insulation, using only a flash light when walking in the streets.

---

55. Original title: Operation Autonomous: with SOE in Wartime Romania

In the spring of 1944, events took a precipitous turn and the Soviet army entered Moldova. It was right before Easter, on the night of April 3, when I suddenly heard the sirens making sinister sounds. This was no exercise; this was for real. My father ordered us to go to the "black cellar." We all went there immediately and seated ourselves on benches. I could hear the planes heading towards us when the bombing began. The bombs were dropped in waves, thudding dully as they reached the ground. I could also hear the sounds of air defense forces. I prayed to God to spare us, just as Haagi taught me. My grandmother kept telling us to keep quiet. Mlle Noel, who had not had enough warning to put on her wig, was wearing only a headscarf. I had never seen her without her wig or without makeup. She looked like a different person. We stayed in the black cellar for about an hour before we heard the sirens signaling that the raid was over.

When we got upstairs, everyone started phoning each other. Nicu and his family were all well, but a bomb had damaged the house of Uncle Ionel, the General, however everyone was okay because they had taken shelter in a detached garage.

"Can we come to stay with you?"

"Sure," said Dad. And so, our house in Armașului essentially became the headquarters of the family.

On the fourth of April, the next day, we found out that the Anglo-American bombers had hit many German targets and the Romanian oil exploitation region. Big agitation followed! Prompted by fear and panic, people were leaving Bucharest and fleeing to other regions of the country considered safer. Meanwhile, thousands of refugees kept coming from Bassarabia, Bucovina, and Moldova behind the advance of the Soviet army.

Under the circumstances, my Central School declared the end of the school year and my father and Uncle Ionel decided that all of us, with the exception of Uncle Ionel and him, should move to Genune In all haste, just before leaving for Genune, I called Ioana on the phone and told her breathlessly, "My parents decided that we should all leave for Genune except my father and Uncle Ionel."

"I'm not surprised," she replied, "because my parents also decided to go to the mountains in the town of Sinaia."

"But still," I added, "it will be a very long summer and it's a shame to waste so much time. I thought I should ask my father to get me an approval to enter eighth grade during these months. What do you say?"

"A very good idea" she said.

Hence, in two seconds we decided that we were going to study on our own for the fall exams, and we would enter eighth grade, and if necessary we would also study for the Baccalaureate.[56] Our intention in going this route was to buy us time, hoping that upon our return to Bucharest Germany would have been defeated, everything would go back to normal, and we would have free time for parties and enrollment in college—not for the sake of our careers, but to satisfy our parents and to increase our group of friends. Said and done!

Immediately after that, I phoned my cousin Cristina and learned she also was thinking about entering eighth grade over the summer. My father obtained a dispensation from the Ministry of Education so that I could condense two years of study into one and take the exams in Craiova.

As soon as I arrived in Craiova, I acquired the book list I needed from the Elena Cuza High School and took them with me to Genune. There I organized myself in an office in the administration building where I could spend my days without being disturbed by anybody. My father obtained a dispensation from the Ministry so I could enroll at Elena Cuza High School.

Being busier than before, I was no longer listening to Radio London; I was hearing about what happened in Romania and abroad from Tante Angela, Uncle Ionel's sister in law, who would give me a daily briefing about world affairs. Thus I learned that:

a) In April, the Germans occupied Hungary and Northern Transylvania entering Sighet, where they caused a Jewish holocaust. In his book, Ellie Wiesel describes how they were picked up by Hungarian authorities and deported to

---

56.   Romania's national secondary school graduation diploma

Auschwitz or to Buchenwald in wagons meant for animals (Wiesel, Ellie. *The night.* Hill & Wang, 1985, 116. p),

b)   The Anglo-Americans continued to bomb Romania. On the sixth of June, the Anglo-American *disembarkation took place* in Normandy (D-Day), carrying out a plan worked out in Tehran. Paris was liberated; all the while, Germans were desperately bombing London with V-1 and V-2 rockets;

c)   In Romania, the socialists and communists started to prepare themselves by forming the National Democratic Front, NDF and the opposition—the Liberals and Peasants—formed the Block of Democratic Parties, BDP.

In the fall, because of the Paris liberation, Mlle Noel decided to leave for good and go to Paris. I felt neither one way nor the other, I wasn't too attached to her, although I had appreciated her reading lessons and the literature, she exposed me to in my education.

One day in early August, we got a surprise visit from Liky, who came riding his motorcycle bike all the way from Craiova. From him I learned that my mother and her husband Alecu Radian had departed for the city of Cluj, where he was diagnosed with cancer in the left jaw. Then my mother took him to Germany where he consulted Professor Dr. Eppinger, who recommended a treatment in a clinic in Vienna. Obviously, chain smoking had contributed to the onset of the disease. Once Alecu entered the clinic in Vienna, my mother continued to commute from Vienna to Bucharest, to Craiova and to Radomir, and then back to Vienna. I felt very sorry for Alecu because he had always been kind to me. He was a distinguished man with a good sense of humor, very smart, who loved my mother and wanted her by his side as long as possible.

My study program was going very well, as planned. I was extremely determined and didn't deviate from the schedule, which was surprising even to me. This effort proved useful, but not for the original reasons I had discussed with Ioana, but future unexpected benefits which would have been then impossible to predict.

Again, one day, Mitică came into the office and handed me a letter. I recognized Ioana's hand writing. Excited, I opened it with a great feeling of curiosity as I wanted to see how it was going with her studies. But the letter dealt with an entirely different topic: her parents had decided to leave for Paris after the city's liberation because they feared the Russian invasion in Romania. I suddenly stopped everything I was doing and rested my chest on the edge of the bureau with my head down. For a long while I just stood there, feeling like a curtain had fallen over me. I was only aware of a feeling of anger that rose in me—a rage that blocked out everything else from my mind. I made a last-ditch effort to gather my thoughts. After some time, I straightened my back and rose to full height. I realized fully, just then, that Hitler's war was going to steal my loved ones, one by one, and I had no way to defend myself from that I had already experienced, twice before, the bitter taste of these separations—with Ioana Herescu and with Haagi. And now, with Ioana Crătunescu! This was another sudden blow that took away a piece of my heart! I wrote back immediately, hoping Ioana would get the letter in time, wishing her all the best in the world. She was such a good and valuable friend. As for Hitler, he gave Stalin the best opportunity to spread his overall influence in Eastern Europe in the shortest time and to cause the deaths of millions of people. There would only be some—those who had the vision and courage—who would be able to leave the country.

I was not allowed time to lament, however. The exams were knocking at the door. It was all about study, study, then study some more. But I made an exception on the evening of the twenty-third of August 1944, when I dropped everything. We were all sitting close to the radio awaiting an announcement of special breaking news. Around 10:00 p.m., we heard His Majesty King Michael's voice, in his typical slow-spoken way. He announced, "To all Romanian men, Romanian women..." gravely bringing to their notice the end of Antonescu's dictatorship, the reintroduction of the 1923 Constitution, the new government, the end of the war with the Russians, and the acceptance of the truce conditions.

We were quite shaken. Joining the Allies against the Germans seemed like good news, but the likely incursion of the Russians was something that we all dreaded. Tante Angela, like the others, said that the German occupation was very damaging to Romania, but all agreed that now we would inevitably face the tragedy of a Russian invasion.

Mitică had hired a number of former political prisoners to work on the property, where they received shelter and food. When they heard the news that night, they were very excited to hear that the country had turned against the Germans. They also got very cheerful, thanks to the plum brandy Mitică offered them, lit a huge fire in the back yard and danced around it. I could see the fire from the balcony—the flames rising like giant tongues to the sky as if to lick thousands of stars—while the prisoners danced to the rhythm of Romanian folk music. Watching them, Tante Angela remarked, "They might be happy now, but they cannot imagine the unstoppable avalanche of Russian troops that will devastate everything in their path with what's left over from the Germans. Poor country!"

She couldn't have been more right! The big red tongues of fire witnessed that night at Genune remained vividly in my mind, foreshadowing the red wrath that would eventually overwhelm and crush us.

The question, often asked, was whether Romania could have escaped her fate? And the answer was, no, she couldn't! Because of Roosevelt's lack of a broad vision regarding Europe, he focused on the alliance with Stalin in order to defeat the Japanese in the Far East. At the same time, China's Mao Tse-toung, the communist, was in the process of taking over the country and ousting Chang Kai-Chek. That was the moment when China began to rise as a great communist power—becoming, as Haagi used to predict, the *"Gelbe Gefahr,"* the yellow danger.

After the twenty-third of August 1944, the new Romanian prime minister, Sănătescu, declared war on Germany, though by then our troops were already fighting the German army. On the one hand, the Germans bombed the capital; on the other, the Russians were invading the country, sparing nothing and no one crossing their path. They arrived in Bucharest on the thirtieth of August.

Tante Lenuţa, being Uncle Ionel's wife, the general, was very worried knowing he was in charge of the Gendarmerie, which cleared Bucharest of the German forces in five days, ending on the twenty-eighth of August. The General mentioned his appreciation toward "the bravery and devotion in the battles to restore the national independence"(Anton, Constantin, *Magazin istoric* no. 8, 1972, page 11–14). But he was severely punished by the Russians for his role. Because Uncle Ionel had worked for the Royal Palace during the twenty-third of August coup, he was imprisoned by the Communists and spent twelve years in jail including two years in solitary confinement in a dark cell.

The time had come for me to take my exams. The plan was that I would make the trip from Genune to Craiova and back in a carriage driven by our coachman Nicolae. Each trip took about three hours. During one of these trips, we were taken by surprise by some airplanes circling over our heads. I saw the bombs falling near us. Nicolae and I jumped out of the carriage and took shelter in a ditch alongside the road, adjacent to a field and trees. The ditch was full of weeds and thistles. My gaze darted back and forth from the sky overhead to the horses and carriage on the road while the planes flew in circles dropping the cargo. Though the raid lasted only about twenty minutes, it seemed endless to me. I knew we were in great danger. I could see the waves of bombs falling close to us, exploding in short succession, while my heart sank. Watching the sky, I fervently prayed for escape. In the end, I was unhurt, and the unforgettable "Liberator" planes were suddenly swallowed up into the sky. Everything became quiet—a silence finally broken by Nicolae saying, "Miss, thank God we are alive and now let's hurry home."

When we arrived home, I heard the news broadcast on the radio and found out that the American fighter jets had flown over and bombed several German targets in the country. Their flight path took them above the military airport on the outskirts of Craiova.

Another incident took place when I returned from an evening exam, again with Nicolae. This time we were caught in a storm right at the top of a bare hill surrounded only by agricultural fields. Nicolae was whipping the horses so that we could arrive more quickly, but the faster we went the more rapidly the sky darkened until finally there was only a dense blanket of black clouds clustered above us. All of a sudden, we were assailed by strong gales accompanied by the frequent crackling of lightning across the pitch-black sky. This was followed by a downpour of rain and hail engulfing the road. The deafening thunder frightened the horses. They reared up, throwing their front legs forward, so maddened with fright I thought they would overturn the carriage. Nicolae was desperately trying to hold the horses in their place while I tried to clutch the canopies to protect myself from the hard-driving rain and hail. We were right in the eye of the storm, fearful we would be struck by lightning at any moment. And totally exposed: there was nothing around us higher than our carriage. It was hell on earth. I was scared, and so I prayed. This unleashed natural forces so impressed me that I was reminded of the fear I had experienced during the 1940 earthquake. But while the earthquake had lasted only a few minutes, the lashing of the storm seemed to go on and on. When the rain and wind subsided, we continued our way into the night. We arrived home very late, soaking wet, much to the relief of everyone who greeted us. I noticed that Liky was among them.

He also had some bad news for me. The events of August 23 caught my mother in the country. She had been unable to leave for Vienna to be at Alecu's side when he was on his death bed. The man died alone in Vienna clinic on the twentieth of October 1944, where he was cremated by the authorities. And Liky also told me that some of his friends left the country after the twenty-third of August to seek refuge abroad, knowing that the Anglo-Americans would not save Eastern Europe from Russia. Liky concluded by saying:"Herescu was so smart to leave the country right in time, and not to expect the Americans to come."

While I was still at Genune, on the twelfth of September 1944, Romania had to sign an Armistice Convention with the Allies. The agreement was, in fact, with the Soviets, establishing extremely harmful conditions. The Convention had been assigned to an Allied Control Commission, which was in fact the Soviet one. (*Georgescu, Vlad. Istoria Românilor de la origini până în zilele noastre,*[57] second revision Oakland Publishing, CA., Scythian Books, 1989, page

---

57.   The history of Romanian from the origins to the present time

272. AR publications). The only positive outcome was getting back Northern Transylvania.

I graduated my eighth grade, and then my only concern was about the final exam called *Baccalaureat* in October in Craiova. While everyone else left Genune for Bucharest, I took all my belongings and books and left for Craiova to stay with Manini. She was very concerned as the Soviet troops were patrolling our street day and night on their way to the Danube. At that time, a Romanian captain had been lodged in Tata-Lae's former office, and since he was pleasant and civilized we often had him over for lunch or dinner. A few days after my arrival, when we were dining, the captain joined us. While Tata-Lae was telling us with disgust in his voice what he had seen in the town after the Russians arrived, suddenly the door from the corridor opened and we heard sounds of boots scuffing along the floor and male voices speaking in Russian. At first we could not see who had entered because the dining room was dimly lit by just one lamp and the far end of the room was in semi-darkness. I got up from my chair, not understanding how a bunch of intruders could have entered the house, but before I could make a move, a Russian soldier seized me roughly by the arm, yelling "*hazaica, hazaica.*" They were all around us now, armed with balalaikas, machine guns, and rifles, and so drunk they could barely stand on their two feet. I was trapped. All I could think about was how I had escaped an earthquake, a bombardment, the storm on Lazu's hill—and now I had to wonder how I would possibly get away from him.

I hoped that the captain would interfere because he was, after all, a military officer! But no way did he not move a finger. The only one who had the guts to do something was Manini herself! She grabbed two pieces of chicken and in a blink of an eye tucked them under the noses of the drunken Russians. It was as if they were sent into a frenzy by the smell. The one holding my arm quickly let go and hastily grabbed the piece of chicken. I heard Manini shouting to me, "You run and hide under Tata-Lae's bed! I disappeared at once, but didn't hide under the bed, only locked myself inside the room.

After a while, Manini came to the room victorious, explaining that the Russian had left. She realized they had entered through the unlocked back door.

"We were lucky they were drunk," she added. "Thanks to the chicken, they forgot about you and that's how I could get them out of the house. They took the bait and we managed not to get shot. And they would have shot us, you understand, if we had done anything to annoy them."

I was thoroughly impressed, this time, at seeing Manini in action. She had gone beyond herself with her quick thinking and calm!

It was remarkable how she always knew what to do—and also when and how to do it. And yet, it seems, she had been unable to take a stand against the mentality of the time when she gave up her aspirations of becoming an opera singer. Fate had given her good looks, a uniquely talented voice and financial opportunity to study with the most famous singers. After this incident, Manini never wanted me to live there anymore. She was concerned for my safety and wanted me to move to Tante Jeanna. Accordingly, I packed my bags again and next morning and moved to the house at Tante Jeanna Drăgoescu. Tata-Lae accompanied me. When I got there, the gate was open. I went inside, where I heard voices upstairs. Following the sound, I saw in one of the drawing rooms three Russian soldiers with their *hazeaicas* (their women, t.n.) and Ileana, Vlad, Tante Jeanna and the doctor. I got in the room, and talked to Ileana and found out that the Russians installed themselves in their mansion that morning.

Seeing these circumstances, with Ileana's help I called Cristina my cousin who was lodged with Tante Sofi, her grandmother (Maman Titi's sister). After I told her what was happening, Tante Sofi said,

"Of course you can come over, Cristina sleeps in a double bed. We're waiting for you." Vlad Drăgoescu showed me off to Tante Sofi Dianu's house.

When I walked in, Tante Sofi welcomed me with a hug. Right away I called Manini to let her know what I found at Tante Jeanna's and my current location. Immediately, Cristina launched into a peroration about the Russians taking hold of all Romania, its lands, telephone services, mail, radio—in short, they now controlled everything. Further, she said, they robbed the country, having the Armistice as an excuse. The Allies had left us in the lurch and were no longer more than a presence on paper. After her talk, we both went to arrange my clothes and books in her room, sharing her massive and spacious dresser and we also scheduled our time to cover all the subjects for exams. Everything went well for a few days.

But, just like it was happening at Manini's where the Russian army was flooding the streets with tanks, or at Drăgoescu's, where the Russian couples had comfortably installed themselves, here, on the third night, we woke up to a huge noise. We heard shouting in Russian following by the thud of weighty boots on the marble staircase. After a while, I heard the piano keyboard, groaning under repeated strokes. As far as I knew, during the previous evening there had been no Russian presence in the house. But I was aware that since the invasion, the Soviets had been requisitioning the most beautiful and spacious houses without the consent of the owners. As it was the case with Tante Sofi's house, when the Russians came in late evening to take over the house, they simply shoved some documents in her face, then pushed her aside and began to carry boxes inside. We both went out to see what was going on. Scores of Russians were carrying away trunks and packed boxes. In the midst of the tumult, a drunk Russian with musical inclinations had perched himself on the chair in front of the piano and was hitting the keyboards not with his hands, not with his fists, but with his boots, alternating the right and left foot. I was stunned. I had not seen such behavior before.

The next day, we found out that the Russians had requisitioned the house for the Soviet command. There was a rumor that Marshal Rodion Malinovsky himself was to be there for a few days. He was the Chairman of the Allied (Soviet) Commission, who was later buried in the Red Square near Kremlin.

In the morning when we left the house, we again saw the Russians and they also saw us. At night the infernal noises continued, making it very difficult to study. And one morning, we were awakened by frequent banging on our door and shouts of "Hazeaica, hazaeica." Afraid and suspecting what they were after, we tried to push the dresser against the door, but it was such a massive monster there was no way we could succeed. The shouting continued as well as the pounding of fists on the door, which was strained almost to the breaking point.

Cristina went to the window to see if it was possible for us to make our escape by leaping over the fence into the yard of the Măldărescu family. She came to the conclusion and said, "We could do it, but we could break our legs." But she had another idea, and commanded me, "Go to bed, pull the sheet over your head, and leave a hand hanging out."

In that position, I could see her through the crinkle, in her pajamas rushing to the door, unlocking and opening it broadly and as she remained in the doorway she shouted loudly while pointing at me with her index finger "Typhus exantematic!" (disease, t.n.). As if by magic, the semidrunk Russians fled from the door in a second. I heard their heavy boots dragging across the floor. Cristina locked the door, trembling and jumping into bed.

My cousin Cristina and I were able to prepare ourselves for the Baccalaureate's oral exam on the thirty-first of October without any other commotion. From Tante Sofi I returned to Manini, who congratulated me for my success in the exam. She then took a beautiful crystal bowl in her hands, looked at it cherishingly, and ran her fingers over it as if she was saying good-bye to her youth. It was a bowl she had bought in Copenhagen. She handed it to me saying, "Take it, to bring you luck from now on!"

I was truly happy to be with her and grandfather Tata-Lae. He told me about a conference in Moscow on the ninth of October 1944, in which Roosevelt did not participate, as he was again running for his third term. At this conference, which occurred between Churchill and Stalin, the two leaders took advantage of Roosevelt's absence. Much later I read in Churchill's volumes, that when in Moscow, Churchill sacrificed Romanian order to ensure free movement of British ships in Greece. Churchill himself wrote, "The moment was ripe to do business with Stalin, when I told him to solve our problems in the Balkans, your armies are in Romania and Bulgaria. I pushed a piece of paper over the table toward Stalin: Romania—90 percent Russia, 10 percent others; Greece, 90 percent England, 10 percent Russia; Yugoslavia and Hungary, 50 percent Russia and 50 percent the Allies; Bulgaria, 75 percent Russia, 25 percent others. Stalin checked with his blue pencil and pushed the paper toward me. The paper was in the middle of the table. Finally I said, "It can be considered cynical that we disposed over these problems, regarding the fate of millions of people, in such simple a manner? Let's burn the paper. No, you can keep it, said Stalin." (Churchill, Winston, op. cit., volume 6, page 227) After this episode, Churchill wrote to his wife, Clementine, "The timing was proper to talk business with the old bear. The more I see him the more I love him" (Meacham, Jon, *Franklin and Winston, an intimate portrait of an epic friendship*. 2003, page 306).

Roosevelt's mistake in 1943, in Tehran, was furthered by Churchill in 1944 in Moscow when Romania, more than any other country in Eastern Europe, was left under the Russian boots. In this way millions of people were sacrificed, deserted by Western leaders, and left to endure under utopian communist totalitarianism. And that was that!

My father called to tell me that Uncle Ionel had organized the return of Cristina and me to Bucharest. We would travel in a big truck accompanied by several military ranked officers, since there was no other way to travel, since the Russians had taken control over all means of transportation including trains and cars.

After a few days, Cristina called me to let me know that the truck had come to pick her up and she was on her way to come get me. Manini and Tata-Lae walked me to the gate, where we hugged each other before parting.

The truck, covered with a canopy, pulled in front of Manini's house. There was a driver and a few military ranked officers who could pass through the Russian columns which were scattered along all the roads, acting as occupation troops and taking everything that came their way. The soldiers were rushing me. "Come on, little lady, the road is long and full of armed Russians!" A sergeant helped me get in the back of the truck. I couldn't see Cristina, though I could hear her voice, and I wondered where she could be. My view of her was blocked by two to three cages with birds, two barrels of wine or perhaps brandy, a cage with several piglets, a few bags, other packages and jars of honey (wrapped in straw), cardboard cartons and other large items all being sent by the administrator at the Foișor estate and by Mitică from Genune. Finally I heard the sound of Cristina's voice, and looking that direction, saw her emerge from between the cages where the birds were clucking and the piglets squeaking. Far in the back of the truck was a bench placed transversely against the soldiers' seats in the front. There I saw Cristina, curled upon the bench, wrapped in an old-fashioned coat, probably belonging to Tante Sofi, with a bonnet on her head, because the cold wind blew inside. When I finally caught full sight of her, she rolled her big eyes as only she could, letting me know about the havoc that was about to happen:

"Well what do you think? You believe that we could escape the Russians before we reach Bucharest, now that we've finally finished with the Baccalaureate? We're in trouble!"

I took my seat next to her, and when I saw her look and observed how she rolled her eyes, I could not help bursting into laughter, and laughed so hard I couldn't stop. I barely managed to say, "I do not know what we're going to do with the Russians, but in the meantime I believe this noise and the awful smell from the cages will definitely kill us before the Russians get a chance!"

After the soldiers climbed into the truck and the driver got on the road, it was even worse. It was hell. The bench was moving, the fowls and piglets got agitated, and the stirred-up scent rose rapidly to our nostrils. Nonetheless, Uncle Ionel's solution—this transport— was our only possible chance of reaching Bucharest.

Of course we were very nervous whenever we were stopped by the Russian, which did happen quite a few times before we reach Bucharest. Luckily, every time they stopped us they could not see us in the back because we stooped down to avoid their eyes.

It was an adventure that I still remember, and even now, every time Cristina's terrified image comes to mind, I burst out laughing.

We arrived safely in Bucharest, first in Armașului, where (at Uncle Ionel's orders) his man emptied the truck and unloaded everything sent by Mitică, all according to Leana's instructions. Then the truck with the remaining load continued to Cristina's house. The trip wasn't pleasant at all, but it had been an education. I knew from Manini how difficult it was to buy meat products, which were rationed and could be bought only with food stamps and only on Saturday and Sunday. Moreover, to get them one had to stand in endless lines. The situation was getting worse and worse in our country; our formerly rich country was sinking into poverty.

In our Bucharest house, nothing was the same as before. Uncle Ionel's family occupied the ground floor. Personally I was preoccupied with becoming a law student, aspiring to follow the same career as my father and Nicu. I went to familiarize myself with the Faculty of Law, the classroom, the great hall, and with those who I hoped would become my future colleagues. The university year normally started in September, but courses were postponed for January 1945. In Romania the Soviet Command, within the Allied Control Commission, was exercising its influence to take over more than the 90 percent that Churchill had indicated. Actually, they had a 100 percent control and had become a de facto government without opposition.

However, with or without the Russians, the youthful enthusiasm of my friends was difficult to suppress. Therefore, without having a governess anymore, I was being supervised by Maman Titi and my father. It was his turn to assume primary care of me. One day, he called me to share his advice, drawing my attention to street demonstrations and counseling me on how to avoid them. He made me understand what was safe and what wasn't, based on the principles inculcated in me over the years by all those around me. I listened carefully to his words, spoken by a man with lifelong experience in these matters. At times, when the opportunity arose, he used to advise me, "Always do your best!" reminding me about everything that he and I had previously discussed.

During that time, I would also pay visits to my mother. After she became a widow, she kept the apartment on Dr. Lueger Str., and when she was in Craiova she stayed at Manini's. The Radomir estate where her car was kept (with the DKW number plate 39) was guarded by Johann Schobel, the administrator. Much later, Johann told me that over seventy-five thousand ethnic Germans of Romanian citizenship were deported to the Soviet Union, and 29 percent died there, one of them being his own brother.

The news coming from Craiova was not good at all. One evening, I received a call from my mother, sobbing as she told me, "Tata-Lae was killed!" Unthinkable news—which hurt my soul and exploded in my ears!

"What, Mommy? Who would do such a thing?" Between hiccups, she said, "Mother sent him downtown to the market to buy carrots and other groceries. He had a hat on his head and was holding it with his hand since there was a strong wind. Just then a speeding Russian truck came around the corner and he did not see because of the hat. He was lifted by the truck into the air and fell on the pavement. The truck accelerated, leaving him there. He was taken (I do not know when and by whom) to a hospital where he gave his last breath before Manini could arrive... You can imagine, Moni, that mother is destroyed and tomorrow I'll go to Craiova, I can't leave her to take care of the funeral by herself. Dănel [his son] is in Sibiu with the army and he must obtain permission before coming back, which takes time."

The news grieved me beyond belief. I loved Tata-Lae as if we had been real blood relatives. And Manini, poor woman, had now lost him forever, an added blow coming with the loss of the Herescu's. It had been only a few weeks before when I first saw him, walking me to the truck before I left for Bucharest. I had never imagined that would be the last time I'd see him alive. I keep counting, over and over again the ones I had now lost—Ioana Herescu, Haagi, Ioana Crătunescu and now Tata-Lae—and all because of Hitler and Stalin.

The news from Genune wasn't good either. The situation was rather alarming. The letters we got from Mitică informed us that *patriotic committees* had been created in villages, and peasant-farmers were agitating for land reform by demanding land allotments from "exploiting landowners." And in Romania, due to pressure from the Kremlin, via the Allied (Soviet) Control Commission, the King was forced to accept the resignation of prime-minister General Sănătescu after his second term, whereupon General Nicolae Rădescu was appointed prime minister. My father and Nicu were very happy with the appointment, since General Rădescu was in a position that allowed him to oppose the dismantling of the Romanian Army, which the Russians had requested.

Also, we heard over the radio, that the Communist Party had been included in the Government, which in the past had never counted in the whole country more than nine hundred members. Most of its leaders were sentenced to prison terms in Craiova in 1936 and later took refuge in Russia. Those who had recently returned from Russia became important communist figures backed by the Allied (Soviet) Control Commission. And the Commission was in full control of the country, taking advantage of the 90 percent influence offered by Churchill to Stalin.

Since terror reigned all over, the oppressive situation compelled Romanians to hope for the "arrival of Americans"! Not only was the Russian presence a problem, but people were being picked up at night and arbitrarily held without trial, an act of sheer intimidation. The only place where I felt more secure from evictions was in our own Armașului house, due to the presence of Uncle Ionel who had stature as Chief of the National Gendarmerie. From his discussions with my father or with Nicu, I learned special classes had been organized for political agitators or organizers. Trade union and party cells were planted in the headquarters of various institutions. Hundreds of new communists were assigned to various important positions with the help of certain opportunist intellectuals.

Tante Lenuța and Uncle Ionel, having no children of their own, loved me very much. Now that they were living with us, Tante Lenuța would often take me to the movies or to symphony concerts on Sunday mornings. But of all things I adored, the best was going with them to the Cărăbuși Cabaret Theatre, where I enjoyed actor Constantin Tănase's lyrics:

"It was bad with *der-die-das*, but far worse with *davai-ceas*" made him famous, meaning, "It was bad with the Germans, but worse with the Russians."

For the next fifty years people would manufacture jokes pointing to facts or aspects caused by totalitarianism.

CHAPTER 5

II Armaşului Lane, 1945-1947

1945

The academic year at the Faculty of Law of the Bucharest University started in January. When I left home to begin my first day of college, Maman Titi and my father were really happy and excited to see me begin on my path to a legal career, in keeping with the family tradition. Already, on my first day I saw many of those who would become my future colleagues. Among them were Istrătel Micescu, Baby Ivanovici, Dinu Tătărescu, and Ion Ioanid, whom I encountered in a discussion group in the corridor. The boys introduced me to two of my future female colleagues—with both of whom I would later establish life-long friendships. One was Anca Tyllo, who went by the name of Aimée among her friends. (She immediately indicated that was the name she preferred to be called.) When I asked her where that French name came from, she explained it was actually an acronym made up of the initials of her five first names: Anca, Ioana, Maria, Elena, and Elisabeta. From our first encounter, I think I got an inkling that Aimée would be part of my life for a very long time. Our friendship was strengthened by the fact that we lived in the same neighborhood, just as my dear unforgettable friend Ioana Crătunescu, also came from the same neighborhood. The other girl I met that day was Lenuş Popovici who was of Armenian descent. She had been a classmate with Aimée at Pitar Moş, high school where classes were led by German nuns.

The three of us entered the classroom together and sat next to each other. When Professor Vălimărescu entered the classroom, we all stood up to greet him. He made quite an impression on me, especially wearing his black robe with white ermine fur trimmings. In fact, that was what my father always wore when he was teaching his courses at the university. After classes, I walked home with the small group of new friends, and we decided to meet again in the morning. That became a routine, and for the following three years—between 1943 and 1947—most days we would walk to and from university as a group.

Soon, I met Aimée's parents. Mrs. Tyllo, called Mamina was very friendly, as was her father, Dr. Tyllo, a gynecologist. I soon saw they would do anything their offspring asked. I noticed how Aimée would raise her voice to an extremely high pitch in order to get what she wanted, which seemed to me quite unreasonable.

Aimée was a tiny delicate girl, with dark eyes, gently shaded with very long eyelashes. As she was myopic, those expressive eyes were often hidden behind thick glasses. When I got to know her better, I noticed that she placed great value on her looks. She attended to her hair, wore discreet makeup, was carefully manicured, and her clothes were perfect, without a wrinkle. She wore impeccable shoes. She was very polite, humorous, and one could always have interesting conversations with her because she read a lot. She was also ambitious, but gave the impression of modesty and innocence. She knew how to show her friendship, using all her charms when she wanted. In time, I discovered that she was also very articulate when she wanted to express contempt towards a person she disliked. She believed that life was meant to be enjoyed. Nothing seemed to be beyond her reach until communism entered the picture. And even then, her cleverness came into play. She understood what had to be done when fate forced her hand, and she would turn out to be a good housewife as well as a determined employee dedicated to her work. Aimée did have a double nature, and it bore no resemblance whatsoever to my good and unforgettable friend, Ioana Crătunescu who was always a straightforward person.

Among the old and new friends, most often I spent time with Baby Ivanovich who lived close to me. We studied together and discussed various legal issues. I also spent time with Ion Ioanid, to whom I was in fact distantly related, his mother being Florica's sister and Nicușor his first cousin.

The parties were still going on. Those of us with houses, who were best situated for throwing dancing parties, took turns hosting them. One of the first parties to which I was invited during university years was hosted by my friend Constantin Alimăneștianu, with whom Ioana Crătunescu used to flirt a lot. My inseparable friends, Aimée and Lenuș, were also invited. When Constantin greeted me at the door, I noticed he had a patch covering one corner of his mouth. He explained that while walking in the downtown area during the evening, a group of Russian military men playfully pulled their guns out and fired a bullet that barely missed his cheek but tore the skin in the mouth area. I was terrified by the story, but happy to see that he was alive and had gotten away only with a scratch.

Soon after, Constantin's older brother Călin started to join our parties, together with his girlfriend and future wife, the beautiful Cici Șeiteanu. Călin was taller than Constantin, imposing in stature, and very handsome. I always thought he looked like an American movie star. Both brothers were dressed in a very fashionable "Sergiu Malagamba"[58] style. When Călin danced with Cici, we all withdrew into a circle and admired their steps. They were a lovely, elegant, and graceful couple.

(Many years later, I reconnected with Călin in the USA. He and his brother Constantin had fled the country, swimming across the Danube to escape the Bolshevik persecution. The four brothers

---

58.   Romanian composer, arranger, conductor, and drummer, who was a fashion trend setter back in those days

as I earlier mentioned, were sons of Virgil, a great landowner, with a forest of 4,500 hectares.)

That evening, in the Alimăneștianu house there were a few people whom I had not met before. One of them was Ioan Șarf, called Lulu, whom everybody invited to parties because he had a big collection of LP's with American music. He looked vaguely familiar to me. He was tall and rather chubby, as if he didn't have any bones, but he was so impeccably dressed, his clothes to some extent masked his figure. Lulu had blond, slightly wavy hair, and blue eyes. His mature behavior contrasted with his childish features. His attitude and lively personality emanated an air of determination and confidence.

Lulu was the de facto DJ who played his vinyl disks in the sequence that he thought to be best. We danced to the tune of records that included such outstanding American jazz musicians as Louis Armstrong, Count Basie, Artie Shaw, Benny Goodman, Tommy Dorsey, Glenn Miller, and Duke Ellington. After a while, I continued to feel as though I had met this guy Lulu before, and indeed I finally realized that we are neighbors on Armașului Lane. The reason I had not recognized him at first was because, that night, he had been wearing a suit that made him look more mature. But the more I looked at him, the more I realized the dressed-up Lulu was in fact the teenager whom I occasionally saw on Armașului Lane, wearing shorts and always riding his motorcycle.

The rhythmic beat of the American jazz music made the windows vibrate. Everyone was dancing. When Lulu invited me to dance, I asked innocently, "Are we neighbors? Do you live on Armașului Lane?" Surprised, he asked, "How do you know that?"

"Well, my house is at the back of the alley, on the left side, while yours is opposite to mine, on the right side. I think you're the motorcycle-guy."

He nodded with a smile and without any hesitation whatsoever, as if not to lose the opportunity, he immediately added, "Then allow me to drive you home."

"I'd be delighted," I said, "but I have two problems. I must get home no later than eleven o'clock, and I did not come alone but with my friends Aimée and Lenuș, and cannot leave without them."

He replied, full of confidence, "No problem, I'll keep track of time and I'll take all three of you in my car, and will come back tomorrow to get the disks, so I won't spoil the party."

I was delighted at his offer, and of course, I accepted.

Just before eleven o'clock, Aimée and I said our good-byes, while Lenuş stayed for a bit longer. While Lulu was driving us home, he gave us his phone number and said he would be happy to take us for a drive anytime—depending on whether the car was available (since he was borrowing it from his father). After Aimée got out of the car, he occasionally looked at me and smiled, but I pretended not to see. His silence and my silence created a very awkward situation. Before I got out of the car, he kissed my hand softly and thanked me for agreeing to go with him. "Will I meet you again soon?" he asked. I shrugged, making him understand that I didn't have an answer. He smiled.

After I got out, he turned the car around and parked in front of his house, which was right across from mine.

Maman Titi had waited up and was pleased to see that I made it in time.

"But how did you get home? she asked.

"Can you imagine? I got a ride from the neighbor living across the street at number twelve."

That night, I'm sure Maman Titi began to worry about possible future problems related to the new neighbor with a car. As I lay in bed, I was smiling in the dark, completely unable to fall asleep.

Not even twelve hours later, the very next morning, Rina the housemaid asked me, "Miss, tell me what should I do, there's a boy from the flower shop with a large bouquet of roses for you. Should I take it?"

It was the first bouquet I had ever received in my life. How was I to refuse it, especially since I knew who it was from.

"Yes, Rina, you can take it," I answered, giving her some change to tip the flower deliverer.

The bouquet came without any letter; just our address was written on the envelope. I arranged the twelve pink roses in a large bowl, and Rina teasingly observed, "What will your grandmother say?"

When Maman Titi came to my room she admired the roses, asking whom they were from.

"I do not know. Maybe from someone who was at last night's party?" I said. I wasn't even lying, because the flowers were anonymous.

"Don't sneak behind my back," Maman Titi prompted me. "I'm sure it's that neighbor, what's his name?"

"John Șarf," I replied.

"Oh, my God! Why did he have to come in our neighborhood?"

But the problem of the flower bouquets had just begun. The next day, the flower-boy came with another bouquet, similar to the first one, with twelve more fresh roses. Thank God for Rina, who rushed to the door, took the roses and replaced the old roses with the newly arrived ones. Then she took the old roses to her room, which was on the last floor of the villa where Maman Titi or Leana never ventured.

Whenever Maman Titi came to my room, she expressed ever more astonishment about those roses. Being myopic and without glasses, she would draw close to admire them and remark, "I do not understand what kind of roses these are. They last so long, don't wither, and still smell so nice!"

I would pretend I was just as puzzled as she was, without offering a word of explanation.

When I had received about the twelfth bouquet of roses, Rina started to become alarmed, saying, "Miss, I do not know what to do anymore." She added, "I have no more vases and no place to put so many roses. Should I throw some of them out? I'm sorry, since they are still so fresh. If you know who sends them, please tell him to stop because the only place left in my room to put them is on my bed."

Laughingly I answered, "Okay, Rina, you can throw away some of them to make enough room for you to sleep."

On that day, when I came back from college in the afternoon, everyone was taking a nap. I picked up the phone and called Lulu, "It's Mona Vrăbiescu."

He interrupted and asked me to go to the window so he could see me while we were talking. Next to him in the window was a very big dog with two paws up on the sill.

"I think it's better this way," he said. Then he asked if I liked the roses.

"Of course I do," I said. "But that's exactly why I called now, to ask you to stop, since I will get in trouble with my grandmother."

He laughed and said that his intention was make me do exactly what I had done—call him. Now he wanted to arrange a drive-out with me and my girlfriends, adding that Aimée had already called him and come up with that idea. He also said that whenever he felt like talking on the phone—if I accepted of course—he would have Rex, the dog, bark at the window to let me know he was there.

Before we ended the conversation, he reminded me one more time, "Please talk to Aimée and tell when you agree to meet us, so I can ask my dad for the car."

Then he added, "Can I call you, Mona?"

"Yes, Lulu, you can."

We said good-bye and waved to each other from our windows. That moment became the beginning of a very long friendship.

Not to be seen alone with him, I contacted Aimée to arrange a meeting with Lenuş. This became a habit. Lulu invited them to come along, and after awhile Cristina joined us. He would take us to Flora's restaurant garden where we usually ate warm croissants and drank cold buttermilk. Or sometimes we went to the movies with featuring unforgettable actors like Leslie Howard, Paulette Godard, and Sonja Henie. Sometime it was pretty hard to get hold of tickets, but Lulu had his ways and managed to get enough for the whole gang. With tickets held between his fingers, he would raise his hand and make us hurry toward the entrance where a cluster of people were still waiting to purchase their tickets.

Whenever I heard Rex barking, I went to the window. Lulu would be there, and after gazing at me for a bit, he would return to his studies. I thought he was studying for college, like I was, until I found out he was in fact in the last year of high school. Because of his height, the fact that he was well-built, the way he had been dressed at the party at Alimanestianu's, and the fact that he drove a car—all had made me think he was older than me. Now it was already too late for me to consider his age a factor. His distinguished looks, sociable personality, attentiveness, and generosity were the qualities that interested me most.

I learned that Harry, Lulu's father, was a businessman in the timber industry and had divorced his mother, Sanda. Harry had the reputation of being a womanizer attracted especially to actresses. Sanda adored Lulu, and he went to visit her often.

The time flew, and I kept myself busy with classes and meeting the girls and Lulu and other friends. In the meantime, events were taking a turn for the worse throughout the country. We were all scared because lots of people were being arrested. Most were taken from their homes in the middle of the night and thrown in jail. Gen. Rădescu, the prime minister, declared he would oppose the communization of the country. To which I often heard my father offer his applause, "Well done, General, well done, bravo!"

Sometimes I was invited when Uncle Ionel had guests. One of the dinner guests, a refugee from Basarabia, told us about the horrible measures enacted there by the Communists in 1940. The first thing they did was to expropriate people's fortunes. Then followed a flurry of arrests and other unreasonable measures, such as the destruction of painted icons inside churches. The gentleman said that communism is based on lies and terror.

After we finished the meal, Uncle Ionel my father and Nicu walked him to the door. After he left my father commented that, "The devil cannot be as black as this person told us."

The truth is that at that point nobody believed Stalin would be able to hold Eastern Europe hostage. Therefore, people avoided facing the danger that was threatening us, believing that some kind of lucky star looked over the country. Uncle Ionel took me aside and told me with an uncharacteristically serious voice, "It is very important that no one knows what we speak inside the house or whom we receive. So we ask you not to talk to anyone, not even with your friends, with absolutely no one, anything about politics, about our views or what is happening in the country, don't mention the church you go to, because these communists have no faith, they don't have any respect for our historical or religious traditions. Or we could all get arrested."

Then my father added, "Even some little conversations that may seem harmless can be a threat."

On the end of February, a big rally took place in the Palace Square. My friend Baby went there and reported that the streets were patrolled by Russian soldiers in tanks and trucks and that there were some dead and wounded. Next day, I heard from colleagues that the pro King and Rădescu's demonstrators were shot during that night. However, according to the Kremlin news report, our army was accused of the crimes. Misinformation had begun.

The Yalta Conference was held at the Livadia Palace at the beginning of February: J. Meacham, reports, "The Big Three signed the Declaration of liberated Europe,...the establishment of order in Europe and the rebuilding of national economic life...which will enable people to...create democratic Institutions of their own choice..." Also, Churchill wrote to his wife Clementine,"...my impression is that Marshal Stalin and his Soviet leadership are to live in friendship and honorable equality with the Western Democracies."

Upon leaving Livadia, according to Meacham, "Churchill... tried to maintain his cheer but found it difficult. He said to his daughter Sarah, I have felt the weight of responsibility more than ever before and in my heart there is anxiety." (Meacham, Jon, pages 322–325). In fact, Churchill's doubts were founded! It is known now that Yalta actually meant the division of Europe and domination of Eastern Europe by the Soviets. These countries became the satellite states of the USSR. The only positive result from Yalta was the recognition, that Northern Transilvania belonged again to Romania, however a fact already mentioned in the Armistice Convention of the twelfth of September 1944.

Right away after Yalta, at the end of February, the Kremlin envoy Andrei Vishinski came to Bucharest where he was received by the King. What followed I have had later the privilege to hear directly from H. M. King Michael. Thus, Vishinski asked in a brutal and violent manner for the dismissal of Rădescu's government, to be replaced by a Communist one. The King tried to resist, but under threats and with Vishinski banging his fist on the table, shouting and walking out of the room slamming the door, eventually he had to give in. That explains how on the sixth of March 1945, the first Communist government was installed with Petru Groza[59] as prime minister.

Now, all that had been left for us was to listen to *Voice of America* and *Radio Free Europe* broadcasts in the hope that Americans would still "arrive" to liberate us.

After Vishinski established the communist government, Churchill's opinions in 1953 were that: "Russia's first violation of the Yalta Agreement took place in Romania…On February 27 Vishinski, who had appeared in Bucharest without warning demanded an audience of King Michael and insisted he should dismiss the all party-government. At the same time Soviet tanks and troops deployed in the streets of the capital and a Soviet nominated administration took office…I was deeply disturbed by this news, which was to prove a pattern of the things to come…Stalin was now pursuing the opposite course in the two Black Sea countries and one which was absolutely contrary to all democratic ideas. He had subscribed on paper to the principles of Yalta, and now they were being trampled down in Romania. *(*Churchill Winston S., *Second World War Triumph and Tragedy,* 1953, volume 6, pages 419–420, 421) And Churchill added that Roosevelt wrote Stalin on March 29 that "I cannot conceal from you the concern with which I view the developments of events… since our…meeting in Yalta I frankly cannot understand why the recent developments in Romania should be regarded as not falling within the terms of the agreement. I hope you will find time personally to examine the correspondence between our governments on this subject" (Churchill, Winston, op. cit., page 744).

J. Meacham explained that the problem was related to the papers signed at Yalta, which were not precise enough and could be interpreted very differently by Moscow. He notes, "At Yalta Roosevelt

---

59. Petru Groza was a Romanian politician, best known as the prime minister of the first Communist Party-dominated governments under Soviet occupation during the early stages of the Communist regime in Romania. His left-wing policies earned him the nickname of the red bourgeois.

was ill, lethargic…tired and sick…jealous of rivals…but he was effective when reminding the world he was the true power believing in friendly relationship with the USSR…(however) in April he shared Churchill's belief that in Yalta…they had taken a great risk there, an enormous risk, and it involved the Russian intentions." (Meacham, Jon, op. cit., 319–328, 338) Further, says Meacham, "Churchill… considered the diplomatic act of Yalta the opening of the cold war when Stalin began to stitch what Churchill called the Iron Curtain." (Meacham, Jon, op. cit., pages 314, 362)

On the seventh of March, my birthday, I invited many friends over. Of course, Lulu was included. I had no problems getting my father's approval, despite all the trouble of the sixth of March. Next day our house was filled with over a hundred youngsters. After everyone had arrived, my father also joined the party. He socialized with people he had known from previous years. Now I finally could introduce him to Lulu, presenting him as "Mr. Ioan Șarf, our neighbor from number 12."

I pointed towards the house across the street that could be seen through the open windows. Father said that he was pleased to meet Lulu, and after he exchanged a few friendly words with everyone, he went back to his room.

The next day my father told me that Maman Titi informed him that perhaps this newcomer, Mr. Șarf, called Lulu, was the one with "the flower bouquets that wouldn't wilt." When I confirmed that fact, my father told me only this, "Always be at your best." These five words conveyed to my ears everything that I knew was worrying him.

"No reason to worry," I replied slowly, but firmly so that he would know that I understood what he meant.

The new Groza government was quick to make its presence felt, which occurred two weeks after my birthday. That's when they enforced the communist ideology and passed the land reform. The act abolished big estates and limited property to only fifty hectares[60] per owner. There was no financial compensation. In addition, our agricultural equipment, including tractors, seeders, harvesters,

---

60.   Approximately 123 acres

threshing machines, were confiscated. Upon hearing the news, everyone in Armașului was crushed. Our ancestral land had been taken away. Mitică was sending quite alarming telegrams to Bucharest, which later I found in 1985, in my father's archives. At least the mansion and surrounding grounds were safe. Nobody and nothing could cheer us up. It was clear that something that started so badly could not end well.

For Easter we went to Genune where we celebrated St. George's day, my father's name day. All the peasants came from the surrounding villages, they were alarmed and concerned about the land reform, not because of our loss but also out of disappointment that they were not given any land from the property that had been expropriated.

When we returned from Genune to Craiova, first I went with my father to see Manini and Dan Defleury, Tata-Lae's son. She had financial problems after the Bârca estate had been expropriated and concerned about the Herescu's abroad or my mother, a widower having problems with the Radomir estate's problems.

The only satisfaction was that Hitler had committed suicide on the thirtieth of April 1945 and on the nineteenth of May, Germany surrendered, so Second World War ended in Europe though the war with Japan was still going on.

As for Romania, Prime Minister Petru Groza went to Moscow to establish Soviet-Romanian companies called SOVROM. After this agreement, the entire Romanian economy was under Soviet control. Thus, the expropriation of land, together with the control over private enterprises, comprised for the time being the most important movements to introduce a Marxist system in Romania.

The state acquired all the power in one swoop, when most of the population was reduced to a status of dependency Social classes disappeared, and the market economy—which had been operating under the 1923 Constitution—was replaced with a planned, government-controlled economy family and friends wondered how it was possible for the West to look with indifference at what was happening in our country.

During that time I was totally immersed in studying for the upcoming exams. Lulu and I would often see each other through the windows when Rex barked. His father bought him a DKW right after he graduated from high school and got him his driver's license. After that, he did not have to borrow his father's car any more. Right after the exams, Paps came to visit us. About that time, Lulu told us that Sanda, his mother, would organize a big tea-party at their home to celebrate his finishing high school. Paps offered to accompany Cristina and me. I had a great time, enjoying the attention received from Sanda, Lulu, and all his friends whom I was meeting for the first time.

At home the atmosphere was more relaxed. The Potsdam Conference took place in August 1945, hosted at the Cecilienhof Palace, an English-style country house. (I would later visit Potsdam Palace, near Dresden, in 2007. I learned the place was chosen so that Stalin could get there by train, since he hated flying, and also because the city was in the Soviet protection zone.) The conference agenda was concerned with the future of Germany and its allied countries and with the revision of the Allied Control Commission procedures, which until then had never before been questioned. But because Stalin's interest was in consolidating his influence over Romania and Bulgaria, disagreements occurred and discussions had to be postponed until another conference. (That one, in September, would be attended only by foreign ministers in London.)

In light of the meeting that was to occur in September, the American and the British Control Commissions informed and advised King Michael not to recognize the Groza government. And as a result, the King asked for its resignation. But Groza refused, and the King refused to countersign any measures taken by this government, which considered illegal. All along, the King was expecting a formal decision from the Allies.

Also then, President Truman, wanted to demonstrate America's exercise of power before the September meeting in London, which he did by approving the atomic bombing of Hiroshima at beginning of August, and immediately after that on the ninth of August in Nagasaki, ending the war with Japan. Truman hoped that this would also bring an end to the tensions of the Cold War in Europe as well.

But, at the London conference of foreign ministers in September-October, they could not agree on the meaning of "democracy" and how that concept should be applied to the Central and Eastern Europe countries. The Russians vehemently opposed any Anglo-American influence in Romania, and although Truman had decided not to accept the new Groza government he caved in to pressures within the Allied Commission and had to compromise. As a result, the communist government remained in power and Romanians lost hope that Americans would impose their decisions. It was a defeat.

Once again the London Conference was postponed. Another one was rescheduled to occur in Moscow in December. Given this time, in Romania and other countries the opposition parties were eliminated and one unique Communist party was imposed.

As Henry Kissinger explained clearly the situation in his book, mentioning that: "instead of putting pressure on negotiations, the Anglo-Saxons had accepted too many conferences: in Potsdam, London, and Moscow…the longer they prolonged the discussions, Stalin had the time to establish one-party governments or the harder it would become to dissolve the unique party system established— under Russian influence as the dominant power in these countries." *(Diplomacy,* New York, Simon & Schuster, 1994, pages 434–436).

In September, Lulu was admitted to the Polytechnic University and I started my second university year. Among the courses I took, I will mention only Civil Law, which I attended with Istrare Micescu (whom I have previously mentioned as a family friend). At the beginning of his course, all students gathered in the great, overcrowded amphitheater. The professor spoke about "freedom, the relation of the law to freedom, and the role of technical progress as it related to human freedom." We were all captivated by his presentation. Suddenly, one of the doors of the amphitheater flew open and a group of girls and boys barged in with their left fist and arm raised shouting insulting words directed at the professor. Several students from the first bench stood up immediately and threw out the intruders. After the door closed behind them, there was a moment of silence before the professor resumed as if nothing had happened. We were all boiling inside, indignant at the audacity and nerve of those hooligans, which I can feel even now as I am writing. At the end of the lecture, we honored Micescu with rounds of applauses, expressing admiration for the substance of his speech, which was full of superb, elegant exposition. We also applauded for what he represented, the former Romanian society that was so threatened now. This was my first personal encounter with those who supported the new communist movement. I will experience a similar movement in 1969 in the USA supported by the SDS students at Columbia University.

After this incident, Istrate Micescu never again taught at our university. He was expelled, as well, from the Bar Association, because he participated in a public demonstration against the land reform in which he referred to "the Constitution of 1923 which ensured ownership" and asked the Supreme Court "to cancel any laws contrary to the Constitution." (See also Micescu Istrate, *Civil Law Course*, Bucharest, All Beck Publishing House, 2000 [Juridica], page 12.) By doing so, he set himself up for becoming a new target of persecution from the new government which ignored the rights and obligations of citizens. One of the accusations involved his being in possession of weapons displayed on the panoply in his house—guns which he prized as a hunter (and which I used to admire when I went to see Istrătel, his son). He was arrested in 1948, sentenced to twenty years, and died on the twenty-second of May, 1951 in prison.

What a shame to sacrifice a brilliant mind for the sake of applying utopian ideas—which only resulted in inhuman terror, subjugation, and destruction! Finally today, Istrate Micescu is considered one of Romania's greatest lawyers in terms of erudition and judicial knowledge. Knowing these qualities of his, I had the great joy of discovering, when I had to go to the Palace of Justice in 2009 for one of my many properties trials, that Courtroom number IX of the Court of Appeal is now called Istrate Micescu Hall. I do not know whether it was only a coincidence, but in 2009, in that Room number IX, I regained my father's apartment in Armașului Lane after fifteen years of law suits, an event which occurred almost fifty-seven years after we were evicted. Without doubt, it was the merit of the lawyer that won the case, but I'm sure Micescu's spirit was also present, as he had so often been a visitor to our house.

But there's more to tell concerning Master Micescu. After many years, I found that one of the hecklers who rudely interrupted Master Micescu's course at the University had become a prominent communist-favoring poet. After the 1989 revolution, the same poet turned into a pro-democracy activist and was a frequent participant at the meetings at the Cultural Center of the Romanian Consulate in New York. I came across one of her poems, written in 1952, in which she expressed admiration for Stalin and Romanian Prime Minister Gheorghiu Dej. She also wrote an anti-American poems in a book entitled *The World's Cancer* (referring to America). Even though she could deny that in 1945 she was part of the anti-Micescu students' group, she of course could not deny that she wrote those poems.

Back to September 1945, the first party during the winter exam session was given by Aimée on her birthday, the tenth of October. Shortly afterwards, on the twenty-sixth of October, Lulu also threw a party for his birthday. My greatest pleasure was dancing with Lulu. With his feet firmly on the floor, his arm coiled around me holding me tight, we started dancing at the first sound of music, moving our bodies in perfect harmony as we followed the rhythm of American records playing the popular big-band songs of the day. We both felt the fun and pleasure of dancing. Lulu gave me what could be called "the joy of life." Those were happy moments that I will never forget. Yes! Moments worth remembering—there are not many like these!

Soon after the two parties, on the eighth of November—on St. Michael and Gabriel's day, which was also King Mihai's birthday—there was a large student demonstration in front of the Royal Palace. My father warned me not to get involved, because there might be incidents. There were thousands of demonstrators, mostly young, shouting "Long live the King!" and singing the Royal Anthem. A communist organization sprang into action. Many trucks came along, and police squads emerged to hit the protesters with iron bars. Two trucks were overturned by demonstrators who were shouting "Off with the government!" There were many dead and injured, and numerous protestors were arrested. The demonstration made it clear that Romania did not want communism.

At the Moscow Conference in December, elections were finally scheduled for May 1946. The King explained to Westerners that the country was in the hands of communists and that if there wasn't a strong oversight with many observer stations on the election day, they would be manipulated.

After Uncle Ionel had returned to his home, my father realized that we had too much extra space. Fearing that unwanted tenants might forced upon us, he decided to give up the top floor so that he would at least have some control over who those tenants would be. So we all moved down on the ground floor. I took the guest room, from where I could see Lulu's window. My father occupied one corner of the dining room and Maman Titi moved in the smoking room, keeping the drawing room and the bureau for friends and relatives who came by—often, to comment on the latest events.

I do not remember how—together with Nicu—my father picked the tenants out of the many who came by. The top floor, now empty, and repainted and the tenants chosen, I was curious to know who would be living in the house. I read the *Book of Property*,(a new government regulation) filled in by my father, because he was responsible for the building and had to keep records of everybody. I shall reproduce the information I read from *tab no. 418*, which I found in my father's archives, because the new tenants will appear further along in this book:

Coloman Kandel—director of Transylvania Bank director, born in Satu Mare 1894;
Rosalie Kandel—housewife born in Borşa;
Stephen Paul Kandel—born in Taşnad 1920, military service, residence in Agigea as a surgeon;
George Kandel—born in Taşnad 1925, student.

The next day I saw the parents when they came down to wait for the driver to get their car out of the garage. I couldn't get much of a glimpse because they were wearing overcoats and hats. (I met them in 1946.)

1946

After the New Year, I accidentally met the new tenant, George Kandel, who introduced himself first and said he had come from the city of Cluj, where he was a law student, to visit his parents for the holidays and organize his belongings when moving in. He told me that his parents would be very pleased to invite me up to meet them. George was tall, slender, had blue eyes and a calm attitude. I was not to see him again until after my exams in June, when I got to know his parents. Rosalie, his mother, asked me to come upstairs, for she had just baked a cake. That was when I saw the apartment with furniture, silverware, and fine crystal. It didn't look overcrowded; the interior looked airy and lovely. George had moved into my old room, right above the one I now occupied. And Stephen, the doctor (who was absent at that time) took over Nicu's old room. Both parents were tall. The husband was a handsome man with straight black hair, dark eyes and gorgeous teeth. His wife had an unusual hairdo: her black hair parted down the middle and pulled back into a small bun. She had greenish-blue eyes, just like George. They were very friendly, and they were happy to have found this apartment which they said they really liked. In short, Rosalie told me that every time she baked a cake, she would be sure to invite me over, even if her children weren't at home.

George came home only during the holidays. Stephen, who was doing his surgical residency as an orthopedic surgeon at the town of Agigea next to the Black Sea, couldn't come home at all, but called instead. I had the opportunity to taste both the winter and spring cakes that Mrs. Kandel prepared whenever she invited her friends to a game of bridge. In time, I found out that the father had heart disease. Though it wasn't too serious, sometimes he had to take a nitroglycerin pill that he placed under his tongue. I felt bad for him, since he was just a young man of fifty-second years, and for her, who at the age of forty-six had to deal with his health condition. It seemed to be a constant threat.

My mother being in Bucharest I went to visit her when she told me that Manini's beautiful house had been almost entirely occupied. The new tenant was Dr. Ion Parhon, together with his wife and two sons. Dr. Parhon was the grand nephew of I. C. Parhon, Romania's Chairman of the Grand National Assembly in 1945, who was also an endocrinologist. With those tenants in place, Manini was left with only one room and a bathroom.

The situation in the country was only getting worse. The King had to sign all previous decrees which were immediately implemented. Romania daily moved closer into the Russian orbit. As a result, everyone from our former entourage began to leave for the West. Now, whenever I walked to the university I saw the streets and avenues overflowing with Russian tanks, obviously placed there to intimidate the population.

What was happening internationally was getting worse as well. Ever since Potsdam, the dialogue between Russian and Anglo-Americans had collapsed. The tension was created by Stalin. Why did that happen? According to Dr. Kissinger, in short, it was because without a preliminary agreement among the three Allies regarding the postwar situation, with the Germans being defeated and the war over, Stalin, no longer needed them. In addition, Kissinger gave an important detail: "Stalin was eager for an arrangement...and a request for quid pro quo'...(But) the price Stalin was willing to pay will never be known because Roosevelt cut short the Anglo-Soviet dialogue before Germany's defeat".(*Diplomacy*, New York, Simon & Schuster, 1994, pages 400, 402–409). We have learned from experience that negotiations with the Soviets have to proceed solely from a position of strength. After Germany had been defeated, the moment was lost!

Therefore, in March at Westminster College at Fulton, Missouri, Churchill warned the world about Stalin's expanding sphere, declaring, "We must never cease to proclaim principles of freedom, an inheritance of the English speaking world...all found in the American Declaration of Independence". (Meacham, Jon, op. cit., pages 361, 366, 369).

At Fulton, Churchill defended the freedom of the West, when the one in the East was doomed. It was already too late for the second chance, because Anglo-American were not able or did not want to follow General George Patton's advice to use their power to suppress the Soviet domination right after Germany's defeat, instead Stalin filled the vacuum.

On seventh of March, my birthday had again arrived. But since we had no room to spare in our house in Armașului, Lulu organized the party in his apartment. That's where I went with Aimée, Lenuș and many other friends, and where Gershwin's powerful percussion rhythms filled our hearts with delight. That evening I met Harry, Lulu's father, an average size man with piercing eyes that kept careful watch over us all.

One morning during Easter recess, when I was in Genune, around eleven o'clock I heard all twenty-two pairs of peacocks go on high alert at the sound of a car engine. Suddenly I saw Lulu's DKW pull up in front of the house. I could not believe my eyes when the two doors opened and Aimée and Lenuș both got out, shouting as hard as they could, "You weren't expecting this, were you? You didn't see this coming?" I found out that it was Aimée's idea to leave Bucharest at five in the morning in order to arrive in late morning in Genune. After the necessary greetings Gică, Nicu and Florica started preparing lunch while Lulu took pictures. They were particularly admiring the peacocks with their fluffy tails. After lunch they took off at once, headed back to Bucharest, a journey that would last at least five hours even if they didn't encounter any Russian trucks on the way.

As always, before leaving for Bucharest, I went to see Manini in Craiova. All the furniture, paintings, silver, crystals and glasses, and dinner sets belonging to her were still in place. Even though they had been sold piecemeal to the Parhons, they were allowed to remain where they had always been. Luckily, Manini told me the Parhons were honest and decent people and she could make a living. Coca Parhon used to invite her to dinner parties—where all dined using the same table, dishes, cutlery and glassware that we had used in the past. Knowing that Manini had a beautiful voice, at the end of the meal the Parhons would ask her sing for them, doing folk songs or *lieds*.

Far too many changes had happened too quickly over the last years, starting with the nationalization of the estates in Genune, Bârca and Radomir, the loss of homes occupied or rented to foreigners, the Herescu's departure and Tata-Lae' death caused by a Russian truck. Anyone would have needed a strong heart to endure all these abuses.

I also went to see Tănţica Naiculescu, my friend, who told me about her great love, Gică Busuiocescu, whom she had married. Tănţica's problem started when her husband began to be chased by the SECURITATE (the Romanian STASI), he being the nephew of Mihalache, a politician in opposition with the communists.

In June after I had successfully passed my law exams, my father wanted to have a talk with me. I suspected what he had on his mind, and my intuition proved correct. It was about Lulu. When Maman Titi found out that Lulu had come to Genune for Easter, she was so annoyed she thereupon launched a campaign against him. She didn't want me, her only niece, to be seen together with him. She was hoping to see me with someone from the high Oltenian society. I was disappointing her by seeing a boy who was not up to "my standards," and she could not appreciate the fact I was only looking for fun. My father said that Lulu Şarf was a nice and mannered boy, but that he was not for me because of his age and because of his family (since his father wasn't an intellectual). I argued that, in the first place, it was not my intention to get married, and, secondly, that Lulu was a honorable student at the Polytechnic University. As I saw it, he was certainly on his way to becoming an intellectual, he always behaved like a real gentleman, and I saw no reason to give up his friendship.

But my father intended to get me away from Lulu. I left with Cristina, in Uncle Ionel's car, to visit the Ercea estate owned by Tante Natalie Ştiucan. She and her husband Uncle Tache received us with joy and warmth. One day followed another with little variation, only the radio and the mail kept us informed, along with any news brought by Uncle Tache, who was very pessimistic about the current situation of the country. It was a place I associate with beautiful memories.

We arrived in Bucharest in early September. It just so happened that when I got out of the car, Lulu was at the window with Rex. I entered the house where I was received with great joy by my family. But their joy vanished within the hour, when a youngster showed up on our doorstep with a beautiful bouquet of twelve yellow-rusty chrysanthemums. It was an explosion of disappointment for my family, realizing that the enforced absence had no effect. I knew that by sending the flowers, Lulu wanted to show me that nothing had changed.

Thereafter I also received a call from Aimée who had found out from Lulu that I had returned to Bucharest. She suggested I pay her a visit the next day at 11:00 a.m. I agreed, suspecting that Lulu would be there. Now I had to work out my dilemma. I knew my father and Maman Titi's dissatisfaction was boiling over, and at the same time I knew how happy I would be to see Lulu again. As far as I was concerned, I had been moved deeply by his care in sending over the flowers the moment I returned. I had nothing to blame him for. On the contrary I rather appreciated the happy moments he always offered me. I fondly remember how he could dance like. No one could compare with Lulu's rhythm. To find an answer to my dilemma, I turned to Haagi's teachings, in which I believed, "Pray and you will receive a solution."

The next day, I went to Aimée's, hoping the solution would come to me. Lulu was there, and we were glad to see each other again. When she left us alone, Lulu hugged me and said with full confidence that he would never allow such a separation ever again. Knowing he had no power to prevent that, I was amused. Laughing, I asked him, "And how exactly are you going to do that?" Very calmly, he sat on a chair in front of me and heard him saying, "Look, this is what I'm going to do." And after a short pause, he announced, "I'm asking you to marry me right now." At the same moment he drew a small box from his pocket—no doubt with a precious jewel inside—which he pressed into my hand. I was flabbergasted; I had not expected this proposal, which certainly was complicating the things. Immediately he continued, "Please do not give me any answer until I finish what I have to say."

He confessed that in my absence he had made a connection with someone else, but assured me he would end it right away if I accepted his proposal, "It is your decision if and when we get married," he continued, "I want to do it as soon as possible."

His tone of voice was very assertive. Naturally, my thoughts were spinning, but suddenly I remembered my father's words: "Be patient and see what Lulu will do until your return…" Hearing about the "connection," my ego was hurt and, conceding this, I already had my answer ready for him. I explained carefully—keeping my composure and taking care not to hurt him I said, "You know you have always been dear to me, but we are too young to get married. You are even younger than I am. We're still students with no personal income, and we would be dependent on our parents. In addition, I wish to finish college first, to be able to have a job and be independent, especially in view of what the Communists are doing to our country."

While I was talking, Lulu was looking at me very closely. I returned the jewelry box, placing it carefully back in his hand. Our conversation had been a shock for both of us. Each of us was now faced with separate issues. He had lost me, but he could now go back to that "connection" he had made over the summer. As for me, I had lost the joys he used to offer me and, it seemed, would be returning to a boring life. But unexpectedly I had found the answer I was looking for. Haagi's advice worked.

Having made my decision, we stood up and hugged as our eyes filled with tears. Eighteen months of my youth had flown away, a time I would never relive again. Our paths had parted, but we were to remain friends for the rest of our lives, both of us holding on to the memory of a very precious story.

When I later talked to Aimée about what happened, she said, "I'm not surprised at all. I know who "the connection" is. She's a colleague of mine from the Pitar Moș high school."

I never told my father about Lulu's marriage proposal. Maman Titi, despite her age, was aware of everything. She had seen Lulu through the window talking with a lady. When Maman Titi asked me if I knew who the lady was, I told her, "Yes, she is a high school classmate of Aimée's."

By this I think Maman Titi understood what had happened during my absence. In fact, I think even Harry, Lulu's father, was pleased with the outcome, because I don't think a marriage prospect was something he would have wanted at that time for his son.

When I returned from Ercea, my friend Baby and I enrolled into the third year of the Law Faculty. Aimée and Lenuş gave up, for no reason at all.

The peace that followed in the house was interrupted by a problem related to the land expropriation in Genune. Both brothers had been given the right to own separate parcels of land—110[61] hectares: 50 hectares for Gică and 60 for Nicu and Florica—by a resolution of a "Commission for the Implementation of the Agrarian Reform in the County of Dolj." But in November they received another letter from Mitică, which mentioned that the prior notice, although final and binding, was not correct. Maman Titi was so upset by what was happening that I even overheard her talking aloud to herself in her room, as I saw she always did when such injustices happened.

We received the above notice on the day when the parliamentary elections were settled, the nineteenth of November 1946. Regarding the elections, some members, acting anonymously, put up election posters during the night. During the daytime, it was impossible for them even to assemble, they were so fearful of being arrested, beaten, or shot. Vintilă Brătianu, my cousin, was taken out of the country by the Americans with a US Military Mission plane; he had been sentenced in absentia to hard labor for life.

And, I heard on Radio London that the British and American military missions had sent urgent protests to Bucharest, objecting to the way the elections were prepared and conducted. But the government took no corrective measures. Communist squads, observing the voting procedures, used brutality as a means of intimidation I was told that, on the one hand, citizens who were registered on the voting lists could not find their names, and on the other, trucks were transporting Communist voters to cast their ballots while opposition candidates were beaten and prevented from reaching the polls. Foreign observers were too few or none. As a result, the elections of November 19 were massively manipulated, as the King had predicted and warned the West, so that the Communist party, declared winning 70–80 percent of votes. Nobody believed the outcome, but

---

61. Approximately 270 acres

we were forced to accept it. Thus, the Groza government reported a great victory on paper, which only intensified the country's Sovietization process.

Although, Radio London broadcast the news that Secretary of State Dean Acheson had criticized the conduct of the elections, that did not do good either. Therefore, even harder times were ahead of us.

Many of the initial leaders of the communist party and government structures were leftist Jews who, faced of the advance of the Nazis, had taken refuge to Moscow where they were radicalized—brainwashed with Marxist ideology—then returned with the Soviet troops to implement communist rule in Romania. These represented a completely different category from those who had been part of the Jewish Community Committee CCER, led, as I mentioned before, by former President Willy Filderman together with Iancu Zissu or Rabbi Alexandru Şafran. Most of those in CCER managed to migrate to Israel or to the West, thanks to Mr. Jacober's diligence in London or with help from the USA Congress through the Jackson-Vanick Amendment. The Jewish newcomers from Moscow, on the other hand, were the ones who contributed to the installation of the dictatorship, the monopoly by a single party—in short, the utopian totalitarianism of Marxist ideology.

1947

During January we received news from Mitică, who wrote us to say that in villages and townships the peasants who were hiding tractors and other tool machines had been arrested. Anyone offering information about this matter was given rewards.

Then followed the day of February 10th, which was a special one for Europe, for Romania, and for me personally. For the defeated European countries, the assembly for the signing of the Paris Peace Treaty was held between February 10 and 16 as stipulated in the Paris Peace Conference of July–October 1946.

For Romania, even though London and Washington admitted that November 19 elections in Romania were neither free nor fair, they signed the Peace Treaty with the Groza cabinet, thus giving stamp of approval to its official legitimacy. The text of the Treaty was not favorable to Romania, imposing hard damages to be refunded to Russia. However, the Anglo-Americans proposed an Allied Economic Committee that should study the possibility of some concessions, but it was rejected by Russia. Again the Anglo-Americans gave in. Also, the treaty permitted perpetual quartering of Russians troops on Romanian territory. Moscow had won all it wanted. Romania remained with nothing more than the inner support of King Mihai and former Romanian leaders, Maniu, Mihalache and Brătianu.

For me February 10 was also a special day. When I returned from classes, Maman Titi said, "George has undergone an emergency operation, he is home now, and asked that you go upstairs about five o'clock in the afternoon."

Usually when Rosalie was calling me, she or the house maid would open the door. To my surprise an unknown gentleman flung wide the door, and for a few moments we measured each other. Then he hurried to say, "I am Stephen, George's brother, and am glad to meet you."

Smiling, I answered, "Likewise," without introducing myself, knowing he knew me and my name.

From the first moment I met Stephen, I enjoyed his friendly ways. He was well-proportioned, rather thin, with a large smile, black hair, and eyes circled with glasses. His teeth seemed very white, particularly in contrast to his tanned skin. (He had enjoyed many hours in the sun near the Black Sea where he was doing his internship as an orthopedic surgeon.) Stephen led me in to George's room. After I exchanged a few words with the patient, I discovered that Stephen seemed suddenly interested in everything that was going on around him. He was interested in the neighborhood, asked all kind of questions, and readily expressed certain opinions. During all this time I observed how he prepared his pipe, taking the nice flavored tobacco from a leather bag, and then striking a match to fire up the tobacco. He drew in the smoke deeply, and upon exhaling, seemed to follow it up with his eyes as if to analyze how it was rising. Conversation rolled on, concerning topics like Rosalie's cakes, my studies, or movies. What else was discussed I don't remember, but I recall he had beautiful hands, with long and flexible fingers, very expressive, with which he gestured, giving weight to his words.

Right there, in my own house, I had fallen victim to a *coup de foudre*, love at first sight. My stay upstairs lasted much longer than I had anticipated.

As I was leaving, Stephen walked me to the door and said in a convincing voice, "When I'll come back to Bucharest, for sure we would see again. I'll call."

I stepped down slowly, knowing I would be subject to Maman Titi's inquiry. Sure enough, she asked right away, "You said you won't stay long, since you have to study. Why did you have to talk so much?"

"George is OK," I replied. "But I met his brother Stephen, who has come back to Bucharest for good to find a surgeon's position."

Her reaction was instantaneous:

"I hope you won't keep going upstairs, instead of studying. How old is he?"

"I don't know exactly, but he is older than George by a couple of years."

I closed the conversation by turning on my heel and walking toward my room. This meeting with Stephen had been totally unexpected, and I kept wondering if he would call me. Though I tried to study, these thoughts certainly hampered my understanding of what I was reading. I clearly remember that afternoon of February 10, 1947, which would weigh hard on my destiny. From that point on, whenever I was home, I was always the first to answer the phone.

Finally, when the phone did ring towards the end of February, it was Stephen. In a cheerful voice he said, "Hallo, Mona! I am back, and mom has made my favorite cake and together we invite you to come around eight evening time." '

Could anyone doubt that I would go? When I left, Maman Titi muttered, "Be sure not to stay too long!" as she closed the door behind me.

As soon as I entered, Stephen put his arm around my shoulders in a familiar way, saying he had finished his internship and, if I agreed, we could now see each other more frequently. I heard myself saying, without hesitation, yes.

Then, to my complete surprise, he kissed me before entering the drawing room. I was impressed! Stephen had been the first grown-up man, with a definite profession, sure of his own fate, with no dependency on his parents, who got so close to my heart. That heart now felt like it was beating randomly, out of control. It was a feeling that has been written in thousands of books, but whose intensity I had never felt before, and which would fill my life from now on. It was instant love for both of us...

Maman Titi, understood that now the situation was much more complicated than the story with Lulu, Stephen being a grown-up man, had stolen my heart. Worse, he was no part of the society from Oltenia which she so desired for me to belong to. Perhaps she was right in her way of thinking. But nobody could convince me to give up Stephen. My destiny was drawing me toward whatever was going to happen. Thus, I was no longer afraid to be seen with Stephen, going to movies, to the theater, to Aimée's or other friends, to a restaurant, to dance at Melody Bar, or to enter Mon Caprice Restaurant with him. When Stephen was dancing with me, my whole being was filled with joy.

Fortunately, the results of my exams were good. My father was pleased and hoped that Stephen would soon disappear from my life as Lulu had. However, he avoided a discussion on this subject, sensing that it would be useless.

In addition, he was preoccupied at that time with more important issues. He had to deal with the wheat prices from the Genune estate and the dreadful drought that had affected the entire country. Rabbi Alexandru Şafran, who at that time was in New York, writes (originally in French) "The famine was such that the peasants were eating the grains meant for sowing." On the eleventh of January (1947) Mihail Ralea[62] had come from Washington to New York to see

---

62. Mihai Ralea was a Romanian left-wing essayist and diplomat who at the time was serving as Romania's ambassador to the United Nations.

me. He insisted I should inform Jewish personalities, and tell them to interfere, asking the American government to send emergency aid for Romania...He acknowledged he couldn't get anything by himself... while the situation didn't cease to worsen...I (Şafran) contacted Jewish personalities, explaining the two aspects: first humanitarian, then political. Finally, on February 10, President Truman decided to help Romania, even though theoretically, the country was still considered an enemy country...On February 16, the USA government, considering the draught, decided to send an aid package to Romania. We couldn't help than wonder regarding the fastness with whom the president has reacted...On seventeenth morning, Ralea was calling me from Washington: "I know"—he said to me—"it is through your unique grace that we were able to get what was considered to be impossible," and he invited me to Washington where he had organized in my honor a big banquet at the embassy." (Şafran, Alexandru, op. cit., pages 236–237)

Hence, President Truman himself had approved giving aid to us, notwithstanding Romania's status as former enemy. Rabbi A. Şafran had wanted to help Romania due to the fact that the Jewish community had been treated well by the then Queen Mother Elena and King Michael.

At home we were lucky to receive goods from Genune, but most of the citizens were eating only marmalade, sold in wooden boxes, with black bread. When we were listening the London Broadcast, Maman Titi would close the doors and cover the phones with a pillow to protect us from anyone who might listen in. Usually we would whisper, being terrified that somebody would overhear our conversations.

For the summer time, in middle of July, I left for Genune with Florica and Nicuşor, but without the company of Nicu, my father, or of Maman Titi who had decided to stay in our Bucharest house. The separation from Stephen was hard, although he mentioned that we would only be apart for forty-five days, during which he would write daily. Coming to Genune had invigorated me, as always. While in the countryside, I heard on the radio news about the Marshall Plan. Unlike Roosevelt, President Truman was not seeking to be conciliatory with Moscow, however he intended the Marshall Plan for Eastern Europe, too. But, the Soviets refused the proposal. It is about then the complete break between the two worlds occurred. The bridges were burned.

Another issue was emerging: the former Romanian war prisoners, who received communist education in USSR now had been enrolled and returned to the country. Also, we learned about the multiple arrests of friends and relatives also in Craiova. We were all terrified by the continuous persecutions.

Moreover, on the fifteenth of August a monetary "stabilization" took place. It had been hell! We had five days to hand over to the banks all our savings, getting instead new lei.[63] As expected, the government did not give equivalent sums in the handover. Instead, we received only seventy-five lei to survive with the promise that the difference would be honored later, which of course never happened. At the same time, the decision mandated that—together with the old currency—each individual must also surrender jewelry, gold, or foreign currencies. And incredible though it was, nobody could work anymore unless he or she had the State's permit. In no time, we had totally become the government's slaves. Days I cannot forget.

But on top on August 16, while I was reading I heard the noise of a car's engine. Raising my head, I saw the Kandel's dark green Fiat with Nicolae the chauffeur at the wheel and Stephen getting out of the car. "Holly, molly! What might have brought him here?" I was thinking. Stephen told me in a hurry that he had come urgently, due to the "stabilization," informing us about the problems caused by it and other troubles.

Meanwhile, Florica who never met him before told me she liked him and that she would take care of the arrangements for lunch.

When Stephen and I were finally alone, he took me by the shoulders and in an extremely serious tone, asked me, "Do you know what is going on in the country? My father is very worried because the former bankers and businessmen are kicked out and he decided we must leave Romania as soon as possible. However, I don't want to

---

63.   Lei is the Romanian plural of Leu, the Romanian currency

leave without you, therefore I came here in a hurry to ask you if you would marry me and leave together?"

I was struck as if a boulder had fallen on my head! Suddenly, I became extremely emotional. It was all too much to digest—the situation in the country, the condition of my family after the expropriation of land, or this monetary stabilization. I was still trying to understand what Stephen was saying about the threat against bankers and their intention of leaving the country, as well as the marriage proposal. It all added up to many problems. When it rains it pours. Within less than a few minutes the foundation of my life had been threatened. I couldn't answer, but the kiss that followed sealed my acceptance.

I have to admit that his proposal gave me infinite happiness, but it was shadowed by having to leave my family for good, as well as by the fact that Stephen was not the man my family had envisioned for me. Hearing Stephen's marriage proposal seemed to make the world stand still. Even the chirping of sparrows, heard through the open window, seemed to stop suddenly, as if they too realized I would have to face strong resistance. I did not care about the family's attitude toward my marriage, but the fact that I would suddenly have to leave everybody and everything I had known since birth was hard to take. I realized that, on the one hand, fate had given me great happiness, but on the other, I felt a shock that seemed to threaten the pure crystal of my love. The problems I was confronted with were real, regardless of whether I married and left or whether I rejected the marriage. Either alternative would crush my soul.

I really cannot describe the way I felt after our short-lived engagement, but for sure I knew that I now found myself on top of a huge wave in the midst of a storm. As always in difficult situations, I remembered Haagi's advice. Accordingly I prayed in my mind, hoping to find an answer to a very unusual and complicated situation. And all the while, Stephen was washing and wiping his hands as he readied himself to face my father immediately.

We both returned hurriedly to the dining room where all were discussing the events of the day. Right away, Stephen addressed my father and led him outside to the big terrace in front of the house.

Immediately he addressed both hot topics—the subject of marriage and the necessity of an emergency departure from Romania caused by the financial stabilization. My father was taken by surprise. I was scrutinizing his face for his reaction, not knowing what to expect. It was a serious matter, concerning the loss of his daughter whom he loved most in the world, and coming so soon after he had lost the land and all his life savings. Too many traumatic events for a single soul to bear! As I knew he would do, my father seemed to ponder for a while, looking for an answer. I could see he did not want to offend Stephen nor to crush the happiness written on my face. Finally, and with a lot of wisdom, he said, "I know my daughter likes you and wants to become your wife. In principle I have nothing against, but I insist that before you get married, she must finish her last year at the Faculty, for she completed three years and has just one left. It would be a pity not to take her diploma. After graduation, in June 1948, you may come and get married then and leave if it will still be necessary."

These were his solid arguments. He was asking for a postpone-ment, which went exactly counter to Stephen's argument—that the marriage and departure were urgent because of the events that were looming, and could not stand any postponement.

However, Stephen seemed to be content that he had been accepted as son-in-law and, further, that I could now leave with him for Bucharest accompanied by Florica. Every word of that conversa-tion still echoes in my ears—Stephen's tone, as he stressed the emer-gency, my father's goodwill, and ultimately the agreement for post-ponement, whose meaning I knew. My father, I'm sure, was hoping that a break of six months would end the affair as had happened with Lulu. Considering all that I had felt and heard in the span of little more than an hour, I felt I had already become a victim of the com-munist regime, which obliged me to choose between my family and the man I loved. I had hated communism before, but now even more so, because it was intruding in my personal life.

In the afternoon, around three o'clock, Stephen, Florica, and I left Genune and headed toward Bucharest. Before getting into the car, I took in everything around me, wishing that I would never forget the look of the house, garden and trees belonging to my soul. I couldn't have guessed then, that it was for the last time. I was sure, then, it would only be a temporary separation. But I was wrong. The sixteenth of August 1947, it was the last time when I stood in my childhood home.

It had been an extraordinary and incredible, day. Since Stephen's unexpected arrival at Genune in the morning, so much had taken place within the span of three hours—a proposed marriage, explanation of the consequences of the financial situation, the necessity of his departure. Everything in the way of my future destiny had been discussed and decided in those few hours.

On our way, we stopped for a few minutes in the oak forest, listening to the song of the birds resounding through the trees. Though alert to everything, I really didn't have a clue what I had in front of me. At a given moment, a Russian truck skidded to a stop in front of our car, forcing us to stop. Soldiers jumped out of trucks and surrounded our car, pushing and jolting it in all directions, even trying to lift it up. The feelings that I had in my soul instantly melted away as I yielded to the terror of those dreadful moments. I could see those faces pressed close to mine, their cheeks puffed out—separated, thank God, by the closed windows—as Russian voices shouted, "*Davai! davai!*"

Sitting in front of me, Florica also was terrified. Stephan held me close as if at any moment, the Russians could have torn me away from his grasp. The entire encounter, with the Russians surrounding us, yelling and gesticulating, seemed to last an eternity. I was frozen, and a cold sweat has drenched my blouse.

Suddenly, the truck that had blocked our way steered sharply to the left, and Stephen yelled, "Speed up!" Nicolae accelerated forcefully, pulling the car out of the hands of those who were prepared to keep us prisoners. With that powerful surge, we got away at high speed, leaving the attackers behind.

We had escaped! Stephen held me tightly in his arms, looking down at me with renewed confidence. We arrived unharmed in Bucharest.

Upon seeing me, Maman Titi immediately asked, "How come you are here and why?"

I explained that Stephen and his family probably would be leaving the country soon and therefore he had come to Genune—and that Florica and I had taken this opportunity to return to Bucharest.

"That Florica came I understand," said Maman Titi. "But you? I think you have taken a wrong direction. Since you are a grown-up person now, I cannot stop you, but I wonder how come Gică has allowed you to come here?"

I answered, "He hopes that the Kandel's will leave and I will get over my feelings for Stephen."

To her this was good news, and it calmed her down.

Next evening, I was invited upstairs. Stephen's parents were happy to hear that I would be their daughter-in-law. Stephen's father said that it would be dangerous for my future to remain here, considering what was happening in Romania. He said, also, that I could be able to complete my studies abroad and, equally important, that we had to hasten the marriage so that he could include me in his application for departure. He assured me he would talk to my father. I left feeling skeptical.

At the beginning of September, I enrolled in the fourth year at the Faculty, and about that time my father was invited upstairs to settle the problem. When both fathers started to discuss the marriage and departure, George Vrăbiescu expressed his opinion in the following way, "How would you feel if you had a single child whom you raised by yourself and suddenly you had to be separated from him or her, without knowing if you would ever see him or her again, or worrying about his or her future amidst foreign people?" Kandel replied, "Yes, I understand, but don't you think about her happiness and a better future outside the country?" Then father opined, "You see, that's why I embraced a golden-middle proposal. I am not closed off to the matter. But she should complete her degree while he manages his surgeon's position abroad. Next year in June, he could come and take her. Then I would be more at ease thinking that both would be able to earn a living among foreigners."

Stephen and his father accepted my father's proposal without anyone asking for my opinion. I realized that what my father requested made sense. I could wait until June, and therefore I did not attempt to intrude in the discussion. We were offered a bottle of champagne which we shared, after the issue had been settled. But, in fact the atmosphere still seemed heated.

Maman Titi refused to meet Stephen. Therefore, I most frequently spent my evenings upstairs. They used to play bridge, with me sitting in a chair next to Stephen. I was happy to be in his presence, breathing the same air, in the same space, looking at him. When our eyes met, we had the same feeling. When Rosalie and the others disappeared from the room for some reason, Stephen used to pass his fingers through my hair. I kept looking at him attentively, trying to fix his features in my memory, knowing that soon he would not be there any longer. I had never loved anyone with such intensity, and I would have been completely happy if it had not been for the awkward situation created by the communist regime. I kept wondering why fate put me through such a trial, one I had never sought. All I wished was to be among those who could just love, without any political interference.

At the end of September, Stephen said that he shouldn't have accepted our father's arrangement and we should have married as urgently as he had wanted to. He had bad feelings about our separation.

But others were having similar issues. Aimée told me about Lulu and his girlfriend who were having same problems, also facing the possibility he would leave the country without her. Tănţca was scared and worried because her husband, being Mihalache's nephew, had fled from home and was hiding from the Securitate [*communist secret service*]. Officers often came to ask her where he was: the Securitate guys suspected that she knew, and they intimidated her during interrogations shining strong lights into her eyes and shouting to scare her. I felt sorry, even scared for her. Eventually, her husband did got arrested, and Tănţica knew nothing further about where he was hiding. The problem was she lacked any other means of existence save for her brother, who did help her.

There never was a peaceful moment. Now, magistrates and professors were threatened with the prospect of losing their jobs for so-called economic reasons (which in fact were political evictions). My father's earnings were our only means of daily support, because the harvest of those fifty hectares from Genune had been threatened by the drought. There were also rumors about future evictions among members of the press, police, and army. Additionally, Prime Minister Petru Groza expelled the representatives of the traditional parties—PNT and PNL—from the government. It was a government that had been approved by the Allies, but Groza was able to expel these people without encountering any opposition from the West.

The month of November was the one when Stephen told me that his family's departure requests were on the verge of being approved and they could get out of the country any day. The news froze my blood. I went upstairs daily. Maman Titi no longer protested at all, being sure that once the Kandels are gone, I would meet somebody else and her nightmare would be over.

One evening, as soon as I entered, Stephen told me that a lady was visiting them who could be of great help in case, God forbid, he was unable to return and I had to find a way to join him. It was about Mrs. Raia Nicolau, the wife of Doctor Ştefan Nicolau, the director of the Institute of Inframicrobiology. He was an academician and friend of I. C. Parhon, who was president of Great National Assembly (like Congress) from 1945. I met her and liked her from the very beginning. She was very friendly and told me she appreciated the Kandels' friendship, that she knew about our engagement, and that could see her if I needed to. She also gave me her address and telephone number…just in case. It was a welcome relief.

Departure day was drawing near. When we were together, Stephen always held my hand, being ever more troubled by the thought of our separation. I was afraid that with his departure, all the joy of living would go out of me. While feeling a profound feeling of uncertainty, I refused to think ahead and project what would follow. I wished to stay optimistic.

The evening of November 26 was the last we were together and when we took pictures. I sat with my hands crossed on my lap, unable to say any word. A wall of silence had risen between us. Stephen told me he didn't want to lose me after only nine short months of happiness. I was interested only in today, this very moment when I still could be with him. I gazed at his hand, just watching the way he held a cigarette. These last minutes were an unbearable torture, a most atrocious ordeal. I said farewell to all four of them that evening, evincing fake optimism regarding the future. My pain was as strong as were my feelings for Stephen.

The day of November 27 was the memorable day of departure. That morning around nine o'clock, I heard their steps descending the beautiful black marble stair. I heard the bell. At once my heart stopped beating, not knowing if I should open the door since I didn't want to be seen crying in Stephen's arms. It was his father, who took me into his arms and promised he would do all in his power to make sure that after I got my Diploma in Law I would be able to follow them. And he told me I would receive a phone call from the airport. I gave him Nicu's phone number, as that was where I had decided to go to avoid Maman Titi. (I knew she was just hoping that this separation be for good.)

At Nicu's, only Florica was home. She understood what I was going through. When the phone rang I couldn't speak. My voice was broken with tears at the sound of Stephen's voice assuring me he would return to take me away. Then, after a while, I put the phone down with a feeling of utter hopelessness. I was crying harder and harder. Florica stayed near me, trying to reassure me by explaining that six months was not so bad. Of course, she was right, but I had so many premonitions I could not listen to her. Life had already taught me what separation meant—all the experiences I'd had parting from Ioana Herescu, Ioana Crătunescu, Haagi, and Tata-Lae. Now it was another kind of separation, the loss of love of another kind, which I felt towards Stephen.

When I returned home, the house looked completely empty without him. And during the following days, even the daylight looked dark and dull.

The rental contract of the Kandels was extended to a new tenant, M. Bacal, a lawyer, who had been retained for the approval of the Kandels' departure applications. Nicu, being the owner of this apartment, had accepted him. I later befriended both M. Bacal and his wife Lydia. Stephen had told me that Bacal could be of help, like Mrs. Raia, and I visited him from time to time and saw how he was keeping the apartment.

Shortly after Stephen's family's departure, another sad event occurred on the thirtieth of December when King Michael was asked by those in power (Gheorghiu-Dej alongside with Petru Groza) to abdicate. They indicated King Michael had two alternatives—either to sign the document which they placed in front of Him, or to sacrifice one thousand young men who would be executed by the armed troops surrounding the Palace. The King signed the abdication document to avoid the bloodshed. Again, I had the privilege to here this episode from H. M. the king himself in New York.

Moreover, the same day, the Grand National Assembly—the new parliament of the country—unconstitutionally ratified the Abdication document and proclaimed the People's Republic of Romania, endorsing at the same time the left-wing endocrinologist professor I. C. Parhon (uncle of the Parhons in Craiova) as president of the new Republic. We all were stunned, since legally the Assembly would have had first to abolish the 1923 Constitution together with the Constitutional Monarchy. But the communists summoned the Assembly in a big hurry to proclaim the Republic, while the 1923 Constitution still remained in force. When the King was forced to leave the country, the Royal Guard broke their swords in protest.

For us, the day of December 30, 1947, was not only when the Romanian Monarchy collapsed after eighty-one years, but also when the *Iron Curtain* finally fell into place, totally separating us from the West. It was a historical mourning day for Romania. Historian Vlad Georgescu and future director of the Romanian Desk of Radio Free Europe opined in his book *Istoria Românilor*, page 284:

"King Michael was obliged to leave Romania at twenty-six years of age. He was a good king, modest and democratic, with responsibility towards the country, but he faced troubled times which no one could foresee. What followed was totalitarianism."

He was right, with the King's departure into exile the last obstacle to the communist totalitarian establishment was removed.

I think, if President Truman's administration, had the guts to bombard Hiroshima and Nagasaki to end the war with Japan, the same Administration could have used America's powerful stance to be more forceful during the Potsdam negotiations. That would have obliged Stalin to abide to the Anglo-American requests regarding the acceptance of earlier elections in the Central and East European countries, depriving Stalin of the necessary time to create the radical-communist one-party system and make the necessary preparation to steal the elections. USA's forceful negotiations in Potsdam would at least have tried to help build democracies instead of Moscow's totalitarian satellites and would have tried to spare the sufferings of millions of people during the forty-five years that followed.

Under the then circumstances I was awaiting Stephen's phone calls, or the mailman's arrival.

CHAPTER 6

II Armaşului Lane 1948–1952

1948

After the king's departure, the communists acted without restraint. The Iron Curtain was real. I felt like a mouse caught in a trap. No one in the house was mentioning Stephen's name anymore, hoping—as they say—that he will be "out sight and out of mind" and that he could no longer return.

A few days later, I received my first short telegram in which the Kandels informed me they had left the country safely! And in early January, I got my first phone call when Stephen informed me that they were in Milan. He was pessimistic about Romania's future after the King's abdication and told me that I would also receive a letter from his father. He encouraged me to meet with the people I'd met in their house. I understood that he wanted me to go to Ms. Raia and to Bacal, because they could help me leave the country. But, I kept postponing my visits; I mostly preferred to be left alone with my thoughts and emotions. I had no inner peace. I often left the house trying to get over the melancholy that had seized me. I was sleeping much of the day, skipping college. I constantly waited for the next letter or for the phone to ring, which was the only thing that kept me alive.

In the first days of January, my father received a letter from C. Kandel. While my father was reading, I was dying of impatience. Eventually he handed me the letter which contained information about what they were able to accomplish that far: "I opened a company so that I can work in Italy with other European countries. As for Stephen, he will soon go to Bologna where he will hold a position as a specialist of Orthopedic Surgery at the Rizzoli Institute."

Then Mr. Kandel insisted in the letter that it was necessary to speed up my marriage and departure. He ended the letter by assuring my father and me that he and Rosalie loved me very much and wanted to accept me as their third child, concluding: "As soon as possible, I hope to get your acceptance of our children's marriage. Warm greetings to all the family members. C. K."

As I was reading, I got all excited and at the same time stressed—thinking I had to leave my family. To me the diploma didn't matter anymore, but my father's immediate comment was, "There is no way I will let you go without getting your diploma first, not after you studied so much for the exams. In life you must have a career; one cannot just leave everything behind…"

His words were like blows to me, and pierced my heart. I replied, "I will study so that I'll get my diploma, but I'll go without it if necessary."

My father took me in his arms, promising that he would not oppose the marriage provided I passed the exams and got my degree. I do not remember how he replied to the letter, but I knew that deep down inside him he was counting on the impossibility of a marriage. I sincerely regretted the trouble I caused everybody, but I was not going to quit. I was beyond being just furious against the communists and all they were doing.

After a while, I received a phone call from Stephen informing me that he had consulted a lawyer who advised him to have a proxy marriage in Italy after which, based on the marriage documents, I would be included in his passport. And after I got the passport, I could begin the formalities for an exit visa for the purpose of a "family reunion." He added that he had already put the procedure in motion and even ordered a pair of wedding rings —as if that was the main problem. His letters were delightful, loving, making my life sweeter. I endured his absence, only hoping we would see each other again soon.

At the same time the government continued its communization with the nationalization of National Bank followed by printing money without coverage, which generated a high inflation. Then they got rid of or incorporated opportunistic members of the old historic parties, merging all into one communist party in order to ensure the dictatorship of the proletariat. At the same time, a treaty of "cooperation and mutual assistance" between Romania and the USSR was signed in Moscow.

As a result the number of those who wanted to leave the country had multiplied, some assuming great risks, even choosing to swim across the Danube just to escape the communist plague. Among my friends, Călin and Constantin Alimăneştianu and my friend from Craiova, Ionică Stanovici, managed to successfully swim across the Danube and escape—later in life we met again—but many others were caught, arrested. or killed in the process.

In February, two months after Stephen's departure, I received the horrible and unexpected news that his father had died suddenly of a heart attack. He was a handsome man, smart and resourceful, the pillar of the family. His death was not only painful but also caused the entire family financial problems since the plans they relied on had not yet materialized.

My birthday gift arrived later by mail on March 15 from Milan. I got the documents for our proxy marriage, which I had to sign at the courthouse. When my father and other family members heard that I had received the marriage documents, they panicked, especially since it was a proxy marriage, something they did not expect. But that was Stephen's ingenious solution. Consequently, they called for a family meeting in order to convince me not to sign anything, saying that marriage had to be based on a more solid foundation and not just on paper. Maman Titi's opinion was that I would be messing up my life.

She screamed, "But...but there's no way you'll marry him. Mona!... This is insane! You ask why?...Because it is just crazy!..."

This was all she could say. Then she mumbled,

"You will never be happy with someone who will only take you away from your family...and away from your country."

There was nothing I could do, except to listen and keep silent!

My love for Stephen had no boundaries, and I wasn't going to give up our proxy marriage, but my love for the family didn't have any limits either. I found myself in a deep mental depression, trying every day to overcome that obsessive feeling I had for him and calm the pressure that took over the entire house. I had no firm ground under my feet, no one to help me escape the stalemate I was in, and I wasn't able to make any mental plans whatsoever. From the moment I received the documents I was confused, so troubled that I couldn't sleep or remember anything. All I could do was lie in bed waiting for the crack of dawn. But daytime wasn't any better. Eventually I found the solution. I went to the Pitar Moş church, sat on the last bench in the back, and begged God to help me make a decision.

When I left the church. I had reached a conclusion. I decided in favor of the proxy marriage, because the power of love was the supreme force that was guiding me, and any logic or reasoning coming from Gică, Nicu, Uncle Ionel or Maman Titi could not convince me otherwise.

So a few days later, I presented myself at the Bucharest Courthouse where I signed the statement according to which I agreed to give proxy to a certain Miss K. S. to appear on my behalf before the Italian authorities and represent me. Then I informed everybody at home that I had filled in the papers and had sent them to Milan. Being convinced I would marry and leave, I concluded, "The college environment became unbearable, professors and students are being expelled because of their family status as big landowner or members of the bourgeoisie, and that can also happen to me at any time. I'd rather leave than get expelled."

Then I added, "Dear Gică, can't you see what's going on in the country? Nothing good will come of it. What will be my future if I get expelled, without any job, a mere landlord's daughter, a 'social pariah'?"

My father could not deny my arguments and replied, "Darling, whatever your fate decides!"

And with that, all the tension in the room faded away.

Maman Titi was so hurt because of me and my actions; there are no words to express my sorrow. I hugged her, I kissed her, it just broke my heart. She was hoping I wouldn't obtain an exit visa. This situation—contrary to my religious belief that one should not hate—only made me hate the Communists more and more. But I could not control myself, and even now, after so many years, I still cannot help hating them for what they did to my country, my family, and myself.

In spring, I heard the news that Mao Tse-tung came to power in China. Stalin helped Mao build the communist regime in China. Haagi's predictions started to come to live.

In early April I received an incredible phone call. Manini, who was in Craiova, informing me that my mother had been arrested on April 2, 1948, in her apartment in Bucharest. I was shocked and so was Manini. I asked her, "Do you know what happened?"

"I don't know anything, except that I was officially informed by authorities. Mancy gave my address and telephone number as her next of kin." I was stunned and all I could do was wait to hear again from Manini.

Another outstanding situation happened on April 11 when the postman brought me several telegrams in which I learned I had been married the day before, on the tenth of April 1948. I received congratulations from the three people in attendance. The proxy marriage took place in Milan, and a religious ceremony was conducted by a county priest in the suburbs of Sesto San Giovanni. Thus, I became Stephen's legitimate wife, and I was glad I had made this step that brought me closer toward him.

Of course, the news produced another blast from my grandmother, who did not want to hear about marriage, either normal or proxy. Everyone was hoping that I could not leave, that I had just mixed up my legal status. Nonetheless, I immediately began to gather the documents that Stephen indicated, which I needed in order to submit a complete application to the Romanian authorities for an exit visa. I consumed a lot of time running back and forth.

Shortly thereafter I got a letter from Stephen, telling me that he had sent his passport that included me. Also, he told me again how much he regretted that he had left without me and said that, if it wasn't for Rosalie and her feelings of loneliness, he would have returned to Bucharest, even at the risk of not being allowed to return.

Indeed, at the end of June, the phone rang and an unknown voice said in Romanian, "I would like to speak to Mrs. Simone Kandel." Initially I was taken aback and didn't realize whom he was talking about! It was the first time someone had called me by my new married name. The call was from the Romanian pilot who was flying between Milan and Bucharest and who had brought me the precious document. We arranged to meet, and he handed me the passport. I stared at the passport as if a miracle had occurred, assuming the authorities would acknowledge my new status and approve my exit visa.

My family was twice stressed out, on the one hand due to my situation and, on the other, because on April 13 of 1948, a new Constitution was adopted after the 1936 Soviet model. The new constitution did not provide for the separation of powers in the state, and it enforced the terror of a police state. Communist activists held all key positions and enjoyed all kinds of privileges unavailable to the rest of the population, which had to cope with food rationing and was deprived of bare necessities.

Bad news kept coming. Following the reorganization and the restructuring of the Army, we got a call from Tante Lenuţa who was crying and could barely speak, informing us that Uncle Ionel had been arrested. After giving it some thought, my father said he knew a few reasons for Ionel's arrest—particularly because he took part in the King's August 23 coup—but he couldn't understand why Mancy was arrested. We all were intimidated and terrorized by what was happening all around us.

Arrests were a daily occurrence all over the country. Police vans circulated through the streets at night, grabbing people away from their homes. Among those arrested were some of my professors at the university, fellow students, and close friends. Baby my friends was arrested merely because he possessed a typewriter that he failed to report to authorities.

I was anxious to know if Manini got news about Mancy. I called her, but all she knew was that the other tenants who were occupying rooms in her apartment were okay. Nothing more.

And then it was the turn of the Justice system to be restructured. About two thousand lawyers were removed from the Ilfov Bar Association for political reasons and accused of being "enemies of the people." Among them was also my dear uncle, Nicu, Nicolae Vrăbiescu.

Soon after, on June 11 the state nationalized the industrial enterprises, the mining industry, the banks, and the insurance companies as well as the national institutes of health. Movie houses and theaters were all closed. The Bârca mansion was set up as a coop for storing heavy agricultural machinery and tractor station, which destroyed the beauty of our lawn and the flower beds. It was another violation of private property.

By the end of June, more terrible news came. A call from Nicu alarmed us, he said to my father, "I'm glad you're at home. Florica was summoned to evacuate her apartment, and we were given a place in the outskirts of Bucharest." My father replied, "That can't be, I won't let you go there. Move in with us in Armașului, we'll see how we'll manage."

As I was hoping to leave, I immediately offered my room to them and moved into Haagi's former small room. The next day, Florica, Nicu, Nicușor, Leanța their housekeeper and Tommy the poodle, moved over. Now there were six people who all shared one bathroom, which was on the ground floor next to the guest room. (When the house was built, the architect did not think that we would ever live on the ground floor: it included mostly living area and only a guest room with an adjacent bathroom.)

During the first six months at the beginning of 1948, our family alone suffered four consecutive strokes: my mother and Uncle Ionel were arrested and Nicu lost his profession as a lawyer and was evacuated from his apartment.

Personally, then, I was preoccupied with getting my application documents for visa approval, scampering from one bureau to another to achieve my goal. Therefore I didn't go to Genune over the summer. I stayed with Maman Titi in Bucharest. As an alternative, I used to visit Aimée or go with her downtown for a walk in the city.

The sovietization of the country continued to speed up, and in August there were other three important changes. The Education Reform Act was enacted after the Soviet model and the private schools were abolished, including Notre Dame de Sion and Pitar Moş, which were changed into public schools. Also I was disgusted to hear that the Central School, was renamed Zoia Kosmolenskaia[64] High School. Furthermore, at the University the fees were assessed depending on parents' wealth, and landowners were threatened with eviction.

I had barely seen Baby since quitting my fourth year of college, and ever since, being totally immersed in my paper fever, I completely isolated myself from everyone and everything. Baby told me that in the fourth year they introduced a new course, an ideological guide to Marxism. Due to the reform, many professors were dismissed or transferred. Others were arrested and convicted for political reasons; many died in prison. I thanked the Lord that my father was still safe, and I was glad that I was no longer an active student because I could have been expelled.

In August the famous Securitate was established. We got information from friends and others that the institution was modeled after the KGB, and stuffed with Soviet agents who were unscrupulous. Their modus operandi was to extract information by brutal interrogations in order to be noticed and to earn the trust and appreciation of their bosses. Over the years we all reached a point where we suspected each other of being collaborators or members of the Securitate. And indeed, there were many people who caved in to pressure and were denouncing others in order to save their own skin. And so, people were taken from their beds in the middle of the

---

64.   A probably fictitious teen communist hero in the Soviet propaganda
       machine

night and thrown into prison. Some of them disappeared forever. The Securitate used cruelty and beatings to intimidate, humiliate, and reach their goals. You were totally powerless in front of them. The active members of the Securitate took a perverse pleasure in causing suffering and cursing, and they were good at "sharpening the class struggle," a typical communist expression. They regularly exterminated citizens and political prisoners, a situation that lasted until 1989. After 1990 they maintained indirectly power to influence the shaping of governments, its policies and the media.

All during that summer, I could not get the documents I needed since most of the officials were on vacation. Finally in September and October, I gathered all required document and submitted them to the Passport Office within the Ministry of the Interior. After a while, I was received by an officer whom I suspected to be from Securitate. I handed him the memorandum and explained my desire to join my husband. He kept thrumming his fingers on the desk; I could see that he had no patience. He registered the papers and told me I would get an answer in writing. I wrote to Milan that I had finally managed to submit the documents in question. By chance, while I was leaving the Passport Office I met Lulu's mother, who gave me the news that Lulu had became a student at E. T. Hoochschule, the famous Swiss Polytechnic.

Incidentally, on November 27—exactly one year to the day after Stephen left—I was called for a hearing at the Ministry of Interior, Passport Service. There I was greeted by a man who I suspect held a leading position within the agency. He was a young man with curly short blond hair and blue eyes—good-looking, as were most of those that the Securitate recruited. I was calm and confident, convinced that my sincerity regarding this real marriage was not just an excuse for leaving the country. With my documents in front of him, the guy started questioning me, and I was surprised that he wanted to know where I intended to go and why, as if it wasn't written in my application form. He seemed not to pay attention to my answers; he was more interested in holding my gaze to see if he could detect the smallest lie. My heart beat a little faster when I told him about the situation. But the ears which do not want to hear are deafer than those that can't hear. Even if he had wanted to hear, his job was not to listen. In the end he informed me that I would receive a written answer by mail. I had no idea how long I would have to wait—days, weeks, maybe months.

On the twenty-eighth of November, the day after the hearing, I felt optimistic, particularly since I had also received a letter from Stephen informing me to expect a golden watch that he had bought and mailed me as a Christmas present. He didn't forget to mention that "yesterday it's been one year since we parted, and all day I have been dreaming about the moment when we shall meet again. If I knew they would have closed the borders, I wouldn't have left you there to finish your studies…I admit I made a huge mistake when I listened to our parents…All my love to you and your family…S."

I was holding the letter, my chest rising and falling with sobs. The tears fell down on my cheeks, and I was surprised how big they were. With trembling hands I tried to catch them in a handkerchief. Yes! His words were beautiful and comforting; I could almost hear his voice and his laughter, I was trying in vain to feel his presence in the room…Those were painful moments of loneliness. Everything he was writing was full of hope, but what I was feeling on the other side of the Iron Curtain was completely different and odious. I encouraged myself to stay calm, hoping for a positive response from the Passport Service.

In December I was sad to hear that the government had outlawed the Catholic Church that was so intertwined with my upbringing and education. They also closed many Christian Orthodox monasteries and forced out many nuns and monks. The Roman Catholic Church was considered imperialistic, a nest of spies and traitors, just because it had connections with foreign countries. Over two thousand priests—Orthodox, Greek Catholic, or Catholic were arrested followed by suppression and many were practically exterminated in the gulag prisons.

About seven days after the hearing, when I got home I found the envelope from the Passport Office. I was very excited, hoping to finally meet again Stephen; maybe I was even certain. Then I read, "Visa application has been denied." Just like that, in short, without any detail or reason. My blood froze in my veins and my whole body went numb. I lay down on my bed, trying to return to my senses.

I remember very well the days that followed. Had anyone asked me what was on my mind, I would have answered with only one word: Stephen! Yet he was not there. However, in my mind I was convinced that as his official wife I had the legal and human right to be by his side. I hoped that one day I will have the opportunity to revenge myself against communism and its ideology. I did not know how but prayed for the occasion.

Then, in great anguish, I decided to turn to Mrs. Raia Nicolau, whom I had met at the Kandels' and who had offered to help us if needed. That was the only way I could regain power. I phoned her and she remembered me; she said that instead of talking over the phone, I should come over. Obviously it was not prudent to talk on the phone.

At the agreed day and time, I arrived at her house. She opened the door and welcomed me inside. While we were sitting in two comfortable chairs, she first asked me in a kind and friendly way if I got news from Milan. Then I had to break the news to her about the death of Stephen's father and tell her the latest about the whole family. Finally, I told her something about myself—that my father was a professor at the Faculty of Law, that my parents were divorced, and I had been raised by my father. That's all. Finally we talked about my current situation, about the proxy marriage done officially in Milan and the negative response to my visa application. I was impressed to see she was following me very closely, truly listening from her heart and expressing her desire to get involved and help me.

I noticed she had a foreign accent, so I asked her where she was from. She laughed and said that she had been born in Lody, Poland, the youngest child of a Jewish family. She had experienced the 1917 Russian Revolution. Her older sister went to Paris before the Revolution, and she succeeded in following her to study chemistry. Back in 1932 she had met and married Dr. Stephen Nicolau. Both returned to Romania, where he became a PhD, a member of the Romanian Academy of Science and the director of the Institute of Inframicrobiology. In that capacity he got very close to Professor Dr. I. C. Parhon.[65]

After she told me all that, I realized Raia hadn't made any comments whatsoever regarding the negative response I had received. Everyone was cautious and careful about what they said, but she was especially so because back in Russia she had been through what we were experiencing nowadays. As I got to know more about her past, and learned what she lived through in Russia—surviving the communist's rigidity—I saw that she was reliving that again in Romania now. I was under the impression that she truly was willing to help me.

Raia confirmed that by saying, "Monuca,[66] I do want to help you and I'll see what I can do before the holidays. Call me after two days."

Then she introduced me to her mother-in-law, her children Claude, who was eight years old and Ketty, who was three years old, both brunettes, and seven-year-old Monica, blonde and slender.

I suspected that Raia Nicolau was a person with great personality. About three days later I called and she told me to come immediately. Arriving in a hurry, I received a warm hug. She gave me a parental glance and said in an encouraging tone, "Monuca, I have arranged a meeting with I. C. Parhon, the president of the Great National Assembly."[67]

I instantly felt a great deal of hope. It was as if my heart were rising to heaven, I was so confident of my future success. I already saw myself in Milan. She knew Parhon because he was a well-known academic endocrinologist and a colleague with her husband, Fanica as she called him. Parhon was almost seventy-five years old, and she believed that at his age he would show understanding for my prob-

---

65. Constantin Ion Parhon (1874–1969) was a Romanian endocrinologist and politician. He was the first head of state of Communist Romania from 1947 to 1952.
66. Term *of* endearment from "Mona"
67. The Great National Assembly was the name of the new unicameral parliament of Romania under the communist regime

lem, which was not of a political but civil nature. It is true the president of the Great National Assembly of Romania was a great personality, but she had her own ways of dealing with a problem—by presenting it from a sentimental view point.

While I was waiting for my hearing with the president, I got a phone call from Craiova; Manini informed us that my mother's trial would take place on December 7, 1948. Her case was attached to a renowned political trial directed against the Romanian resistance. This was a trial meant to destroy the class enemy. Obviously, the judges were communists and had already been trained to view such convictions as a necessity.

Uncle Nae (my grandfather's brother) who lived with us in Armașului passed away mid-December 1948 without being sick, at the age of eighty four. (He is also the one I mentioned who wrote the letters to his sister Pauline about his travels, which were published in 2007.) I would miss him!

After his death, the Locative Agency immediately occupied the space for a family. The fact that they were unpleasant, didn't greet anyone, made a lot of noise was less important than the big problem they will cause later, when big spacious houses placed in the center of the city were spotted. Obviously, ours was not an exception.

After the middle of December, I went with Raia to have my audience with President, I. C. Parhon. I took with me a copy of my statement and the refusal that came in response to my exit-visa application. The protocol was not complicated; we were soon announced. The president was very polite and shook hands with us, we each took a seat, and Raia explained that she was a friend of my husband's family and asked the president to kindly understand that this case was one of family reunification. He listened, occasionally glancing at me. He kept my memorandum. I thanked him, and Raia told him she hoped he would work out the situation.

I thanked her from the bottom of my heart for her kindness. The truth is that not many people would have done what she did for me, her being a foreigner and on top of that, knowing I was part of the enemy class. This lady had courage and a very big heart.

While I was waiting for an answer, I anticipated it would certainly be a favorable one. But fate had other plans for me. The negative response from the Ministry of Interior came in an envelope just before Christmas. Now I was desperate and my desire to get revenge against the communist system only grew stronger. I did not know how but prayed for the occurrence.

Although everyone from my own family showed sorrow for my suffering, I knew that the news could only be good news for them. So I called Raia, the only person to understand and console me. She invited me over straightaway.

When she heard my news, her only comment was: "Monuco, I did what I could; I really wanted to help both of you."

She still didn't know me well enough to say what she actually thought, but I could read it in her big, black, piercing eyes. She expressed her regrets and invited me to come and let her know what I was going to do in the future. I left her, but knowing that I was leaving behind a true friend.

Back at home I had the difficult task of writing to Stephen about the second refusal.

When my father heard my exit visa was turned down for a second time, he insisted again that I should resume the fourth year. He argued that there might come a time when I would need the degree, so I shouldn't postpone my exams. Besides, he might also be kicked out with the second batch of evictions from the faculty. In conclusion, he added that he would pay my credits—which had been substantially increased since August 1948—and advised me, "Please consider what I said and don't postpone it any longer."

* * *

By the end of December I found out about my mother: Mancy Radian was convicted on December 31, 1948, to five years of rigorous imprisonment, five years of civic degradation, and twenty thousand lei trial expenses for the crime of conspiracy under Article 227 of the Penal Code issued by the Bucharest Military Tribunal. Now I knew it was a ploy.

The year 1948 brought a new Constitution also based on the Soviet model, followed by many arrests, evictions, purges, nationalizations, trials with convictions, repressions of churches, and suppression of personal freedom.

Churchill was right when he wanted negotiations with Stalin as long as America was a strong nuclear monopoly. He expressed his views some time before October 1948 at Wales, repeating that "the Wests' bargaining position would never be better than it was at that moment." He asked what would happen when the Soviets got their own atomic bomb. "No one in his sense can believe that we have a limitless period of time before us," Churchill declared. (See also Kissinger, Henry, *Diplomacy*, page 466.) How right he got it!

1949

After the great drought of the former years, the 1949 winter was excessively cold, people got sick due to the lack of fuel to heat their homes. Inside the house it was unpleasantly cold and I dressed in many layers of woolen clothing. Wrapped up like that, one evening I went to Bacal to tell him of my troubles and the negative responses I had received. I asked whether he could help me get an exit visa through his connections, knowing he was part of the elite of the day. He said that as soon as he heard anything from one of his connections, he would let me know when to file another request. Thus, there was still one more slim hope.

At that time I also considered my father's advice about going back to the university. He had already paid the fee, leaving a hole in the household budget. I didn't hesitate and resumed the courses that I had taken before—when I still could benefit from normal courses and the old professors, before the Faculty started to consider the students' social background. To motivate myself, I reminded myself that the diploma would be of use abroad, if I could leave. Studying had a positive aspect—like a drug, it replaced the avalanche of desperate thoughts. All I could focus on were my studies.

Of course, this was not to say that I wasn't expecting phone calls and letters from Stephen, who kept encouraging me to keep submitting more applications. I wrote him about Bacal and about the fact that I had resumed studies to finish the fourth year—which I was ready to suspend as soon as I would get the visa. His letters gave me strength to study with a purpose.

After my mother's sentencing, Manini intended to send packages to Mancy. Therefore, she came to our house to buy bacon, sugar cubes, nuts, cigarettes, face cream, and DDT and hoping to be able to see her at the visiting room. My father and Maman Titi welcomed Manini in a very friendly way, hosting her in our still unoccupied drawing room.

When they saw each other in the visiting room at prison, Mancy told Manini why she had been arrested and then Manini told us. The story had begun on January 1945 with the persecution of over seventy-five thousand German ethnics, Romanian citizens, who were deported to the USSR. Johann Schobel's brother, Hansi, was deported to Siberia where he died. Being scared, Johann refused to stay at Radomir but could not go to Medias either, so my mom offered him a room in Bucharest, the free room next to Erji's, the former cook who lived there with her husband. Johann let one of his helpers replace him at the Radomir estate.

What happened? It was back in the day when the Allied Control Commission was still functioning but did nothing to curb the Russian interference into the internal affairs of the country. And the Romanian General Military Staff headquarters, not far from my mother's apartment, requisitioned some of her rooms for three officers. It was then that one officer told Johann about his apprehension regarding Russian actions which he and his colleagues Staff headquarters could not comprehend, because the ninety percent Russian's influence on the basis of the Churchill-Stalin bargaining was not yet made public then.

As a result, the officer came one day with a request for my mother to hand a letter to the United States Allied Commission in his place because it was easier to follow him and track him down. The letter contained information about the expansion of Russian power in the country. My mother accepted this mission, although she knew it could put her in danger. Even though the prospect of a prison term did not appear to my mother, she showed patriotism taking the risk to take the letter to its destination. This was allegedly the reason for mother's arrest and conviction for conspiracy. Now we knew why she had been arrested.

We were all living under terror, especially after the establishment of the Securitate in August 1948, when the intensification of the country's Sovietization became a very busy agenda on domestic and foreign policies. The Communists acted unscrupulously against their own people. The police introduced mandatory identity cards for all citizens; there was harsh punishment for crimes against state security. Political prisoners had to endure especially harsh conditions as they were not allowed to receive food packages and correspondence. Meanwhile, foreign radio broadcasts—the only source of propaganda free information—were jammed.

However the most unbearable decree occurred on March 2, 1949: it was a follow-up to the former nationalization of large areas of agricultural land. This time, the mansions of the estates were also expropriated and the process of forced collectivization of agriculture started. Agricultural associations were established.

My Genune with every living soul was gone! And the Vrăbiescu's old dispute with the State for the 110 ha no longer had any meaning; it ended the countless notices given by various committees and councils, or memos written to the Ministry of Agriculture. This last expropriation as well as, the one of March 29, 1945, was a theft, being done without any financial compensation.

The expropriation was not only directed against landlords, but also against petty landowners and peasants. On the night of March 2–3, 1949, at two o'clock in the morning, across the entire country, the activists came and in an inhuman and ruthless way threw out the owners, whether landlords, kulaks, or peasant. Robbed of all their possessions and belongings, some left in some carriages while others were delivered to railway stations to be dispersed, empty handed, in faraway directions. After the decree, the former mayors and councilors were replaced by activists, unskilled villains. Many of the remaining peasants threatened, but those who showed resistance were arrested, imprisoned, deported, or killed. A vivid example was

Aunt Natalica's case. She was sent to a faraway location, with the status of "forced domicile" stamped on her ID, and with her husband and cousin assigned to one room, without any pension rights, where they all lived on a neighbor's charity until they received money from relatives. They remained there the rest of their lives.

Luckily for us, we were in Bucharest when they were doing the forced collectivization of our estate. Otherwise, we would have been among the thousands of people driven out from their houses, mansions, and estates. The victims were Mitică with Silvia, who were ousted from Genune from their beds and forced to leave when the party activists barged in. The activists took everything they found in the house and in the warehouses, including the barns with animals. Mitică and Silvia fled to the village of Ciutura, but Mitică was taken by gendarmes who delivered him to the Craiova Police for the crime of being himself a petty land owner and having been Genune's administrator. After being released, he sent us desperate telegrams, informing us what had happened and how. He had only two words for that: robbery and theft.

Losing the mansion at Genune hurt me as much as losing a beloved creature. I could not handle any more breakups. I felt sorry I didn't spent the last summers there instead of running around to get the documents which, in the end, had not done any good anyway. I thought about Joc, Hep and Tom, the dogs, horses and all the livestock that had been stolen. I wondered where they were and how they were treated.

Manini was also in Craiova, but after this last expropriation she did not have any more income, having lost the fifty hectares from Bârca, and she had no pension. She could barely make a living from selling, one–by–one, the objects in the house to Dr. Ion Parhon (I. C. Parhon's nephew) and his family.

Concomitantly with the expropriation, many arrests followed keeping us under terror. I also had to experience in another way terror. One evening Aimée told me about her fiancé, a pilot nicknamed Papanuș. I had once seen him at her place at the beginning of 1945, but now I was told he was a refugee. He joined the partisans hidden in the mountains who represented the anticommunist resistance.

Aimée told me that Papanuș had come to her house a few days before to inform her he had fled from the mountains because Romanian and Russian soldiers had begun searching for the partisans. He gave her two revolvers to keep until he could find a way to let her know where to deliver them. Aimée added she could always be suspected or followed, being his fiancée and was afraid of being subjected to a possible search of her apartment by the Securitate and was afraid to keep the guns. She asked me if it was possible to bring them to my house until she was told where to take them. I thought I would help her. The next morning she brought the handguns in a bag and I hid them in my closet.

But, when I heard one afternoon the front door bell ringing, I got scared. Previously, I wouldn't have reacted to the bell, but now, having Papanuș' guns in my closet, I felt under pressure, also because friends and relatives would knock at the door in a special way to be distinguished from who knows whom. Thus, I tiptoed to the door to hear the voices. They were of my father and Nicu, but there were others I didn't recognize coming from the staircase. They were some strangers and I wondered what they wanted. Who knew what kind of information they were after! I suddenly got the idea that maybe they had come to inquire about my mother and may be to search the house. The sky fell on my head, my heart stopped beating, and fear got hold of my body from the stomach down to my feet and back up the spine to my head. At that moment I wished I had never been born. I turned around and stood motionless in my room, paralyzed by fear and guilt. I was the only one who knew what was hidden in my closet. Guns were forbidden by decree, and their discovery would be followed by imprisonment. As the conversation kept going on between father and those strangers, I got the feeling they were asking for something, using their official authority. I suspected they had come to search the house.

That was when I started wondering whether it was worthwhile to put my family and myself in danger out of friendship for Aimée. We all could end up in a desperate situation because of my poor judgment. My *blood pressure* was going up, my heart pounding so hard I could barely hear anything. However, suddenly I thought I detected footsteps going down the stairs, and as the door closed, I heard Gică quietly addressing Nicu. It looked like I had got away with it!

I looked for a towel to wipe my sweat. I was so exhausted I felt as if I had run a marathon. I sat down on the nearest chair. When I finally came out of my room and saw my father, I was told that those strangers wanted to speak to the owner of the building, who happened to be my father, asking him if everyone had ID cards in accordance with the new decree. I recovered my peace of mind and thanked God. Immediately I went straight to Aimée. She had just had found out through someone where she was supposed to bring the guns. She came back with me to my house, took the guns, and left. When I saw her leaving our street, I was somewhat relieved, but did not entirely recover myself until I heard her voice in the evening on the phone. Thank God, again! We have both got away with it!

Again, I have to mention another unfortunate event, the start of the Danube–Black Sea Canal construction. The main purpose for building the Canal was to use it as a labor camp for the elements considered reactionary and—through inhuman labor conditions—to exterminate tens of thousands of prisoners. My beautiful Lausanne educated mother was one of those interned to toil in the Danube-Black Sea labor camp.

* * *

And during 1949 three major international events took place: a) April 4, 1949, the Westerns signed with the North Atlantic Treaty Organization (NATO), an agreement whose most important point was Article 5, mentioning the use of force in case of aggression against a signing state; b) Soviet Russia detonated it first atomic bomb on August 29, 1949, which marked the end of the US monopoly over this weapon. c) On January 25, 1949 Romania became a member of the Council of Mutual Economic Assistance (CMEA), an organization of international trade set up to exchange information among all communist countries wanting to imitate the western Marshall Plan.

Regarding my exit visa, Bacal was not of much help. Either he couldn't get that approval, or he didn't want to compromise himself by putting in a good word for a person wanting to leave "the communist heaven." The only thing left for me was to study for my degree.

My exam session began and I passed the first four exams successfully. The last one was the one Marxism as my friend Baby indicated. I was annoyed that now I had to absorb propaganda and about the existence of class enemies. But I did not really care; I had in mind the final goal, my diploma.

On the day of that last exam, I entered the examination room and quietly sat on the bench waiting for my turn. Suddenly the door opened and I saw through the crack my former professor of Constitutional Law, Mihai Oroveanu. It seemed he was looking for someone, and then, when he spotted me, he nodded and waved, inviting me to leave the room. I got up, exited, and closed the door behind me. Outside in the hallway he whispered, "I heard there is a group of students in this room who came especially because of you. So when the teacher mentions your name, they will intervene saying you have no right to take the test because you are the daughter of a landlord. I recommend you consider postponing your exam." I thanked him, and he disappeared like a ghost.

Because I was so nervous, I really needed to go to the rest room. There, alone, I had some time to meditate. I spent a lot of time inside, praying, asking God for help. After a while, I felt a kind of indifference, then a bit of courage, and finally a hope that luck would be on my side. I decided not to postpone, and went back to the classroom. Leaving the restroom, I looked around and saw a group of noisy young people coming out of the classroom. Perhaps they were the ones, or maybe not. Anyway, I let them pass, reached the door of the classroom, and held my breath as I opened it. In my absence the room had almost emptied out. I approached the professor, who raised his head inquiringly. I told him my name and told him I missed the call because I did not feel good.

"Can you take the exam now?"

"Yes, Professor."

"Please sit down."

Suddenly I was calm. I answered the questions, I got a B. I made it! I had to pay the price for the emotions I went through, being Professor George Vrăbiescu's daughter, a former landlord!

I felt exhausted due to the effort I had gone through. I thanked God for saving me by helping me to return to the class room and giving me a way to justify my exit. I left the Faculty building feeling very satisfied, not so much because I had finished my fourth year and graduated, but rather because I had managed to circumvent the group of students who were allegedly poised to heckle me. Yes, it was a great satisfaction!

As for Professor M. T. Oroveanu, he protected me from evil, which influenced my future and therefore, remained forever grateful to him. My diploma and those of my colleagues were not issued in 1949, however. We did not receive them until 1953.

After I finished the exams I was free, I had nothing to do, nothing to study for, no documents to chase. I had only to hope for a miracle for getting an exit visa. I went back to the bridge parties at my neighbor, the Swiss Ambassador Walter together with Aimée, Sandu Negri, and others. Sometimes Georgiana, Lulu's connection was also at Aimée's, and I was glad to hear good news about Lulu who had successfully passed his exams at Polytechnic in Switzerland.

At that time, via Liky, I met some of his friends from Craiova and Târgu-Jiu, such as Mişu Vaias, M. Pleşoianu and Chuck Sadoveanu (who had adopted his English first name while studying in the past at a university at London). Mişu and Chuck tried to flirt with me a little bit, knowing I was a desolate lady. But emotionally I was not ready to give up the hope of meeting Stephen again. Two years had passed, and I thought I had proof of my love, due to stubbornness I had shown, trying to overcome all obstacles put in my way by the communist system that tried to impose on my life, like a prisoner. If I had it to do all over again, I still would have done the same.

One day Liky—who knew my problems and was proud I had taken my degree in law despite my unrest—advised me to see his friend Pleşoianu, who was a friend of Grigore Geamănu, Secretary of State in the Ministry of Domestic Affairs. Liky believed that comrade Geamănu could put in a good word for me and help me obtain an exit visa. I accepted the proposal immediately; Pleşoianu arranged my meeting with Geamănu, not at the ministry but at his home, not far from Armaşului Lane.

I went with Ioana, Liky's daughter. Grigore Geamănu welcomed us in a very elegant way, with caviar sandwiches and a glass of champagne. After he listened to my situation, Geamănu seemed willing to give me a hand. He told me to submit a memorandum to the Passport Service in which to dispute the rejection of my exit visa and to communicate to Pleşoianu my registration number and the date of submission. I left a little more optimistic. When I returned home and told them about my new attempt, the atmosphere became tense again. It was because I had finished my law degree. As always, Maman Titi did not believe my departure would offer me a better life in the West; she still was much convinced that the Americans would not leave us under the Russians forever, and she thought my place was with them here in Romania. And that was that.

I submitted my memorandum and gave the registration data to Liky, who in turn passed the information to Pleşoianu. Again I found myself waiting for a letter providing the date and time when I would be having an audience at the National Commission for Visas and Passports. In late November 1949 I was received by a Securitate officer who, after he had investigated my case, asked me, "Why are you in a hurry to leave?"

This question got me furious! That was plain mockery! Though I could hardly contain my feelings, I replied calmly, "You have a folder with all the documents which show that I have been waiting for the last two years to be able to join my husband."

While I was answering, he gazed at the stains on the ceiling as if he was expecting them to help him listen to my lamentations, which I considered to be reasonable. Regardless of my arguments, he probably knew that my pleas were not even worthwhile. After pouring my heart out, I was weary. I waited for his reaction. Finally, in a relaxed tone, he told me I would receive an answer at home. I stood up and asked when, and he replied, "Soon."

After hearing his answer, I left the office puzzled. Perhaps, after all, the magic answer would arrive, thanks to Geamănu's intervention for a case which seemed to me to be fair, apolitical, and human, but not to them. In any case I felt sick as I stepped into the street.

The waiting period was short. The answer couldn't be anything but negative. And that's how it was again!

Until then, when I had received a negative reply I tried to fight back my inner demons of discouragement. But this time it was different. It was the final act, which destroyed me. I could not see any other way out. I had fallen into final despair.

Either Geamănu or I. C. Parhon had not intervened on my behalf, undoubtedly for fear that they might compromise their situation, or else their actions were not taken into account by the Passport Office that followed the "Iron Curtain" policy. *Iron* is a good descriptive term because I felt my soul crushed by an iron bar. This is where Churchill was right.

Distracted by my despair, on my way home I almost got hit by a city tramway. Being deep in my thoughts, I had crossed without looking and heard the driver swearing because I had jumped in front of the tram like a rabbit. That evening, I went outside the house to think about the situation I found myself in. Then, for the first time, I considered the possibility of dropping the proxy marriage. I wrote Stephen, letting him know about the third negative answer.

I had lost any faith in any further success. I believe Stephen felt the same way. In his reply to my letter, he confessed he was having financial trouble with his stay in Italy; he said our difficult situation seemed hopeless, and he was having a hard time dealing with it. He told me how much he loved me, more than ever, but it was hard to wait for my arrival in Italy. He had to go to take care of Rosalie at her brother's in Tangier.

I answered his letter by telling him that I understood the situation and that I couldn't have done more than what I already tried many times in my efforts to escape the Iron Curtain. I added that I still loved him, even from the bottom of the hell in which I found myself. What else could I have written? All our efforts to reunite had turned out to be futile.

I thought that the main culprits responsible for my situation were Hitler, who unleashed hell in Europe, as well as Roosevelt and

Churchill who couldn't find a way to overcome Stalin, while we in Eastern European countries remained hostages to the Russians. Romania had lost its identity, its wealth, and its freedoms.

Looking back, I can say now that, thanks to Stephen, I experienced the great joy of a love without limits, but also the terrible pain, which was not our fault but was due to a system that ignored the individual, even though its social ideology claimed to be for the people. Now my desire to get revenge against this political system had no boundary, it grew bigger and bigger hoping. I hoped that someday I will be able to react, impossible, though, to know how. But that was what I felt.

Since Stephen's departure, many months full of agony had passed. It was a failed romance. I was left with a burning wish to see him again one more time, but had lost all hope that that would be possible. Then, in great pain, I promised myself that I would make it happen although I didn't know how—not only because of him but because I desperately wanted to defeat someday the communist system, just as I had fooled that group of students during my Marxist exam. My desire for revenge was real and has remained the same, strong and permanent, over the years, now and forever!

After the last negative reply from the Passport Office and after Stephen's letter, peace had returned to the family. I knew I no longer had anything to expect, nor anything else to hope for. It was clear I had to understand who I had become after this experience; I had to do something for myself, to transform and escape my obsession with Stephen. But, I did not know how to start or where to go, considering the suffocating political environment that engulfed the country. I started to pray for an answer.

1950

Maman Titi kept insisting I should forget the past and start a new life, but I could not even use my law degree to practice my profession. On the one hand, this was because I had not yet received the diploma; and on the other, it was because of my social origin, being classified as the class enemy or "enemy of the people."

Whenever I felt emotionally overwhelmed, I would listen to Grieg's Concerto for Piano and Orchestra. I imagined the music as a cry of rebellion, a big *no* thrown in the face of all restrictions I had to put up with. I had done what I could for a decent marriage and for a decent profession, but I was denied both. The solo piano silenced the agony; each sound was hope for a brighter future.

Mid-January, Liky and Mitzy came to see me. Liky had divorced and remarried Mary -called Mitzy, whom I had met before. She had a nice figure, raven-black hair, big black almond-shaped eyes, and very white skin. She was a good Catholic who loved her mother and her two daughters from her previous marriage, and she was quite a resourceful woman. I was glad to see them. We talked about what was happening in the country, about the exit visa denials, and about Stephen's intention to leave Italy. Then Liky said, "I know you're angry because of so many failed attempts to get a visa and because you cannot practice law. You have to forget about your profession."

I stared at him wide-eyed. I told him I did not want to give up the effort I made to get that degree, believing I deserved it as, to me, it was my sole reason for not following Stephen out of the country. He asked me to keep a clear judgment in view of the times we were going through and listen to what they had to suggest.

Then Mitzy interfered, informing me about a training course for a new communist profession called normator,[68] a course offered by an organization called Sovrom Construction no. 6, and advising me that I should take advantage of such a course. Sovrom enterprises came about in 1945, after several agreements were signed by the new prime minister Petru Groza with Moscow. They were joint Soviet-Romanian economic ventures, intended to control Romanian production and transportation managed by the Soviets. Sovrom no. 6 was the one for road and highway building enterprise.

---

68. A cross between a supervisor a foreman and a bookkeeper who was in charge with keeping track of standardized work quotas and who would accordingly set up the deserved monetary compensations based on how each individual in the organization fulfilled those quotas.

Mitzy assured me that "the Russians are not interested in the origin of their employees, and they only required people who are qualified for the job." She added that such training courses had been organized before and were now being offered again due to increased demand. In her opinion this kind of job was a Godsend for those considered enemies of the people, and indeed most people who held those positions were former lawyers or other professionals who couldn't work in their former fields. She added that she intended to sign up for a two-month training course which was scheduled for February to April. For her that was one of the few options: it would assure her of a future salary and allow her to earn a living for her girls and mother. Liky told me that in the interim, in order to make a living—since he was a former landlord himself in Craiova—he had accepted the position of truck or car driver at the same Sovrom no. 6.

Their proposal somewhat appealed to my desire to get out of my room and apathy. But I still hoped to work in the legal field, plus I knew I wasn't even going to work in Bucharest. I would have to go somewhere in the country to build roads, an occupation that had never occurred to me. When my father heard about it, he seemed concerned I would leave home. Maman Titi, far from being opposed, wanted me to follow the course, thinking the distance from the capital would prevent me from making another attempt to follow my husband abroad.

After spending several nights thinking about my options—as French say "*la nuit porte conseil*" ("night is a good counselor")—I decided to go, see what it was all about, and possibly sign in for the course, knowing I had nothing to lose. One morning I woke up feeling somehow more enthusiastic and went to the designated address where I would meet Mitzy.

The head of the training program was a former lawyer, Nicolae Ciocâlteu, whose family was originally from the town of Craiova. I introduced myself as Simona Kandel, which gave him no clue about who I was until Mitzy mentioned that I was the daughter of professor G. Vrăbiescu from the Law Faculty. That generated an instant bond between us, partly because he had been my father's student and partly because we both came from families with roots in Craiova. So

I filled out the paperwork required to sign up for the training course, and Mr. Ciocâlteu was my instructor. I really saw him as the embodiment of the solution to the situation I was trapped in—one in which there was no prospect for the future because of the stigma attached to my family—maybe it was the answer to my prayers.

As a former lawyer, Mr. Ciocâlteu was a good teacher, tactful, cheerful and clever. He was also a good organizer, agile and with a quick mind. The classes lasted from February 13 to April 15, 1950, and I missed none of them. The environment was quite nice; most of the students were former law students or other professional who had been unable to pursue their professions. Like me, they were there to acquire new skills that held out the promise of a future steady income.

At the end of the course, I got a Graduation Diploma in April 1950 from Sovrom Construction Enterprise No. 6—the Road Transportation Division. Nicolae saw to it that Mitzy and I were assigned to the same building site. On the twentieth of April 1950 I was assigned to work on a road building site not far from Bucharest, with headquarters located in the small town of Urziceni. Thus, I joined the labor force of the People's Republic of Romania. That day, I took a bus to Urziceni and reported to work.

But I cannot omit another communist calamity. The day before, on April 19, 1950, in the morning, we heard over the radio that we were no longer the owners of our home following a government decree regarding the nationalization of private houses. So overnight and with no prior notification, we were turned into tenants in our own home, which was now owned by the state without compensation to the owners. The nationalized houses were listed in a so called Annex to the Decree. At the same time medical offices, restaurants, and shop were nationalized as well. My family was truly outraged, because it had been a significant financial effort for them to build that beautiful town house. It was the first time I heard my father saying, "The Kandels were right to leave when they did. There is nothing more to live for here."

On that day, after dinner, many of our relatives and friends came over to vent their frustration at being dispossessed of their homes. Our drawing room soon turned into a veritable lamentation choir. The Decree essentially completed the communization of the country in accordance with the Soviet system. I continued to pledge revenge against it!

In the evening, I packed a few things for my next day's early morning trip to my new work place.

On the bus I was physically present but my mind was elsewhere. I was thinking about Stephen. I wondered what he was doing, where he was. The driver, who looked quite shabby, made many stops to pick up peasants who were carrying all kinds of bags, boxes, or live chickens. It was a pitiful sight—a world entirely different from what I had experienced. But my thoughts were interrupted when I arrived in Urziceni, where I had to face reality again.

The Sovrom enterprise divided the length of the road in three sectors: Alexeni—Căzănești —and Andrășești. The chief engineer in charge of the three sectors was Alexander Roșculeț, a tall man with glasses. He had a gentle look and slow movements; to me he seemed like a person of character. Mitzy remained in Urziceni while I was assigned to Alexeni. After a while, my friend, Dinu C. Giurescu also joined us. He was a historian, a professor at the University of Bucharest. I had known him before the coming of the communists. Dinu was the one who calculated his own reports and also checked hours before sending them to the headquarters in Urziceni.

At Alexeni I lived in a farmer's house without electricity or running water. During the summer, when it was getting very hot during the day, I used to wash myself during the late evening hours at the backyard fountain to remove the dust that had gathered during the day. Then I would be down on a straw mattress that was deeply concave in the middle. Plainly said there was a whole.

The office was situated at the end of the road just before a T intersection with the highway. That is where all action occurred. On one corner there was a pub used by the villagers, workers, and staff. We, the staff, ate in the cafeteria, but only after the workers had finished, leaving behind an unbearable sweaty smell that ruined my appetite, even though I used to be very hungry after walking along the road for hours on end.

The menu included either a bean soup with a potato stew or a potato soup with baked beans and, rarely, cabbage stew. Even more rarely we got bread, but more often than not there was polenta. Because the square of polenta was rather dry staying on its own next to the plate, I used to scoop a piece from the middle which was untouched It was a big hit when we could find chili peppers or feta cheese at the pub.

When inspecting the workers alongside the road, I noted that every single day two freight trains passed by at approximately the same time, one in the morning and one in the afternoon. Each was about 150 wagons long filled with agricultural products and timber or pulling oil tanks heading toward the port of Constanța and, from there, to the USSR. The loads were part of the reparation payments determined under the Armistice with the USSR in September 1945. But when the trains passed, we all pretended to pay no attention because to make any comment about them could mean many years of prison sentence.

At the end of each month, we worked for three days and three nights straight in to finish the calculation of the amount of work performed and compared to the normative tables with the specified quotas. Of course, every team wanted to inflate the amount of work per time unit to get more money, so they were submitting the sheets at the last minute, on the one hand. On the other we had strict dead-lines to hand in the calculations that would allow the payroll group to do their work and collect the money to pay the salaries on pay days. That was the reason which forced us to stay in the office and late into the night. I remember how, one time, the four of us were almost beaten by the workers because the ministry had delayed sending the money and they suspected that we had taken it.

On Saturdays after lunch, we were driven to Bucharest in open trucks. We were brought back to work early Monday morning in time to begin the work day, which started at seven o'clock. On those trucks there was a lot of noise because some of the commuters were bringing home live foul in cages (chickens, ducks, turkeys, geese, you name it) that they had bought from the locals. So there was little room for us who were forced to sit in very cramped positions all the way to Bucharest. Because I was quite thin and not too heavy I was often asked to sit on top of a cage. I used to lay a towel over the wire cage to avoid being pinched by the birds. My hair was dusty and I was sweating. In short, I was a mess. But nothing mattered to me anymore; I was no longer bothered by anything. Reaching home I was worn-out by the sun, full of dust, thirsty, and dead tiered.

At home, although now being tenants in our own house, I enjoyed my family and my bed with a straight mattress in good shape. I was delighted to be able to take a warm bath, and eat at a table with china ware, glasses, and silver cutlery. Well, what a luxury! But Maman Titi, seemed quite depressed. I had never before seen her in such a low mood. Nevertheless she seemed relieved that my leaving the country was finally out of the picture and that I could come home on weekends. She was very apprehensive about the black, windowless police vans roaming through the streets during the night. People were arrested, picked up from their beds in the middle of the night, and thrown into those vans with only the clothes on their backs. The sound of those vans kept Maman Titi up at night as she wondered which of the neighbors were targeted or whether—God forbid—they might also stop at our house.

Maman Titi told me about the massive arrests that had occurred on the night of the fifth and sixth of May while I was on the job. I went to see Bacal, who was well informed and gave me further news. He tried to comfort me by saying that most of those arrested had occupied ministerial positions until 1945.

*   *   *

An international event took place which I do not want to overlook because it explains the roots of what is happening while I am writing. In June 1950, the communist forces of North Korea crossed the thirty-eighth parallel into South Korea. President Truman did oppose the expansion, based on a containment policy. Then, General MacArthur in charge of the US military suggested that the US should occupy North Korea, which was being provided with weapons from both Russia and Mao. The general's proposal was opposed by politicians. Had MacArthur been given a free hand, North Korea wouldn't have become the issue that it is today (now notorious for its nuclear program as well as the fact that it helped build the Syrian reactor in Kibar and helped the communist expansion in Northern Vietnam. Also, had General Patton been given a free hand in 1945, to defeat Stalin, Central and Eastern Europe would have been freed and may be the Russian expansionism in Eastern Ukraine would not unfold in 2015.

Then too in Romania in 1950 were established units of labor camps with the declared purpose of reeducating hostile elements through labor. In truth, the sole purpose of those labor camps was to exterminate the opponents to the communist regime. Anybody could arbitrarily be labeled hostile. People who survived these camps later testified that they were forced to torture and humiliate one another, both physically and mentally, in order to crush their personalities.

Regarding our acquaintances, Aimée hadn't heard from Papanuş since he had been arrested, nor was there word about Ion Ioanid or about many others who formerly attended our tea-parties. The only good news came from Georgiana regarding Lulu, who continued his studies in Switzerland. During all this time, Stephen neither called nor wrote again. And on top of everything, although I had managed to get my law degree, I was denied the possibility of getting a judicial position. I realized that fate had other intentions for me. To make things worse, on a given Sunday before leaving for Alexeni, Gică told me that doctor Missirliu (Sandu's father) diagnosed Maman Titi with lung cancer. She had never been sick before. I was sorry I could not stay with her. I had to be in Alexeni until late autumn—when it turned very cold—and the building of the road had to be put off until spring of 1951.

1951

Gigi Sescioreanu had been a good friend of the Vrăbiescu brothers ever since they were studying Paris at the Sorbonne getting their PhDs in Law. Dinu Sescioreanu, his nephew, was a friend of mine and also a lawyer who could handle the marriage annulment. He said he would handle my case just for the sake of our friendship, even though that case was a dangerous one as it involved foreign countries. Indeed, I was very moved by his intention to assume such a great risk; I thanked him warmly for his proposal and said I would think about it. What complicated things was Maman Titi's desire that I should marry Dinu. He was a gentleman and a landowner at Craiova—exactly what she wanted for me. But I continued to think about Stephen. My thoughts were as fixed as a minute hand stuck on the dial of a clock. Since Maman Titi was sick and I didn't want to upset her, I said I agreed with the annulment of the proxy marriage, but I could not yet think of another possible marriage partner. His help seemed to me appropriate because I had a new job outside Bucharest and could not handle the case myself.

Dinu took the application to the Law Court after I had signed it with the following justifications: "Dr. Stephen Kandel went for one year to Italy to improve his orthopedic studies and to return afterwards, which did not happen."

So in papers I was separated from my husband and the blame was on him; it wasn't the fault of the communists. I had to accept this demeaning statement because I couldn't tell the truth. Under communism one could not speak the truth.

Later Dinu got married to my cousin Cristina. She had asked me, "Do you mind if I interfere?" I had given her the green light on the spot. Their wedding took place next spring. They were both from Craiova and former landowners, which was just the marriage my grandmother would have wanted for me.

Though Maman Titi knew she had cancer, she refused to go to the hospital even after learning what was wrong with her. She lay in bed more than four months, from November to February. Over the winter being more often home I realized that her condition was worsening. Holding her hand, I asked her to squeeze mine tightly, and she tried. That was her last gesture. On February 13, 1951, she gave her last breath. After the funeral, occasionally, I brought flowers and candles to her gravesite and also to Uncle Nae's.

Several days after the funeral, when I was taking a nap, in my sleep I thought I could feel Maman Titi taking her seat on the edge of the bed. She leaned over and kissed me on the forehead. Suddenly,

I woke up, shaking. She was not physically present, but I'm sure she was next to me. I was so impressed that even today I cannot forget her kiss and her undeniable presence at my bedside.

Maman Titi had been a beautiful and courageous woman. She married young, had children immediately, became a widow when she was still young, and raised her boys on her own. She also took care of the mansion and the Genune estate. She sent the boys for university studies in Paris and during the war expressed great pride that they were fighting for their country. Then she became a loving grandmother, who could also be very severe. I almost laugh when I remember how, one evening when I came home late she slapped me so hard it made my head spin.

What hastened her end were all the devastating historic events she had to go through during her lifetime. First there was the loss of Greater Romania, then there was the Iron Guard rebellion, and finally came the communists—with the painful land nationalization and expropriations—including the devastation of our Genune estate and the stabilization which left her without the money she had saved. Not least among her misfortunes was undoubtedly the prospect of my leaving the country for a man who was not to her liking. I was really relieved to let her know that I had handed-in the petition for the annulment of my marriage, but I could not forgive myself for being at least partly to blame for the tumultuous last years of her life.

I moved into her room. I could almost hear her whispering in the house by herself, her lips moving slowly, words that need not be heard about the adversities she had witnessed. Without her in the house, everything seemed strange and desolate. I could not imagine life without her. She had been the pillar of our home, and she had supported all of us; she was always there for us; she was the steadfast anchor of her family and friends. Now I was sure she would help me from above.

* * *

I knew that Mitzy wanted to find a job in Bucharest to be closer to her children and her mother. At one point she heard from a nephew that the Sovrom Designing Institute was hiring people with our qualifications. She informed me that she had gone there, that the information was correct, and that she spoke to Mr. Comino, head engineer, who was willing to recommend her for one of his available positions. And then she added, "I told Comino, without even consulting you, it's not just about my transfer but also about you, my niece, with whom I worked in Urziceni-Alexeni."

I embraced and thanked her. Of course, I preferred to have a job in Bucharest, not to mention the fact that the Institute was very close to my house.

When fate intervenes, things can be really easy, and that proved to be the case with our transfer within Sovrom from one enterprise to another. Mr. Comino got the official approval, and both of us were transferred starting March 19, 1951. The assignment was signed by the Russian director Kopâlenko and, Brenner, his Romanian assistant director. Mitzy was appointed to the Planning Department under Comino and I was appointed to the Employment and Payroll service, with Chief Poliacoff and Viorica Ruja-Stein his assistant. My colleagues in the Norms Department were assigned to various internal departments.

At the beginning my assignment as normator was shared with Fănică Niculescu at the Architecture Department, a nice fellow with whom I got along very well; he was cheerful, skillful, friendly, and funny. The Institute had over eight hundred employees, many of whom I befriended over the years.

Getting to the office in the morning was a piece of cake. It took me only twenty minutes to walk there. As far as my job was concerned, I had to adapt my knowledge from road construction to blueprints and their standards of specific norms. In time, I got to work in three departments—Architecture, Roads and Bridges, and Resistance—so that at the end I knew almost all of the eight hundred employees, and most of them knew who I was.

I believe fate gave me a bonus through Mitzy. Thanks to her, I found my first job and it is to her I owe my transfer to Bucharest. My personnel file was not so bad either, because I knowingly omitted in my resume what was not acceptable. For example, I wrote that my mother was just a "housewife."

From my salary I was able to put aside a certain amount to send to Manini and for Cristina's aunt Natalica and her husband who had been ousted from the Ercea estate and were without any pension. It was not much, but better than nothing.

I have to mention my colleague, Viorica Ruja-Stein—with reddish brown hair, brown-green eyes, a distinctive profile, and nice legs. She was a very quiet person in the office. I never quite knew what she was thinking. This was not surprising because, in general you protected yourself by remaining quiet since you could not trust anybody you had not known for a long time. (And even with those you knew well, you sometimes had to be careful.)

The country's overall environment had become detestable. You suspected everyone. So my friendship with Viorica was slow to develop, and it was only much later that we really became close friends, which we remained the rest of our lives.

Regarding my personal problems, in March 1951, Dinu told me he had filed the papers for the proxy marriage annulment on the following grounds: "SK, the husband, did not want to return to Romania after having been in Italy for a program of specialization in surgery…" and People's Court mentioned that I "asked for the annulment of the marriage—which actually never existed, because it was not consumed as such, thus it didn't exist under Romanian law" and "by working at Sovrom Enterprise I proved that my purpose was to remain employed, thus actively working to build socialism in the Romanian People's Republic." All irony and lies! But it was the only way I could get the annulment.

After that, the Department of Civil Status had released on April 13, 1952, the "Cancellation of the Marriage Certificate Act" of April 10, 1948."

Four years of my youth had been spent under the spell of Stephen. After I first met him, ten wonderful months followed with a tremendous amount of love, then lots of running around to obtain the necessary documents, and three applications filed for exit visas, all with lots of hope to get permission to join him. I'd had two audiences with the president of the General Assembly and with a Secretary of State from the Department of Interior, with three negative responses.

Without question, I felt that all hope was lost, except of the hope on revenge one day!

In fact, everything was lost—my beloved land estate Genune, my marriage, my professional career. All was due to the inhumane communist rule. I had a deep desire to take revenge on the communists for ruining my life. Although I did not know exactly how that would be achieved, I hoped that in time, one day, I would succeed.

What was left? For sure, it was Mrs. Raia Nicolau's friendship, that of her children and the good relationship with Bacal and Lydia his wife, whom I occasionally visited. Although he had not helped me at all, I was pleased to realize that he was very disillusioned with what was happening in the country, being too smart —that, in spite of the fact that he was considered to be a communist believer.

Despite the marriage annulment, Stephen was still on my mind. I kept thinking if fate would ever decree we should get together, it still seemed possible, regardless of annulment. Thus, I tried to use the comfort of harboring a doubt about the finality of it all, since the certainty of a final separation made me lose my taste for life.

Only a month had passed since I got my job in Bucharest when we got another big blow. Luckily, God had taken Maman Titi in due time. After losing the estate, our savings, and our home, my father, Professor George Vrăbiescu, was dismissed from the Faculty of Law to which he devoted his soul and sacrificed his marriage. Also, he was dismissed from the position as Consultant from the Legislative Council, after twenty-two years of service. The Council itself was abolished by the communists on April 21, 1951. All my former teachers were dismissed, their careers destroyed by a political ideology alien to the Romanian nation, an ideology that destroyed our historic tradition!

But George Vrăbiescu was a resourceful man. Realizing that we no longer had any financial means to survive, he started to look for any kind of job, not only for the money but to prove to himself that he was still active in the work force and thus avoid an eviction from the apartment, because these two aspects were sort of related. Meanwhile, Nicu, a former lawyer, had also become a normator in order to be able to contribute to the payment for water, electricity, heat, and food (which we needed as we no longer received any food from Genune). We were dead broke, but at least we lived in our house.

Unlike in Urziceni-Alexeni, here in the Bucharest Design Institute we were required to attend all meetings, in the presence of the Chief of Staff, the Trade Union's Chief, and the Party Boss. I was physically present, but my head was somewhere else, since all the speeches sounded the same. Invariably, every speaker praised the Communist Party and its economic achievements. It was all propaganda, but of course most of us knew that the truth was different. All meetings exalted the economic achievements under the 1951–1955 Five-Year Plan.

All religious holidays were outlawed and replaced with such Communist holidays as May the 1, the international workers' day, or November 7, the anniversary of the Bolshevik revolution. On both these days there were big parades that everybody was expected to attend.

At home in late November we received a call from Uncle Costinel, my father's cousin, who was recently been released from prison where he had spent about two years—years in which nobody knew anything about him. He had been arrested after the August 1947 stabilization because he hadn't submitted his gold coins to the bank as required by decree. I believe he held out hope that Americans would rescue us while in the meantime probably somebody denounced him, and when the militiamen came for searching his apartment—they found "capitalist coins." Costinel was arrested and the coins were confiscated.

Now he told us that his family received an eviction notice and were summoned to move to Bucharest's outskirts. Poor Costinel was desperate. My father and Nicu thought we might also be in danger of eviction, having still too much space. So Gică told him, "Dear Costinel, you should move-in with us. You and Margueritte can take my bureau and your son Ion can stay in the drawing room. With eight people in the apartment, it will be more difficult to be evicted or send other foreigners to stay with us."

And that was what actually happened. But, on the spot I asked my father, "Well, Gică, there are already five of us sharing one bathroom, isn't it difficult enough? What about eight persons?"

"It will be much better than having strangers among us," was his reply.

"We already have the fellow from Securitate living in the basement, that's enough threat as it is. With Costinel we would be better protected!"

I kept quiet. He was right, although the situation was becoming impossible. One bathroom being used by eight people was something awful. I remembered, longingly, the time when I once had my own bathroom on the first floor.

Costinel's family moved in. My cousin Ion was a great bridge lover, and after he moved in with us he started having friends over to play the game. Among them was Dr. Dan Poenaru, Ileana's brother and Alecu Radian's nephew, Dr. Mircea Alexandrescu (both from Craiova), and Dr. Cecil Poppa, a colleague from the medical field. I presented Ion to Aimée. The tea-parties had been replaced by bridge tables. I played with pleasure; it was a way to keep my mind busy with something other than the failure of my former projects.

When guests were expected, everyone knew how to listen for a familiar knock, assuring us these were not some strangers at the door. If we weren't expecting anyone and the entrance doorbell rang, everyone got worried. We lived in eternal fear. For the same reasons we did not celebrate the holidays with big parties.

1952

On the afternoon of seventh of March, on my birthday, just before a bridge game session, while I was getting dressed and combed my hair, I happened to glance into the mirror that had formerly belonged to Maman Titi. The sight surprised me. What I saw now was a woman who had reached an age when both my grandmothers were already mothers with two or three children. Gazing longer, I realized I was wasting my youth waiting for—what? I was not very happy with what I saw in the mirror. The Communists had defeated me, and

I could no longer restore the former balance I'd had in my life, nor could I replace Stephen's memory.

This was my state of mind when I lost myself in bridge games with Ion, Aimée, Dan Poenaru, Mircea Alexandrescu and Cecil Poppa. Except of my job I had no other interests.

Aimée told me that she liked Ion very much and about that time, I accepted her proposal that we should enroll in a cosmetics course twice a week in the afternoons. It began on April 5 and continued for a year.

Finally, in early June, my father got a job as the manager of the cafeteria of the national society of PLAFAR, an enterprise manufacturing and distributing teas with plant extracts. He knew all market prices and the food needed for the daily menus—matters that had never concerned or interested him previously in his life. Nevertheless, my father did not feel humiliated by this position. On the contrary, he was rather happy because he thought this was the way he would save us from eviction. (He knew that if we were evicted, the new tenants would damage the house.) Moreover, both my dad and his brother had the conviction that the utopian communist system could not last. So in my father's view, the least of the problems we faced right now was the overcrowding of our own house.

One evening early June, as Ion and I were listening to classical music, he told me that his friend Dr. Cecil Poppa liked me very much. I asked him to tell me more about him. I learned he was a highly respected doctor. The hospital's patients appreciated him, and so did his hospital boss, Professor Dr. Costel Nicolau, who was also director of the Institute of Hematology, where Cecil served as his assistant doing research in the field. Besides being exceptional in his studies, Cecil was also a very well-read person. In fact, Ion told me he had procured an encyclopedia and read it through from beginning to end in alphabetical order. Along with an exceptional memory, Cecil had encyclopedic knowledge in a variety of fields and an outstanding memory. That explained why he was such a good bridge player.

I saw that Cecil knew how to conduct a conversation and how he loved to impress his audience. He was tall, with straight light-brown hair, white skin, green-tinted brown eyes, a beautiful nose,

and a mouth that was very expressive whenever he spoke. He had
not been and was not married; he lived with his parents. If it had not
been for Ion telling me about Cecil's feelings toward me I would not
have noticed anything. There were no bouquets of roses, like those
Lulu used to send me and no *coup de foudre* in the doorway of the
kind I had felt with Stephen. There was only one similarity—the fact
I had met him in Armașului, my house.

Shortly thereafter, Ion asked me if I would agree to go out with
him, Aimée, and Cecil. I said I had nothing against it. So we all met
one day in Armașului and went to a restaurant. A few days later,
Cecil invited me to meet him at a pastry shop. When I went there,
he told me about his student life, about his parents, and about his
sister who had died in an alpine ski accident. And he even accompanied me home. Undoubtedly, he was a presentable, smart man who
appeared to be quite successful; he was of appropriate age and very
polite as well.

Right after Gheorghe Gheorghiu-Dej became prime minister in
June 1952, immediately a monetary reform took place (on June 28)
that was not announced beforehand. In short, all our hard-earned savings, representing a mere safety net in case of layoffs, was gone. The
savings were stolen from us just like the house and the estate with its
land—without any compensation or equivalent cash. Luckily, Gică,
Nicu and I each had a salary. The aim of the reform was to bring our
currency, leu, at par with the Russian ruble; and to destroy or ensure
that people would have no other means than the salaries or pensions
paid by the state. At the same time, the state enriched itself, further
becoming the Leviathan controlling everyone's life.

* * *

One afternoon in late July, the phone rang. When I picked up the
phone, the voice at the other end asked, "Moni, is that you?" I recognized my mother's melodious voice. The surprise was huge. I was
very happy. She told me that she had finally been released, after
four hard years, from the Danube-Black Sea Canal labor camp. She
gave me an address where I could find her, adding that Manini had
made arrangements for her to reside in Bucharest with one of her old

friends from the boarding school for girls who had offered to share her apartment. Being able to show prison authorities that she could have a Bucharest residence, they released her to that address where she was consigned to serve the balance of her sentence under house arrest. Part of her obligation was to report once a week to the Police precinct, to be home no later than 9:00 p.m., and to stay within a fifteen-mile radius of her domicile at all times.

When I saw her, she was very weak. Her hair was too long, her face very pale, but altogether she was glad she could serve her house arrest sentence in Bucharest instead of who-knows-where. Mrs. Alexandrescu, my grandmother's friend, was a gracious lady—small, hunched-over, with white hair pulled back into a small bun, and always moving slowly. Manini also came from Craiova frequently to see her daughter and myself.

We were happy to be together and brought each other up-to-date on our lives during her imprisonment. Mancy gave us chilling details about the prison life she had endured since her arrest on April 2, 1948.

Below is an excerpt she wrote many years later in New York, "On the twenty-second of April at 6:00 a.m., some soldiers rang the doorbell, entered and searched the apartment, but found nothing. Around 12:00 a.m. they asked me to grab a few necessary things, we went to the car which took me to the Ministry of Domestic Affairs (A TERROR AND TORTURE place) This was the location for the interrogation of political prisoners, a living hell where militia men carried out inhuman interrogations.

"And there I was sitting on a chair in the middle of a cold room, to be seen by everyone who was passing by. I stayed there until they took me to have something to eat and after they searched me I was taken to one of the several detention cells in the basement or 'studios' as they mockingly called them. At about 6:00 p.m. I was moved to 'Studio no. 5.' In the cell everything was dirty, even the food looked like dirty water. The interrogations were taking place every morning starting at 2:00 a.m. We all were accused having affairs with foreigners and we were convicted on mere false accusations with no back up evidence.

"On April 17, 1948, I was transported to the Văcăreşti prison. The interrogations were conducted while I was blindfolded, with one of the guards pulling me by the sleeve or pushing me. On the way to the inquiry room I could hear screaming along the corridor from the cells. The interrogation was very long, it lasted for hours and there were many questions. Whenever I thought we were done, we would start again from the beginning. Afterwards they took me back to my cell. In the evening the investigation continued, when they'd ask me about the many other people my husband was meeting with. Towards the morning I'd be back in the cell, and in the evening I'd come back for the investigation, which was their system used to destroy the prisoners' will and mental strength.

"TRIAL. December 7, 1948. Military Court.

"The trial lasted for six days. I spent the daytime at the Court House and at night I was taken to the court-martial. They carried me from one place to another with dark windowless vans. There was a panel of judges, with a president. The main hall was very crowded, full of armed guards. I was taken to the stand and I could see the other people who were on trial, and also a small room also full of guardians.

"On December 17, 1948, after my conviction, I was brought back to a prison hospital in Văcăreşti, where the church had been turned into a warehouse and the prison had several floors. I had been informed we had to be transferred to the Mislea prison (a *convent* building *converted into* a *prison* for women *prisoners*). At one o'clock at night a van took us to Băicoi, where militiamen threw us out of the van in the middle of a freezing night and accompanied us to the train station toward Mislea.

"From December 31, 1948, to April 2, 1951, I was imprisoned in Mislea; we were taken there by a train with armored cabooses and bars, then by a truck which dropped us into the big yard of the prison. There we were received by Elena Tudor, the odious director, welcomed up with a spit in our face. The windows here had bars; the rooms had two beds and there was a stench in the air from unwashed bodies. There was only one bathroom and a dining room.

At Mislea, it was mandatory for us to work, making rugs or embroidery. I embroidered three Romanian blouses.

"From April 2 to May 20, 1951, I stayed in the Mislea Camp. When I left I was the only one escorted by armed militiamen. The militiaman made a mistake and instead of taking me to Ghencea jail they took me by truck to the famous Jilava prison. In the truck there were some men lying down facing the bottom of the truck, with their backs to the sky. I was ordered to do the same myself. In each of the four corners of the truck was a soldier armed with a gun ready to shoot. Since they weren't expecting me at Jilava they put me in a separate room until someone came with a warrant to take me to Ghencea. That man was a monster. He made me run on a half a meter path on the top edge of a fifteen-meter earth embankment. I do not know how I managed to keep my balance while this policeman wouldn't let me slow down and kept punching me in the back. It was a great terror and physical pain. On top of all I was also carrying my luggage while having to gallop on a land full of weeds. It was hell on earth. Even today I still cannot forget that dirt and mess.

"From May 21 to May 24, 1951, I spent four days at Ghencea. Over there, gypsies were in one barrack and us, the political prisoners, in another one.

"From there I was taken by train to the town of Cernavoda where I stayed from May 25 to July, 1 1951; the commander in charge with the camp was Florian Cormos who was extremely cruel. Ultimately, I ended up at Saligny—situated a few miles from Cernavoda.

"From July 1, 1951, to February 4, 1952, I was interned at Cernavoda-Saligny, near the Black Sea. The camp director was sub lieutenant Georgescu, helped by the well-known torturer Bogdănescu whose reeducation method was torture. The 'Danube-Black Sea Canal' or the "death canal" project began back in 1949–'50. Here I was exposed to direct sunlight from six in the morning till sunset. In the evenings after work, when the trucks took us back to prison and I put my feet on the ground I was hallucinating, I saw the earth with fluorescent grass. I used to bend down to see if I could grasp the grass I was terrified. I asked someone why I had those visions, and that person answered, "We all went through that; it is because you are exposed to direct sunlight." Also, because of the sun my arms were swollen and it was very painful. From the Medical Center, where I could go at midnight and where doctors were also detainees, I acquired a cotton roll to wrap my arms. It was extremely difficult. I was digging for hours removing carrots, beets or potatoes from the ground or digging earth, or carrying wheelbarrows with heavy rocks until I fell down on my knees powerless. There was no mercy, even when I was sick with a high fever due to cold and lack of clothes, coughing until exhaustion, the Securitate would force me to do things faster. And when I fell on the ground they hit me with their boots or the rifle butts, accompanied by demeaning swearing and trivial vocabulary. Only God helped me to survive.

"On February 2, 1952, we received news that we will be released in alphabetical order. My turn came on February 6 when, after spending a day and a night without moving in the van, I arrived at the Târgşor prison.

"From February 8 to July 20, 1952, I was kept for six months in Târgşor near the city of Ploieşti. In that prison the work was divided into two teams, one worked twelve hours a day, the other twelve hours at night. What we intertwined rope nets to cover cannon-pods. My team worked for twelve hours a night. If we fell asleep we were awakened by getting slapped and hit with fists by the women supervisors. My hands bled from thick wires of strings. And in order to cope with the gypsies, I tried to behave and keep them away from me. In this jail there was an environment of fear and suspicions. Even executions took place. It was an extremely difficult time.

"On July 29, 1952, I was called for release with others. We went by van to Ghencea, when in the morning we were taken in a separate yard waiting to be released. The doors were opened only at five in the afternoon when we were pushed out like animals. The people with carriages passing on the road took some of us to Bucharest! I served a total of four years and three months in seven prisons."

We were all extremely moved listening to what she had to get through. It was hard to believe that a woman with her upbringing had resisted. She said it was her severe education from family members and school that mostly helped her.

* * *

A few days later, on August 3, I invited Manini and my mother to our Armașului house. That was a real family reunion. It was an opportunity for Mancy to exchange with Ion's mother about the good times in Craiova and with Uncle Costinel prison memories. Among those present to greet my mother was also Cecil Poppa invited by Ion for a bridge party. It was quite emotional for him to be present with all of us. I knew he liked me, but I thought our beautiful and centrally located house was also a factor in his fascination with me. It is true he was good looking, but sort of stiff in manners.

While my mother was catching up with different family members including my father and Uncle Nicu, Cecil kept trying to join the conversation. Struck by his attitude, Manini asked me who he was. I told her he was Ion's friend, when she replied, "It looks like he's interested in you."

"Maybe," I said with a dry voice. I knew she was right.

After those long conversations, we felt a degree of peace. For all that had happened to us, at least we were still living in the house without strangers among us. I accompanied Manini and my mother on their way home.

Three days later, when I was already home from the office, I heard voices on the staircase, and then the sound of somebody climbing the steps and ringing the doorbell. The Romanians have a saying, "One cannot get away from what one is afraid of," which was also true in our case. My father opened the door and found himself in front of militiamen, who announced that we must evacuate the apartment by the following day. My father said he refused to talk to them until they showed an official order and closed the door. More than likely, our apartment had caught the eye of some party or secret police boss, and as owners we were simply regarded as a "nest of vipers" that had to be annihilated. Those in power wanted better, centrally located housing, and the communist bosses would stop at nothing to reward—in fact, to bribe—their supporters. These abuses came at the expense of homeowners considered "enemies of the people" and had to be imprisoned, destroyed or at least marginalized. They were to be deprived of their property in favor of the working masses, the proletariat, or the newly empowered and privileged ones, who were part of a mafia-type leadership structure.

After the militiamen left, Ion took the initiative to cancel the following day's bridge game in our house, explaining to our friends what had happened. He also asked me where he could find me in case we were evicted. I told him I would leave my phone number with Aimée, who also knew where I worked, having been there a few times.

Shortly thereafter, Cecil called. In a worried voice, he said, "Ion informed me what is going on in Armașului. Since time is pressing, I would like to ask you if you would consider marrying me and coming to live with me and my parents, instead of getting a lodging who-knows-where on the outskirts of the city."

Cecil's proposal took me by surprise. I had to take a deep breath. It wasn't enough that we had just got an unexpected eviction notice; now, on top of that, came this marriage proposal!

Hearing Cecil talking about marriage reminded me about Stephen's marriage proposal, one that also came in exceptional circumstances caused by the financial stabilization. Now was Cecil's proposal, caused by losing our Armașului home.

I replied by thanking him for his care and for the proposal, but I asked him to understand that I was too excited to be able to make such an important decision in this particular moment. I said, "Let's see what happens, if we shall be evicted after all." Then I added, "If we do not get evicted and if I accept your marriage proposal, would you move in with me here?"

He did not expect my reaction, since he was very close to his parents, as I was to my father and Nicu. He answered, "You're right, let's see what happens, but in any case please let me know where I can find you if you have to leave!"

"Okay. I shall let you know."

And that was that. Although I was very troubled by the possible eviction and by the unexpected marriage proposal, I did not mention Cecil's proposal to anyone.

I couldn't sleep that night. In the morning I called the office to tell them I couldn't come in. At the Institute I was working at the Resistance Department in the same room with the chief engineer Gustav Vianu, his assistant engineer Tudor Dinescu and with Radu Petrescu, the Department's secretary. I shared the same desk with Radu and had become very friendly. So I called him and told him, "Radu, I cannot come today because we are threatened with eviction."

"Oh! My god! Monel, where will you go?"

"We do not know yet. It's likely they'll come again today with an official order of eviction, and then we shall know for sure."

"Monel," Radu said, "if you aren't given a decent location, and you're sent to who knows where, you should turn down their offer and come to live with us until you find a solution."

"Thanks, Radu, that's what I'd do. I shall call you as soon as I know something."

I told Gică about Radu's suggestion that we shouldn't agree with any location that we didn't like. I also informed my father about Radu's offer to stay with his family until we could find another place to live and suggested to my father that he too might move to Florica. (I have to mention here that Nicu's wife and Gică's girlfriend had the same name: Florica.)

Around noon, the doorbell rang. I suspected who it was. I went to the door, my father behind me, but opened only one window pane in the door. There they were! I told them I would not let them in unless they showed me an official eviction order. One of them pulled out an official eviction order, rolled it into a tube, and passed it through the bars.

At that point, my father and Nicu had to open the door. We were given three addresses to move to. Nicu and his family and Uncle Costinel and his family were assigned to convenient locations, but my father and I had to move somewhere in the suburbs. The location to which we were assigned, we learned, had no running water. There was a water pump in the back yard, along with a toilet.

Discovering all this, I refused the repartition. In earnest, I was even afraid I might be attacked by hungry wolves in winter time as I was an early riser who had to leave the house at dawn in order to make it to the office by seven o'clock. When we objected, the angry militiamen said they could not give us another location. We had to hurry to leave the apartment. The trucks were already waiting outside with workers ready to help us move the furniture. They informed us the space had to be empty within three hours for the person who was to occupy it, and the militiamen had to return to home base by a certain hour, so there was no time for bargaining.

I looked outside the window and saw the driver who formerly rented the Kandel's garage for his taxi. He was looking at our windows to see what would happen. When I went to him and explained the situation, the man, with a big heart, told me that we could put all furniture that we could not take with us in his garage, and that he had no problem waiting with his taxi outside.

We were at a loss deciding what to take and what to leave. Nicu and Florica loaded their truck, and so did Uncle Costinel. (The furniture of both of them had been stored already in various places since their previous eviction.) Gică was happy to see that our furniture could be stored in our former garage, now the taxi driver's. And in the meantime took a large suitcase, not to pack clothes, but to save all diplomas earned in Paris or Romania, including the medal decorations received, all kinds of official documents, family letters, property and estate deeds, and graduation diplomas. His cloths were tucked in other suitcases. I followed my father's example and did the same thing, putting besides my cloths the letters and telegrams from Stephen.

Then I phoned Radu, told him what happened, and said I accepted his offer and would come to his place with my suitcases in the evening. He had already talked to his wife and told her that I might be their guest that evening. He gave me his address and home phone number.

I gave my dad all the information about the place where I was going to stay. My father got in touch with his girlfriend Florica and decided what furniture he might be able to bring over in her apartment and basement. Then my father made arrangement with Tante Lenuţa Anton to receive Rina and with Tante Cornelia to receive Leana, our maids. Before leaving, I promised Leana that I would let her know as soon as I found a place to live and would take her to live with me—to which she responded with a single cry, "Miss, please don't forget me!"

Before our departure, we met the new residents. The apartment was going to be occupied by the family of an engineer called Zamfirescu, who assured us that we could temporarily leave the four thousand volumes in my father's study with him, and gave my father a note to that effect. So a ridiculous situation followed. George Vrăbiescu ended up by thanking the man who had in fact thrown us out of our home. Later on I have found out that Zamfirescu was in fact a highly qualified professional from the city of Braşov, and the Communist oligarchy wanted him in Bucharest for some government-sponsored project. So they provided him with a spacious home in the center of the city while mercilessly throwing us out. In our beautiful house in Armaşului, Bacal remained on the first floor where the Kandels used to live, so far nobody dared to evict him.

When our truck was loaded, my father took a seat next to the driver with the archive suitcase at his feet, containing the only evidence of our former properties: that was all that remained! I embraced Leana and Rina. The three of us were crying, and Leana said, "Good thing that the old lady isn't alive to see this."

I climbed onto the open platform of the truck, sitting perched on the things my father took with him. That was my triumphal exit from Armaşului Lane in August 1952. Then again I promised myself revenge that I hope will be possible one day against this inhuman treatment.

First we stopped at the home of Mrs. Florica Arghirescu and her sister Viorica, whom I met for the first time. From there we went to my colleague Radu's house on Puccini Street.

It was past seven o'clock in the evening when I arrived at the apartment of Radu and his wife Mieta. They welcomed me with open arms while their daughter, Roxane, stood watching me inquisitively with wonder in her big green-blue eyes. They hid my suitcases behind some curtains and invited me to sit down for dinner. First thing, I called my father, who thanked Radu and Mieta for receiving me. I was hungry and tired. The eviction emotions had drained me. Even though my nerves were shaken, I felt kind of relaxed. At least

I did not have to worry about Uncle Costinel and Nicu. They had found a place to stay, and so had my father. Nor was I worried about my mother with whom I could keep in touch by phone.

By the time we sat down for dinner, I thought there were no more surprises in store for me that day. But after I took one bite and had a glass of wine, while Radu and Mieta wished me welcome, Radu relayed some further information.

"Monel, I want you to know that after you called me and I announced to both Vianu and Turică [which was how Tudor Dinescu was called by everyone] why you missed work, they felt very sorry about your situation. But then, when I was alone with Turică, he told me again how much he liked you, and told me that for a long time he had pondered whether to say anything or not. I'm pretty sure when you come to the office tomorrow, he'll make you a serious proposal. What do you think?"

I instantly remembered again August 16, 1947, and Stephen's marriage proposal and leaving Genune for good, all in one day. Today, August 7, 1952, I had experienced the eviction from my house one night before a marriage proposal. Being very surprised, I replied, "I am very fond of Turică, he impresses me very much. He is the best resistance engineer in our organization. I love his friendly smile and beautiful teeth, but I think he might be a little old for me. How old is he?"

"I do not know for sure," Radu said. "But yes, he must be at least twenty years older than you. And it also happens I know that he constantly receives calls from a lady. Apparently he has been in a long relationship with her."

I instantly said, "I do not think I am interested to get into a threesome relationship. In fact, a very good friend of my cousin, hearing about our imminent eviction called me right away and proposed marriage."

After filling all the glasses, Radu lifted his and said, "Bravo, Monel, what's the name of the lucky guy?"

"Cecil Poppa, a highly regarded doctor."

Apparently what I said touched a tender spot with Mieta who asked, "I think everything seems to work out for you, but tell me, do you feel anything for this man?"

I had to think before replying.

"I respect his qualities, but no, I'm not in love, and moreover I cannot overlook the fact that I'd have to live with his parents who are total strangers to me. And I do not know what kind of people they are."

Well, by the end of the evening I knew I could count on their moral support and friendship. They advised me not to make any commitment in a hurry and suggested I should pay Cecil a visit to get to know his parents. But I knew that it was time for me to make a decision.

Next day, in the office Tudor Dinescu didn't say anything to me, while I kept asking myself whether I should marry Cecil or not. Finally, I called him. He was thrilled and invited me to his home to meet his parents.

Cecil and his parents lived in a one-story house with a yard and with a basement that was inhabited by some of their relatives. The house belonged to another family, Georgescu, where the wife still kept a room. Cecil's mother, Muțuleana as he called her, was an elderly woman with completely white wavy hair pulled back into a bun. She had blue eyes and a pleasant smile and still had beautiful features. Cecil resembled her. She seemed to be very kind, open-minded—a caring mother. His father was rather short, with small but very lively eyes. He was balding, with gray hair. I learned he was a descendent of a family of shepherds from Transylvania. They had acquired some wealth, but everything had been seized by the communists, an act which turned Cecil's father, "Uncle Gogu," into a fervent anticommunist. That was something that I definitely had in common with him. It seemed that, for both of them, their son was at the center of their existence. Later on, I would learn that they'd had three children, but Cecil was their only surviving child.

Back at Radu and Mieta's place, I voiced my opinion about the visit, "I saw the house and met his parents. They are good, hardworking people from Transylvania, and they are very proud of their son and his career. However, there is a big difference between the climate in his family and mine."

Radu responded, "Monel, it's not like you're going to be stuck with him forever; if you do not like him or his parents, you can always divorce him and you will have plenty of time to find a place to live."

After one more night of thinking, I drew the line and reached the following conclusion: everything I loved was gone—Haagi the two Ioana, Genune, Armașului Lane, and Stephen. Though Stephen still held a place in my heart, I had nothing else to hold on to and, moreover, I had promised Leana that I would take care of her.

Next day, I called Cecil, told him that I agree to marry him and added that I would like Leana to stay with us. He told me he would first have to check with Muțuleana, although he knew there was a spare room in the basement. Then he asked me if I could bring the large sideboard from our dining room which was now stored in the taxi driver's garage. I replied I would check with my father about it. Indeed, I did not like the cupboard I saw at their house. In fact I did not like any of the furniture in that house, but I especially disliked the dark wallpaper in all rooms.

The second time we talked on the phone, he told me I could bring Leana and, in turn, I said he could come with a van to take the sideboard from the garage and also pick up Mama Titi's cupboard. Once we sealed the deal, Cecil informed me he would submit the forms for our marriage. Everything went smoothly but I was kind of detached as I felt that everything that was happening to me was in fact what fate had in store for me. Perhaps it was fate that had prevented me from leaving the country—a goal that I had fought so hard to achieve without any result. There must have been a good reason.

I remember the horror of the night of fifteenth to sixteenth of August, on Saint Mary's day. I spent that day at Radu and Mieta's; it was the day of mass arrests. The streets were crowded with police vans going back and forth, taking thousands of people out of their homes for investigations and convictions.

When I saw my father, I broke the news about my decision to marry Dr. Cecil Poppa, whom he had met through Ion in Armașului.

He seemed content, but I felt no emotion inside me. My heart did not react. Instead, the many arrests made me very depressed and anxious.

I also informed my mother about the wedding. She kept a neutral face but in no way did she seem excited. Finally, I met with Raia Nicolau, who knew what was in my heart and what to say to encourage me. She shared with me the past experiences she'd also had to face during her lifetime.

Later on, I called Leana (who now lived with her niece) and asked her to come to live with me in Cecil's house and letting her know that Muțuleana would from that point on replace Maman Titi. She agreed for my sake. I was glad, finally, to have one of my own among so many strangers—someone who had worked for us from before I was born. Also, the sideboard went into the dining room and the cupboard fitted perfectly into the larger bathroom, which would be the only place where I could keep my personal belongings under key. Then there was my Recamier bed—narrower than a regular bed—-that I managed to fit in across Cecil's bed. The Recamier was the only piece of furniture, given me by Bacal that had in fact belonged to Rosalie Kandel. (I had to sleep on that Recamier because Cecil told me that he wasn't used to sharing his bed with someone else. And neither was I for that matter.)

And so my fate was decided by communism which rolled over me as a bulldozer crushing my soul.

My marriage to Cecil took place on August 21, 1952, at the People's Council in the presence of Cecil's parents, my father, Nicu, and Florica. Also in attendance were Aimée and Ion (she was still much in love with him), Mitzy and Viorica Ruja-Stein (whom I had meanwhile befriended), Radu and Mieta, as well as Raia Nicolau. Leana and Rina were also there. I still remember Raia's bouquet of red gladiolas and the way she hugged me with great warmth.

The ceremony was simple; we just had to sign the marriage certificate issued by the People's Council of the Stalin District, which was very remindful of all the papers I had to sign to apply for my exit visa. This event marked the beginning of a new life, for which I didn't have to struggle at all. Some of those present at my wedding knew what was going on in my heart but gave me their warm hugs. Leana, overwhelmed with emotion, was crying.

Getting married to Cecil felt like I fulfilled an obligation. It was similar to the feeling I had at the end of each month when I'd finished calculation of the work quota reports. From City Hall Cecil's parents and my father came to Cecil's house where everything seemed new to me except Leana, the sideboard, and Maman Titi's cupboard. Apart from them, I still kept in my mind and heart Genune, Armașului with Lulu's and Stephen's elegant, warm manners. All I had now were good memories and an empty heart.

CHAPTER 7

48 Scărlătescu Street 1952-1958

1952-1955

After the civil marriage we arrived in Scărlătescu Street. Muţuleana was concerned with getting the table ready. Leana would serve. With my father and Leana near me, I felt more comfortable. Cecil and his parents were very kind and went to a lot of trouble to circumvent the food shortages, offering a meal that included meat and fish. The general climate was not particularly festive, given the arrests that had occurred four nights previously when thousands of people (especially students) had been picked up from their homes.

In the end, when my father stood up to leave, he invited both of us as well as the in-laws to pay him a visit. His departure left me with sadness.

Not being used to the noises in the neighborhood, at night I was weakened by sounds as insignificant as the squeak of a car's brakes. I was especially alarmed when Cecil would stand up and go to the window to find out what was going on in the street. The terror was nerve-wracking. Being cautious by nature, Cecil avoided any possible conversations with neighbors; he did not want anybody to know what we were eating, what our schedule was, where I worked, or what I did every day.

The day after the marriage, when I got to the office, Radu, with no comment on his part, handed me a newspaper. I read about the Council of Ministers Decision of August 1952, which indicated seven categories of crimes against the State, and a Decision that established a Commission charged with incarcerating people in labor colonies. The situation was worrisome.

The house in Scărlătescu Street—formerly the property of the Georgescu family—had a backyard and a garden. At the far end of the backyard, Uncle Gogu had set up a cage where he was raising a pig (a good thing to do, considering the meat shortages in the market). Mrs. Georgescu remained in the house with a room to herself. The in-laws also got their own bedroom (the former parlor) that was decorated with pink-red wallpaper. A door connected their room to ours, blocked with hanging carpets on both side. The wallpaper in our room was dark blue with a design depicting bouquets of flowers, which made the room seem dark. Though not very large room, it held a very big wardrobe. Cecil's bed and my sofa were between the two windows that were hung with curtains. There was also a big bookcase, a desk filled with medical bottles or boxes, a chair, a tiled stove in one corner, with a door leading to the bathroom. Basically, in order to go to the bathroom, the in-laws had to go through our room. That had been okay when Cecil was not yet married, especially since he was not home most of the time. Unfortunately, I could not change anything in the room to suit my liking. It was even a long while before I was able to move the bottles from the desk to the bathroom because Cecil was very particular about where he kept his things and, at first, objected to them being moved. For the same reason, I was not able to take down the wallpaper and paint the walls a brighter color as I wanted to do. I felt lonely. To cheer myself up, I consoled myself with the thought that what fate had offered me was, at least, better than the location that had been signed to me by the State. But I did not like my new home either.

I realized that Muțuleana was extremely busy. At her waist, she carried the keys to the pantry where the family kept the goods that had been bought by Uncle Gogu. During meals, Muțuleana spoke only when necessary because Cecil wanted to be listened to and did not like being interrupted. I became aware that his attitude had been encouraged by his parents. All their attention was on their son, the only surviving child out of three, and they were very proud of him.

Uncle Gogu had acquired a certain amount of wealth in the past. Considering his age, he was extremely active. He devoted himself to the household, to his wife, whom he obeyed and respected, and to his son. Outside the house, however, he was a kind of philanderer, and never shy to brag about it, knowing that his wife was not jealous. She allowed him to do whatever he pleased as long as he kept doing his duty around the house. All was forgiven, because he would wake up early in the morning, go from one shop to another and buy everything he could get that day. This was a valuable service, considering that, in those days, one could rarely find anything that one needed or wanted. One could only buy what happened to be delivered to the store. He would wait in line to get bread, seltzer water, dairy, meat, eggs, cornflower, and corn beans (to feed the pig), and so on. The in-laws never invited other guests, with the exception, now, of my father, because of the difficulty of getting supplies. When my father did visit, it was about once every two or three weeks. My mother came only once.

After the marriage, instead of three mouths to feed, there were five of us, including Leana. She did the cleaning, helped in the kitchen, and served two meals. Leana's discontent was in seeing how Cecil got all the attention while I —the girl she had known ever since I was born —was now treated as second fiddle.

The meals were the center of activity, and each was a solemn event. There were two meals a day, one at half-past three when Cecil and I got back home, and the other one at ten o'clock at night when he would return from the Institute of Hematology, which was just around the corner from our house. At the hour when Cecil was supposed to arrive home, the table was already set and we all had to wait for him. The opening of the front door announced his arrival, alarming Muțuleana and Uncle Gogu, who then would yell through the kitchen door, "Leana, the doctor arrived! Make sure the food is hot! You can bring it in five minutes."

"Yes, right away!"

(Never had my father received such a triumphal welcoming when he came home from the University or the Legislative Council.)

Then Cecil would tell us what he had done and we would listen. The atmosphere was so different compared to what I had been used to in my families, or in Vrăbiescu's or Mirica's. Not always, but often, I stayed silent, convincing myself that fate has brought me here to live with those hardworking people, being aware how they had to stand on endless lines to get whatever food was obtainable. My contribution was almost my entire salary, which went to cover the daily needs.

Cecil was not a man of the world, but he was a very good professional and focused on his career as a doctor and researcher. He had a winning way, both with his presence and with his words. He was respected for the way he had met his obligations as a doctor. He was dedicated to his profession, a good diagnostician, and careful with his patients. He worked, on average, twelve hours a day, if not more. He was very meticulous, well known for his pedantic style in the Institute's laboratory. In short, in both the positions he held, he was highly appreciated.

I could not measure his ambition. Cecil persevered in keeping up with his reading, and he seemed to have an opinion about everything. I was fascinated by his erudition; he seemed familiar with any topic that came up and he would discuss it giving many details and examples. Asked about a single city, he could give the history of a whole country. He had an extraordinary memory, like an elephant. Whenever we were socializing, he aired his opinions as if they were final and irrefutable, impressing his listeners. This, people found admirable, and that made him happy.

From another angle, considering how much he appreciated my cousin Ion's friendship, I think his interest in marrying me was related to and motivated by my family's origin. He was aware of my family's former wealth, which eventually might be recovered.

I was impressed by his reputation as a doctor, by his good looks. But his behavior did not compare well to Lulu's, or Stephen's. With Cecil I did not enjoy any feeling of togetherness. I would leave early in the morning, before him. At noon we had lunch with his parents. After resting for an hour, Cecil would leave for the Institute, returning after ten o'clock in the evening when we were again all together. I couldn't wait to get to bed since I used to get up at five-thirty in the morning in order to leave the house at six o'clock. It was a fifty-minute walk to my office where work started at seven. Due to the constant presence of his parents, Cecil seemed to think he had to impose his will on me in order to be able to show his manhood.

Cecil had been used to the fact that his opinions were always accepted, and my in-laws were dismayed whenever I did not agree with the ideas he put forward. Even if they happened to disagree with him, I knew they would never express their opinions. Later I found out that there was an explanation for this. Muțuleana had been married before and had a son. At the age of twenty, her son had gone hunting and was accidentally shot in the head by a fellow hunter, dying on the spot. And there was a further tragedy in the family. Alina—Cecil's sister and Uncle Gogu's daughter—fell into a ravine while skiing and was not found until three months later after the snow had melted. Given the premature death of those siblings, Cecil now got all attention, care, and affection from his loving parents, to whom he was bringing happiness via his profession and reputation. I had been accepted only because I had been chosen by him.

Since my in-laws had no friends or a social life whatsoever, they had a different perspective. They must have asked themselves why I was taking cosmetology classes. Or why I had to leave home in the afternoon to meet Mitzy or Viorica? Wouldn't it have been better to stay home and wait for Cecil? But I have another kind of personality and received a different education; I was sociable. I had to go out and meet people; otherwise, I would be overwhelmed by the thought I was wasting my youth (especially after keeping myself separate for so long when I was vainly hoping for a reunion with Stephen).

At Sovrom-IPSR I was very compatible with my colleagues Radu, Mitzy and Viorica, but there was no time for friendly chats.

Some afternoons, Viorica and I would go out to see a movie or would stop by her place; there, I got to meet her husband Mircea Stein and her red dog named Seta. Another place to visit was Mitzy's, where Liky appeared sometime.

When Cecil and I happened to be alone together, I could have a normal conversation with him, as he was relaxed. On one occasion—the only time the in-laws were absent for three days—we even invited in guests for dinner. After two years of marriage, his parents bought him a car, using their savings, or so I was told. Now, on Sundays, Cecil kept tinkering with the car, fussing over it, polishing it —he always found something to do—and almost a whole day would pass while he lay under the car working on it. During meals on those days, he would proudly recount stories about how he managed to fix it without calling a mechanic. We never went out for a drive—or very rarely. What was this car for?

Cecil had no friends except a former colleague, a gynecologist named Pupi Rădulescu. The bridge parties stopped after our marriage and after Ion married Aimée, who didn't invite us because she did not like Cecil. The feeling was mutual. Cecil considered Aimée a very shallow person.

My father had moved in with Florica Arghirescu, a general's daughter, in an overcrowded, three-story house that had no elevator. My dad and Florica occupied a three-room apartment that had a kitchen, bathroom and a small balcony. Living in the same house were Florica's sister Viorica, and her cousin Ziguța with her daughter Coca—whose husband, Titi, a former judge from Iasi, was now in jail. I was surprised to see, in a corner of their balcony, a blooming oleander. My father told me that the plant had grown from a branch imported a few years previously from Genune. It was hard for me to keep away from it. Part of the furniture and chairs had been brought from Armașului, while the remainder of the furnishing were in the basement storage room.

Florica was shorter than Dad, with red hair and deep blue eyes. She was cheerful, very well-read, and seemed to be quite fond of my father. I became friends with her at first sight—and with Viorica and Ziguța as well. It felt good to visit them, as their house now essentially replaced our lost house on Armaşului Lane. Costinel came there every day, as he lived nearby, and so did Nicu. On Saturdays, Florica prepared many sandwiches with salami and cheese along with a salad à la ruse with homemade mayonnaise, whipped beans, and sausages (when available).

I dropped by with Cecil every two or three weeks; it was always a pleasure for him to show off everything he knew. I don't recall Florica ever visiting us.

One day when I had stopped by to see my father Gică on my way home from work, he told me that he had just received a phone call from Vintila Dongoroz, his former penal law colleague and friend, who mentioned that, after being dismissed from the Faculty of Law, he had found a job with the Institute of Juridical Studies that had been newly created by the communist leadership. He also mentioned that Institute paid pretty good salaries, and he suggested that my father apply for a position there, since his chances of being hired seemed very good. My father's pension was really meager.

"And what did you say?" I asked.

"I refused," my dad replied.

"I told him I cannot accept working under this new communist orientation, because I have fought in the First World War for a greater Romania and I have dedicated more than twelve years to write the Penal Code. For these reasons, I do not want to change the legal system I had studied and worked with, no matter how big a salary they offer. It's about principles. I have thanked Vintila for his intentions and that was that."

"Have you found out what the payment would have been at the Institute?" I asked.

"About four time greater than my pension."

I turned and looked at Florica to see the expression on her face when my father turned down such a tempting opportunity. But she sided with him, saying, "Principles are principles. And the communists will disappear one day, while George's reputation will remain."

I left feeling very proud of my father, and I appreciated Florica even more.

In September 1952, a new version of the Constitution was adopted which resembled the Russian one even more and in November, Prime Minister Gheorghe Gheorghiu-Dej substantially consolidated his power. The terror continued. One evening in December, Cecil reported that on his way home from the Hematology Institute he had seen the body of a man who was probably shot by the Securitate. Cecil was really shaken by the sight.

1953

I cannot forget the day of March 5, 1953, when Iosif Vissarionovici Stalin's death was announced when about that time Romania started a gradual rapprochement with the US.

For us Romanians, Stalin's death was marked by three days of mourning and a grandiose military parade. I remember being summoned to appear in front of the Institute early in the morning. We were stationed in perfectly aligned in rows, each row having a commissioner accounting for our attendance. We joined other groups of people, thousands being gathered listening to speeches followed by a twenty-four cannon salute.

On my way home after the parade, I stopped at Radu and Mieta's house. We were wondering whether the transition from the Stalin era would bring about any improvement in our country. They asked me then how my married life was, and I told them that I was okay, but I mentioned nothing, though, about the torments of my soul.

After three years, in March I got my Law Diploma from the Faculty of Law, which was now called C. I. Parhon University. I stared at it knowing that because of it I had to sacrifice my marriage with Stephen, not leaving the country with him in November 1947. Now, with my diploma in hand, I couldn't even get a job in the legal field. It seemed to me that my sacrifice was useless and had led me nowhere. Disgusted, I hid the diploma between the linens in Maman Titi's cupboard.

I received another diploma one year later, in April, when I finished my cosmetology classes. As with the Law Diploma, this one didn't do me any good either, because here there was no place to practice. Cecil and my in-laws would have been horrified if I had brought strangers in the house. I took that diploma and put it next to the other one, to keep each other company.

Finally, in June, I had a moment of joy. My father succeeded in changing his job, assuming the position of Legal Counselor and Head of Legal Department at the Ministry of Agriculture. He would work there for about seven years, from 1953 to1961. This joyous moment was followed by one of sorrow when I heard that my good friend Ion Ioanid had again been arrested and thrown in prison.

At some point the subject of a child came up. Cecil did not even want to hear about paternity because of the times we were living in. I am convinced that, actually, he didn't want to be number two in the house. He was afraid of any possible change in the rhythm of his professional life. He knew he wouldn't have time for a newborn because it would disturb his sleeping hours he needed to keep him alert at work. I was also fully aware of the drawbacks of my own résumé that put me at a disadvantage. I did not have the ability to ensure the steady resources necessary to raise a baby, nor could I feel sure that the child would be provided with a solid education at the level that I had received. All I was left as a dowry was my education; the rest was taken away by the communists.

Given my overall situation, I accepted the facts and, each time, I had to consider an abortion. In short, the communist system again was bearing the guilt for the situation I was in.

That brings me to religion. On this topic, I was Cecil's opponent. Being a scientist, he considered himself an agnostic, i.e., "one who says we cannot know if God exists because His existence cannot be proven." Like Voltaire, Cecil rejected metaphysics; for him, that chapter didn't exist. But he liked to argue with me. He supported his ideas with strongly supported arguments, trying to convince me to abandon my prayers and opt for reason instead. I hated the confrontations and controversies, but I couldn't always keep my mouth shut, and on this subject I was actually very vocal. The firmness of my position always disappointed him.

Being always so busy, Cecil never thought about vacations. He couldn't imagine being separated from the hospital or the Institute.

So for many years in a row, I went with my friend Viorica to the Black Sea—or, once, to the Tuşnad resort in the mountains. When we were in Tuşnad, Cecil came to stay, but it was only for only one night, and the following day he drove us back to Bucharest in his car. It was then I noticed that when he was away from home he was in unusually high spirits. Once we went together to a Black Sea resort in September. We stayed nearly ten days. I noticed, at the time, he could eat almost anything at the restaurant without any problems, in contrast to conditions at home when he often suffered from severe colitis.

1954

Aimée married Ion secretly, and without giving notice to anybody. He moved in with her, which made me happy. Not long after, Aimée called me in desperation, informing me that Mamina had died from an intestinal occlusion. I went to her funeral. She had been a rare breed of mother, wife and friend, and I cared about her very much.

Just as one sorrow so often comes after another, a few weeks later, Aimée told me on the phone, "Last night they arrested Ion. I'm desperate."

"Why?" I asked.

"I don't know, but after a serious search of the house, the soldiers told him to grab a few clothes and follow them. You know what a phlegmatic fellow Ion is. He asked me to call his father, Costinel, and tell him he 'went on a trip.'"

It was quite a blow also for me because I cared about him a lot, and I remembered the time we had spent together in Armaşului Lane, listening to my favorite Grieg piano concerto. I found out there had been a series of arrests involving Romanian employees who had been working at Embassies. Ion was a translator at the British Embassy.

When Cecil came home and I told him what happened to Ion, he felt very sorry and scared. He asked me to avoid going to see Aimée because her apartment could be under surveillance and the Securitate would find out who was coming in and out. Later Aimée found out what Ion's sentence would be. It was ten years.

I was satisfied with my job at IPSR, where I was with Mizty, Viorica and Radu as well as many others who had become my friends, including Mario Navarra from the Finance Department.

But nothing lasts forever. My relative bliss was interrupted by the abolishment of Sovrom enterprises, which were sold back to Romania and became State enterprises. Thus, the State organized the transfers. On the fifth of May 1954 Mitzy and I were transferred to the Engineering Institute for Roads, Bridges and Hydrotechnical Works within the Ministry of Transportation. Viorica became part of another institute and Radu Petrescu ended up in a cooperative. Separation brought a lot of sorrow.

The new institute to which I was transferred, IPHD, was on the top floor of the Ministry building. The Institute's director was Ion Iepureanu—tall, thin, with a friendly smile—who was considered a skilled engineer. After I got to know him, I could say without hesitation that he was a gentleman.

The Planning Office where Mitzy had been assigned, and the one for Work and Wages Office where I was working, were in the same spacious bright room. My new boss was kind and well-mannered, a good colleague who was pleasant to work with. The quantity of work was enormous. There, just like as in other places, the engineers were handing us the data the last days of the month in a hurry and we had to stay late at night to finish calculating. I also made friends there, all being very good engineers who had helped design massive bridges throughout the country.

At home together with Cecil, we often listened to Radio Free Europe or Voice of America in our room, with the volume turned low and the doors shut. The transmissions were often so jammed that one could barely hear anything. But we were able to find out that from April to July 1954 there had been a Geneva Conference on Vietnam with participation of representatives from the USA, UK, France, and the USSR. Regarding these conferences, the representatives of Russia were persistently promoting their goals, which were always offensive, while the West was constantly on the defensive, making compromises such as the ones in Tehran and Yalta. Again the conference ended with the hope that free elections would allow people to express their will. I was wondering how it was possible for the West to believe that elections might help stop the communist expansion, given the rest of Eastern Europe's experience in connection with so-called free elections. They simply never happened. The communists are well organized and not deterred by elections, knowing that outcomes could be manipulated.

The London Conference marked the "end of the occupation regime" in West Germany, which was now recognized as a sovereign nation. So Germany, which had been defeated, ended up a part of the Free World while we were unwillingly caught between the dictatorships of Hitler and Stalin. Despite the fact that, on August 23, 1944, Romania had turned its army against Germany, we ended up being the losers who paid a heavy price both financially and in human lives.

1955–1956

Toward the end of 1955, Mancy—who said she was missing Manini—submitted an application to the Police requesting approval to visit Craiova from the first to the thirtieth of November. When I told Cecil, he panicked, "Tell her to be back on time," he said. "She can't play around when it comes to Obligatory Domicile."

He was right. In fact I talked to my mother and Manini by phone several times, warning my mom that she was supposed to be back in time. By the end of November, Cecil urged me to go and bring her to Bucharest. I took the train on Friday and went to visit Manini.

That's when Manini told, for the first time, about the letters that the Herescus had sent her and that they settled in Paris, however, after graduating from high school, Ioana settled in London.

Then my mother told me something that got me worried. Namely, together with Manini's friend, they had been practicing "spiritism" to find out through a friend, Jenny, when Romania would escape from communism. I realized that this was why mom was reluctant to return to Bucharest.

While I was in the house, I revisited Dănel Defleury, Tata Lae's son, and his wife, Aurelia, called Bobo, the tenant Ms. Constantinescu, as well as the Parhon family who were very kind to Manini.

The next day, Jenny arrived at five o'clock. She was tiny, skinny, and feeble, had white hair, a thin voice, didn't speak much, and was dressed all in black. The three of them prepared a small wooden table—specifically one with no metal nails—and we took our seats. I was impressed to see how Jenny gradually lost the sense of reality and, at some point, she fell into a trance. She remained sitting straight upright with her head erect, maintaining a dignified, controlled attitude. Mother, with notebook in hand, was ready to take notes of whatever Jenny would say. When the table began to move, rising slightly from the ground, horizontally. I looked underneath to see if somebody had produced the movement while Jenny was having a conversation with someone who had passed away long before. Considering the way she greeted that person, it seemed like he was someone important; when she called to him, she raised her head upwards towards the ceiling, at the same time inviting a connection with any other spirits who wanted to come. Suddenly, a general began to communicate through Jenny's mouth. She borrowed his serious, deep baritone voice, which was completely different from her own. I could not believe my ears! As the general started speaking, the table stopped moving and my mother began taking notes. Our sole interest was strictly related to Romania and communism.

In short, the imaginary "General" said that "what we are suffering" would last a long time. Romania would no longer be what it had been. Then Jenny, at Manini's request, called the spirit of another friend to ask about the Herescu's, and she replied they would remain where they are. When Jenny came out of the trance, her back was restored to its bent position, and she was sweaty. She used a tissue to wipe off. She was exhausted. Once again, she spoke in her own voice, which was thin and barely audible. Manini offered her tea and coffee with cakes. Jenny asked about what she said, because she couldn't remember. My mother read her the notes; all three were disappointed with the overall message, that the communist misery would last, Romania would not be what it was, and the Herescu family would not return. Manini was saddened.

I felt sorry to see them like that. I didn't quite believe what I had heard, but I was intrigued by the movement of the table as well as by Jenny's transformation, which really impressed me. It didn't seem like she was faking.

After Jenny's departure, I urged my mother to pack but she said; "I want to stay a few more days because I am invited to..." I replied, "Do not play with fire. You have already spent almost five years in prison."

"I will come to Bucharest in three days, not now."

All I could see was how unrealistic she was.

Later, I saw Bobo, who pulled me aside and told me to leave as fast as possible, because the Securitate might find out about the spiritism sessions in our house.

I asked her, "Who would tell them what Manini is doing in her room? And how come you know about that?"

"Well, Lucreția, has told me." (She was calling Manini by her real name, Lucreția.)

I gave my opinion: "No one knows about this except you and the two of them, and Jenny isn't crazy enough to talk about her."

"I beg you. Leave," she insisted.

On Sunday afternoon, I took the train to Bucharest without Mancy; I could not convince her because she absolutely wanted to go where she was invited to another "session." To her that seemed very important! At home, I found Cecil on fire, and for good reason.

On Tuesday, December 6, 1955, just after three thirty, during lunch, I received a phone call from Craiova. It was a man from the Radomir estate calling me, someone who had, by chance, passed by to visit Manini. At her request, he informed me that my mother had been arrested by Securitate men, who had come to Manini's on the fifth of December and ransacked the room and hallway. They found my mother's notebooks. Regarding Manini, they declared, "You're not under arrest."

Of course I was shocked by the phone call, but what had happened was predictable. My concern, now, was to find out whether the Securitate had come because my mother hadn't returned to Bucharest according to the rules of house arrest or whether somebody had denounced the spiritism episode. And most of all, I was concerned about how my mother would survive if she had to go back to prison again. This time she had not done anything "against state security," like the first time, but the notes reflected her desire to get rid of the current communist power. The worst mistake her taking those notes; no matter how well hidden they were, Securitate found them immediately. It was as if someone had given them prior information.

I felt so bad for Manini, who had to go through this.

After I hung up the phone, which was in our room, I returned to the table, where all looked at me inquisitively, especially because I had spent quite a long time on the phone. Cecil looked as if he knew that what he feared had become a reality, and he asked, "Is something going on with Mancy?"

"Yes, she was arrested yesterday!"

"I knew if she didn't make it back in time something bad would happen to her and to us as well," he replied.

I didn't say anything about spiritism, because the mention of it would have raised a storm. The reason for the arrest did not matter anymore. The in-laws kept silent. There was nothing to say.

When I told my father, his comment was, "Good thing you came on time from Craiova. I'm sure someone has been an informer there. I'm sorry for Mancy, but she brought it all on herself again."

When I had been living in Armașului, I rarely caught colds, but that was not the case on Scărlătescu Street. There, I would often have a sore throat, high fever and feel a lack of physical strength. This was the case in January 1956 when Cecil took me to the ear, nose and throat specialist at the Hospital who said, "There are pus-filled spots on her tonsils...she must be operated immediately."

I was hospitalized and underwent an operation with local anesthesia, being fully aware of what the doctor was doing. After the surgery, I was taken into a room with two beds, one occupied by Muțuleana, who stayed with me overnight. After five or six hours, I got very sick, my liver having a very bad allergic reaction to penicillin. I was hospitalized for three days, not from the surgery, but because of the medication. I could not eat; even the smell of food made me sick. When Cecil came to see us, Muțuleana briefed him about my condition, which was obvious. Then he sat on the edge of the bed and asked me why I didn't want to eat.

"I can't, I can't even smell the food."

He was annoyed. And before I knew what was happening, he slapped me in the face! Surprised and angry beyond measure, I wanted to get up, but I could not. I turned to the wall and started to cry. I did not understand his ruthless reaction.

Muțuleana, surprised, said to him, "What are you doing, Cecil?"

"Never mind, Mother, she'll get over it; crying is good for the body."

I burst into tears—weeping all the tears I had kept inside for so long.

Cecil forcibly turned me to face him and said, "Mounette," as he liked to call me when he was in a good mood, "I'm sorry, but I had to force you, to create an impact." And he kissed me on the forehead.

I must admit, though I do not know by what miracle, that scare combined with crying actually worked. When Muțuleana brought lunch, I was able to swallow.

The next day we went home and life returned to normal. I convinced myself he was an efficient doctor! I just hoped he wasn't slapping his other patients too!

One day when my father came for dinner, as I walked him to the tram station I told him that I thought it was time for him to marry Florica. My words had an effect, since they got married in the spring, soon after making it official in the records. I was happy for both of them.

Autumn brought important changes in Romania. On October 3, 1955, Gheorghe Gheorghiu-Dej was promoted from prime-minister to member to the Presidium of the Grand National Assembly— Communist Romania's Parliament, emphasizing the need for Romania to forge its own individual brand of socialism that, especially regarding trade relations, outside the Communist alliance. Unusual measure which will later affect me personally.

Furthermore, in 1955, Romania became a member of the military Warsaw Pact along with other satellite countries, a counterweight to the 1949 NATO treaty. And on December 14, 1955, Romania was admitted as a member to the United Nations and other UN agencies.

But the most important September 1953 event was the election of Khrushchev as First Secretary of the Communist Party. He was the one who issued the October 1956 order that Soviet tanks should invade Hungary, a response to Imre Nagy, the Hungarian leader who—in defiance to Moscow—opted for a multiparty electoral system and for the Hungary's withdrawal from the Warsaw Pact. As a result, Imre Nagy was tried, sentenced to death and executed in June 1958.

During the Hungarian revolution, thousands of people were killed, especially young people, and more than two hundred thousand Hungarians went into exile. The West did not interfere; it just took in refugees. Henry Kissinger's view was that Truman's policy of containment would have been definitely indicated in this case to prevent Russian expansionism into Hungary. "What, after all, was containment if not an attempt to surround the Soviet Union with forces capable of resisting its expansionism?" he asked. (Kissinger Henry, *Diplomacy*, page 565).

Since Stalin no longer existed and the Soviet army had retreated in October from Austria, there was no longer any reason for the Soviet Army to remain stationed in Romania. These events encouraged Dej to ask Khrushchev in 1956 to withdraw Soviet armed forces from our country as well. But Khrushchev did not act until 1958.

The following three events: Romania's trade relations, outside the Communist alliance, the Hungarian Revolution; and the withdrawal of Soviet armed forces, will have an effect on my personal life.

1957

My mention of the Hungarian Revolution had a purpose, because in its aftermath in Romania Dej and its Interior Ministry took drastic measures against anybody who threatened the "people's democracy." Over 2,200 citizens were arrested, most of whom were students and intellectuals.

Cecil was increasingly pessimistic. Indeed, the Romanian reaction to international events came just when he was thinking he could fill the position of director of the Institute of Hematology, following the retirement of the current director. Cecil's parents were equally concerned about his promotion and, obviously, because of the tightening of the internal policies as well as Mancy's arrest. I personally wasn't too concerned since my Curriculum Vitae or résumé records were clean, by omission not having mentioned our properties nor the many arrests of family members.

One afternoon when the in-laws were sleeping and Cecil was gone, Leana came to talk to me. "Miss, I have something to tell you."

"Leana, what is it?"

"Well, you see, every time the doctor comes home before you at lunch, he and his mother begin talking. I don't know what they're up to, but every time they do, Mrs. Mancy's name keeps coming up. I don't understand why since she doesn't come here anymore!"

I hadn't told Leana about Mancy's arrest, and neither had my father.

So I said, "Who knows, Leana, maybe you didn't hear right. Why would it be their concern?"

"Well, that surprised me too, but I wanted to tell you because you should know what happens here in your absence."

I thanked Leana, told her not to worry about it, and embraced her. After she left, I immediately phoned and spoke with Florica and Gică. Again I reminded them they shouldn't talk to Leana about Mancy's arrest because Cecil didn't want anybody to know, for fear that neighbors or other people might find out. Of course Leana had heard my mother's name correctly; her arrest was an obstacle to Cecil's contemplated promotion.

I had to reflect on the issue. Muţuleana was probably already thinking I was an obstacle in her son's career. Leana had also told me that Cecil kept silent during these discussions, that he would just listen. There was nothing I could do. I knew he loved me in his own way, despite his selfish and reticent attitude in front of his parents.

But what upset and annoyed me was that whenever I had a conversation with him and my views were different than his, he would tell me that my thinking was the result of a "bourgeois" upbringing. He claimed it was my origins that prevented me from seeing things differently, as if he hadn't known, before our marriage, that I came from a bourgeois-landlord environment from Oltenia and had been raised in a different milieu than his. He had been flattered by Ion's friendship, which he considered as a way to enter into a more highly educated society. Nor could he pretend not to know what the exact situation with my mother was when he saw her in our house a few days after she got out of prison the first time. I usually avoided defending myself by stating these truths, which would have done nothing but lead to the extension of unpleasant discussions. After all, I knew whom I married; he was a smart man with enormous professional qualities, but lacking in manners and delicacy in many respects. After such discussions, I tried to remember Lulu's roses and how I had felt when we were dancing or to remember Stephen's letters with the sweet words that had warmed my heart. How many women could boast such treasured memories?

Cecil began expressing his reactions against my origin more and more often, and sometimes I snapped back. I told him my viewpoint, and of course we argued in front of my in-laws. Then Muţuleana would offer me her advice, "You know Cecil he has a golden heart; it's true he can be moody, but you know that. So don't argue, what good does it do? Let it go."

"Okay," I would reply. "But I also have my opinions I want to express them. You want me to be afraid of him?"

When I discussed how little time we spent together, Muţuleana gave me more advice, "Don't try to change him. For so many years he was unmarried and had his own habits, which you will not change. He likes to do what he wants in his free time, to read, to fix the car... If you love him, seek to please him more."

To that I replied, "Okay okay, but doesn't he think maybe I want to do something else when we're together? As if it isn't enough that he spends his whole week at the Institute and doesn't come home until late—and I don't get to exchange a single word with him!"

I had appreciated these conversations with Muțuleana—that is, until Leana informed me about what was happening in my absence. Now I had mixed feelings. I realized she was a mother defending her last remaining son. She wanted him to make progress and be promoted in his profession. It was normal. On the other hand, I was young, and I wanted a husband; he shouldn't consider himself single once he had made the choice to get married.

In addition, more recently, Cecil had developed the habit of coming home later and later, occasionally close to midnight. Then his excuse would be "You know when a man is truly engaged in his profession, it also gives him satisfaction. This is when he forgets to leave the workplace and come home."

The late hours began to intrigue me. Therefore, one evening I intentionally got back late after I had visited Florica and Gică. On the way home I passed the Institute (at the corner with Scărlătescu) and could see his office window from the street. The lights were turned on. So I decided to go in and take him home for dinner. At the entrance, I told the doorman, who did not know me, that Doctor Poppa was waiting for me, and went up to the third floor. The last time I had been there was back in 1952 when he took me, once, to show where he spent his afternoons.

When I knocked on the door, I heard a rustling. Cecil immediately asked, "Who is it? Just a second!"

Why would the door be locked, and why didn't he unlock it right away? I didn't like what I was witnessing and didn't want to create an awkward situation. So I got away from the door, returned along the hallway, and took the stairs down to the next elevator, on the second floor. Since it was late at night, I didn't meet anyone on my way; all were gone, except the doorman. Returning to the street, I headed home, where Uncle Gogu and Muțleana were waiting.

When Muțuleana saw me all by myself, she said, "But what if Cecil had been already home and wanted to eat? Was he supposed to wait for you?"

I didn't reply. An unpleasant thought had planted itself in my head. A doubt had been planted in my head, and now it grew steadily. I went to my room and washed my hands as if water could clean the thoughts away. I decided not to talk about what had happened. Cecil, not knowing who might have been at the door, didn't mention anything either.

After this incident every time I looked at him, I was filled with an indescribable inner rage thinking how he kept us all waiting for him at the evening meals. And all the while, he would come in with explanations about the satisfactions his job was giving him, and how his preoccupation with that made him forget to come home on time. I didn't buy it anymore. As far as I was concerned, I knew that what he said and what he did were two completely different things. But I could not take a stand unless I could prove something. And I wasn't prepared to do that anyway. I didn't have money, nor was I able to find another place to stay. But this was a new complication, and eventually I realized where I was heading.

I found my strength by closing my eyes and remembering Stephen. Sometimes the image of him was so strong I tried to keep my eyes closed so as not to lose it.

Towards the end of September 1957, I had to face some challenges; perhaps it was fate, perhaps the time was right. So one day, I was called to the Staff Service Institute. The chief had my résumé in front of him and told me while looking over it, "Comrade Poppa, the ministry will open an International Relations Office, whose head will be Comrade Gheorghe Tănase. He's looking for qualified personnel, and you were selected out of many because you have a law degree, you speak foreign languages and have a clean record, and also your father has worked at PLAFAR and at the Ministry of Agriculture, and you have a husband who is a doctor and deputy director at the Institute of Hematology. We have requested you transfer from the Institute to this new Office."

What I heard should have made me happy, but it didn't since a transfer meant having my family records checked. In addition, the political climate was still dangerous after the Hungarian Revolution, and God forbid if they found out about the "mother issue."

So I said to him, "Please let Comrade Tănase know that I thank him from the bottom of my heart, but I'm very happy here at the

Institute and I don't think I can cope with international relations; I am used to working with numbers."

A few days later, my boss Zwergel answered the phone. Apparently impressed, he said, "Yes, Comrade Gheorghe, I'll send her to you."

Then he asked me, "Why does the Ministry Head of Personnel want to see you?"

I told him what was going on and that I hoped they would leave me alone.

I went down to the ground floor where Comrade Gheorghe was waiting for me. He was a tall, stout, slightly bald, red-faced man, who invited me to sit down and then went straight to the point, "I know you prefer to stay at the Institute, but Comrade Tănase thinks you are exactly what he needs, and he will come here to see and speak to you."

All of a sudden Tănase appeared in the doorway—a short, plump, white-haired but young-featured man with short legs. His eyes were big, black, and penetrating, and he had long eyelashes. Judging from his lively appearance, he seemed a jolly fellow. And it was just my fate that he would be the first person to contribute to the coming changes in my life.

Tănase shook hands with me and said, "Comrade Simona Poppa, I hear you want to stay at the Institute, but at Relation's Office you can use your law diploma and foreign languages, which we are in need of. You can put them to the Ministry's advantage. You will receive an appropriate salary, twice what you have now. I hope I have convinced you."

Gheorghe added, "I think so too."

Tănase was telling me what I had wished to hear for a long time. But knowing the real situation of my social background, I was forced to say, "Thank you, Comrade Tănase, I have listened to all you had to say, but still I prefer to stay at the Institute."

Neither man said anything. Tănase, however, seemed a little annoyed. Sporting a furtive smile, he turned off on his short legs, leaving with swift, sure steps.

As I was taking the elevator up to my eighth-floor office I felt anxious. It was what a skydiver must experience on his first jump when he's keenly aware of the danger. On the one hand, had I accepted the offer, I would have risked being in even greater danger. And yet, by refusing the offer, I had lost the opportunity to use my law degree and begin making more than double my salary, which would have given me more independence.

Arriving upstairs in my office, I informed Zwergel, who was happy I had refused.

But in the afternoon, the chief of Personnel of the Institute cracked open the door to my office and poked his head in.

"Comrade Poppa, you are expected to see the Transportation Minister. But go first and see Comrade Gheorghe."

After that, he disappeared, closing the door behind him. Everyone in the office was surprised by what they had just heard; Zwergel and Mitzy were the only ones who knew what was going on. I looked at Zwergel without saying anything, and took the elevator downstairs.

Comrade Gheorghe told me right away, "You see, Comrade Simona, if you had taken the offer from the very beginning, you could have avoided disturbing the comrade minister [the Secretary of State to the Transportation Department]."

He led me to the end of the hall and presented me to the secretary, who showed me to the Minister's door. It was in that spacious and rather dark room that I first saw him, sitting at his big desk—comrade Blumenfeld, our almighty minister. He was a handsome man, about fifty years old, tall, with very dark hair and black eyes. He stood up, shook my hand, and with a calm and compelling voice, invited me to sit on the chair before him.

"Comrade Poppa," he said, "I heard from Chief Tănase you have a law diploma and you speak foreign languages. I believe the ministry has more to gain from your qualities by sending you to the new International Relations Office than by keeping you at the Design Institute. I shall issue the transfer order today!"

I realized the difference between us: he had the power while I, having no rights, was the one to be blown by the wind. In addition, he was a very busy man in a great hurry, as was apparent from the many memos piled on his desk and on the tables next to it. Before replying, I had an instant to weigh the situation. My instinct told me that if I refused—by telling him the truth about my real social situation and the danger if my background would be checked—I probably would not get his understanding, especially considering the politically harsh situation after the Hungarian Revolution. I would be expelled or purged immediately. If I agreed to the transfer, I'd live with a permanent insecurity, in prolonged agony, knowing it would sooner or later be discovered, but at least I would profit in the meantime from an increased salary. So I got up without making any comment, when he added, as if it was a matter of course, "You will receive a phone call from Comrade Gheorghe, from the Ministry's Personnel Office."

My case was not a problem of any consequence for him—whereas, for me, it was just the opposite.

So I was forced to agree, against my will, in accordance with the policy of the day. In the communist system an individual is just an insignificant cog in the wheel of an enormous machine. Nothing more. The individual must listen to orders, remain submissive, and accept any situation, even those contrary to one's own interests. Freedom of choice does not exist. Tănase had the power to acquire what he wanted, and he succeeded by having Blumenfeld let me know what was desired by the Ministry—that is, my transfer.

The establishment of an International Relations Office hadn't originated with Blumenfeld nor with Tănase. It had all begun with Gheorghiu-Dej, right after the December 1955 Congress when—as I mentioned above—a new direction in Romanian trade relationship with the West. Blumenfeld had to implement Dej's foreign policy establishing an International Relations Office, and the Personnel Office was supposed to come up with qualified people within the Ministry, with "clean" folders. And yes, this is how they found me—however, with my file omitting the essentials!

On October 1, 1957, I received the transfer to the International Relations Office. Cecil was proud and satisfied, and so were the in-laws impressed with my appointment. Now I was a wife in a high position, promoting the new foreign policy of Gheorghiu-Dej. My promotion happened about the time of the launching of the Russian Sputnik satellite in October.

Having to change my office and move from the eighth floor to the first floor, I realized how genuine my former colleagues' friendship to me was. They all expressed their regrets for my departure and congratulated me for my promotion. I said good-bye to director Iepureanu, a gentleman and a man of culture, and to my coworkers. Mitzy urged me to come more often to her home.

The International Relations Office was right next to the Personnel Office of the Ministry, the Communist Party Office, and Blumenfeld's office. In our Office there were only four employees in three smaller rooms—one for Tănase, one for M. Vardan, and the third, a little bigger, rectangular, facing the street, for M. Făgărășanu and me.

I was very lucky to work with Făgărășanu, a somewhat older intellectual who had been my father's former student and then the former Romanian ambassador to Iran before the Communist era. I was in a distinguished company. After a while, when we became friends and when we were alone together, we didn't use the term *comrade* anymore. I'd call him "Mister Făgărășanu," and he'd call me "Miss Simona." A delight! Every day we brought sandwiches that we ate in the office. Tănase, after running all kinds of errands in the morning, came by to inspect our offices. He would cheerfully stride in, ambling toward the windows to talk with us while he chewed a toothpick stuck between his teeth. He would inform us about future projects we needed to handle, which he was already in the process of organizing. At the beginning, there was no work; however, I had a salary double that at the Institute. Not bad at all, I thought. I hoped it would last. In the interim, I had ample opportunity to make conversation with Mr. Făgărășanu, and ask him questions about Persia, the current Iran.

Mr. Făgărășanu explained about the Iranian population's mentality, whose roots go back to the Quran, their holy book, which dates from the year 632. The frequency of their prayers—which are done many times a day, even at work—meant that Muslims took time from actual work. I'd listen to him with interest, but, at that time, I believed what was happening over there was strictly "their business." How could I know than that that I will hear more in 2015?

Sometimes I would meet with Comrade Gheorghe in the corridor or with Colonel Buzescu, head of the Communist Party Organization, a tall man, downright handsome, with black eyes and black hair, sociable, who liked to make conversations. Knowing that the ministries were infiltrated with Soviet advisers, I was cautious to avoid any conversations which were not of a professional nature because I didn't want to cause suspicion about my identity or want people to suspect my inner thoughts. One could pay a dear price for imprudence; I had learned that from Mancy's experience.

1958

Due to Dej's foreign policy, the relationship with Moscow began to cool while ties with the West began to grow a little stronger, explaining the establishment in many ministries of departments like the one I was working in. And as a result the internal measures got stronger, too.

Often, while I walked to my office in the morning, it happened that Comrade Gheorghe with Colonel Buzescu, passed by in his chauffeur-driven car Comrade Gheorghe was sitting next to the driver while Colonel Buzescu sat in the back seat. Either one, when they happened to pass me, would ask the driver to stop and invite me to join them. Sometimes I'd tell them I preferred to walk, but I couldn't always refuse. It was awkward given my mother's situation, and besides I was embarrassed to get out of their car in front of the ministry building and be seen by former colleagues who might think I had become friends with members of the communist regime.

With no work to do, I had time to weigh my own private life. I knew from Leana that Muțuleana continued to have discussions in my absence. Cecil kept coming home very late, and in his spare time he would either read or work on the car. From time to time he'd ask me whether I had any fresh information about Mancy. I hadn't told him about the sentence she had received (the previous year) as

I didn't want to add to his fears related to his possible promotion. Mancy's situation was very serious, she was sentenced by decree in 1956, as a previous offender without extenuating circumstances, to ten years imprisonment for the crime of spreading prohibited publications under Article 111 and 325 Penal Code.

* * *

After Khrushchev had been appointed prime minister in March and agreed to withdraw the five Soviet divisions from Romania in June— July 1958, a total of twenty-five thousand Soviet soldiers. This was another reason for internal policies to become increasingly strict, with Dej seeking to maintain firm control over them. The wind was blowing a communist terror, which required every one of us to be even more careful about our behavior.

Also, in October 1958, when Khrushchev came for a vacation in Romania, he persuaded Dej to allow Jewish emigration to Israel under a barter system. Henry Jacober, whose name I mentioned earlier—a Jewish businessman living in London—had initiated an exchange program under which Jewish families in Romania would be allowed to emigrate for four thousand to six thousand dollars per person. At the suggestion of Khrushchev, the Romanian authorities chose to accept agricultural products instead of money. Then, Jacober brought animals from the Netherlands, sending them to Romania in exchange for giving permission to Jews to emigrate. (Ioanid, Radu, *The Ransom of the Jews*, pages 83–85).

* * *

One day, comrade Tănase entered our office with his now familiar quick steps and cheerfully informed us we could begin our work in September. A French delegation was scheduled to visit for talks regarding their former interest in the Danube navigation. Our office would participate in the preparatory work within NAVROM (the Romanian Navy) whose offices were on the sixth floor. He also said he would bring us materials from NAVROM to read about the legal status of the Danube. He also asked us to plan our vacations one at a time, in July and August, before September.

I chose mine from late June until early July. But I did not know where to go. As usual, Cecil was not available, and Viorica couldn't come either. I decided to go to Drăgăşani and see Tan Natalica. I'd go alone, far away from Scărlătescu where I did not feel at ease. Tan Natalica was happy to see me.

*   *   *

In the train on the way to Drăgăşani, I could hear the rhythm of the wheels, transmitting to me a kind of peace that I was much in need of. In the railway station Uncle Costica Emion was waiting for me. He took me to Tan Natalica's place where we had dinner. They rented a room for me at the neighbors' house. Here I regained my personality; I returned to my normal self. For several days in a row I went to the shore of the River Olt and into the cool water. It was as if I wanted to wash away all of my past, together with the most over-whelming present. On other days I'd take walks through the famous vineyards of Drăgăşani. Even now I can picture myself sitting on a rock under the clear sky on one of those hills, pondering how my youth was passing by like the flow of the River Olt.

In this silence I was able to summarize my past. Lulu had offered me nothing but roses and happiness. Stephen had given me supreme happiness and, equally, great suffering. Cecil, through the diligence of my in-laws, gave me a life free of household chores. I was appreci-ating his professional level, but with him I felt lonely. I wanted some-thing else—to live in my own house next to a man who had time for me, not when he decided to allocate a few minutes. It was up there, in that vineyard of Drăgăşani, where I decided I needed to change my life. I wanted to live my life to the fullest as long as I was still healthy, cheerful, and energetic. I remembered Grieg's Concerto —the one I played when I was seeing no way from the stalemate caused by my separation from Stephen. I could hear that piano sounds filling the air, crossing from the River Old to the vineyard and back again. I also remembered Haagi, who had taught me to pray because she always believed the Lord would find a solution. Up there, suspended between the clear sky and the vineyard, that's exactly what I did.

I went down the hill feeling a great relief of mind and an even greater appetite. I left with regret, and returned to Bucharest. When I re-entered the Scărlătescu house, it was with the certainty that I would find a way to escape the monotony of my life and prevent my mother's situation from being a threat to Cecil's promotion.

* * *

When I returned to the office, Mr. Făgărăşanu was away on vacation. Comrade Tănase gave me some documents related to the Danube's project, reminding me that the delegation was coming in September. I looked through the documents to familiarize myself with the international legal status of the Danube navigation and its maintenance established by various treaties. I also gathered information about the delegation, namely Société Française de Navigation Danubienne (SFND). Their coming was related to the new direction in foreign policy.

Tănase also brought us a list of words and expressions specific to navigation, and a Romanian-French dictionary. I might have known French, but not the terms associated with rivers. So I memorized them. I didn't want to stumble when it came to translate unfamiliar words. He informed me that before the conference with the foreigners he'd introduce me to NAVROM's director and to the members of the Romanian delegation. (I was to go out to dinner with all of them at the Lido Hotel restaurant that had live music.)

The day finally came, at the end of September, when I went to greet the French delegation at the airport and drive them to the Lido Hotel. The conference was held that afternoon, and the following day, in the Great Hall of NAVROM. Following conversations among members of the two delegations, I gathered that the Frenchmen wanted to feel the pulse of NAVROM, the ministry's department, which dealt with inland navigation on the Danube. They noted that France was the only non-riparian country which had sailed from the Lower Danube all the way to the Delta, under the 1921 Treaty which they considered still valid—regarding which, they wanted to find out Romania's position.

NAVROM was aware of the Soviet interests in the area, and understood the fact that the Russians wanted exclusivity for riparian countries only. The ambiguity of the situation demanded diplomacy on behalf of NAVROM to keep a balance between the Russian reality and the recent Romanian foreign policy forged by Dej, the leader who continued to desire greater contact with the West.

Tănase worked intensely to organize the last dinner at the hotel. Before that, Tănase called me into his office. There he whispered close to my ear, "During the meal with the French people, don't talk about anything compromising. You know the tables are equipped with sound recording technology. Do not say anything about our internal difficulties."

"I know the situation," I replied calmly, "and anyway, I am not interested in having such a conversation."

"Yes yes, of course, but I figured it does not hurt to remind you about that."

I left the office of Comrade Tănase convinced he was not "one of them," just as I had figured.

Each of the three Frenchmen took turns asking me to dance. One of them, a fine gentleman, asked me how I had learned to speak French. I told him I studied in high school with the nuns of Notre Dame de Sion. This encouraged him to ask me if it was true what they had heard about the terror in Romania. I answered, "Obviously you live in the West and this makes it easy for you to ask such a question."

There was nothing he could say, but at the end of the dance, when he kissed my hand, he added, "I feel terribly sorry for you!"

From the way he shook my hand, I realized he understood my ambiguous but clarifying answer.

In fact, I really wanted to tell the French about how the domestic policy had tightened after the Hungarian Revolution, about the withdrawal in the last two months of the Soviet troops, about the mandatory study by all citizens of Marxism-Leninism, about the trials and convictions for all sorts of imaginary crimes, and so on and so forth. The next day, I accompanied the delegation to Sinaia together with Tănase, who took care of the lunch. (On that occasion there was no music, no dancing, and no dangerous questions.) The third day, I accompanied them to the airport when they left. With their departure, I began to feel safer—though I probably was not.

During October and November, the ministry building was full of rumors about intense personnel purges. Everyone was tense. Around that time, Comrade Gheorghe met me in the hallway and told me in a friendly tone that the delegates from NAVROM had been satisfied with the services provided by our Office. Also, Tănase told me in a hushed tone, secretly, that he knew that Comrade Gheorghe was checking my file since they want to give me a promotion. I tried to conceal any anxiety. At that news, my blood froze in my veins. I would have flushed bright red except that my blood was no longer flowing. There was no way I could defend my bourgeois-landlord origin or my mother's independent actions. I was resigned to the idea that happened will happen! And that was that!

At home, I did not mention anything about the situation. On November 25, on St. Catherine Day, Maman Titi's name day, the phone rang at ten o'clock in the morning. It was a call from Comrade Gheorghe. I knew what would follow. I got up slowly and walked to his office with lagging footsteps, trying to compose myself and decide what I would say. Upon entering, I found him sitting at the desk with my file opened in front of him.

He invited me in and shouted, "Well, Comrade Simona Poppa, I would have never believed it! How is this possible? You didn't mention anything, absolutely nothing about what is recorded in your file; so many estates belonging to your father, your mother, your grandparents, and uncles and even to your stepfather, Radian, which now have been found after the investigation family—your mother who was arrested two times. But even more serious are the arrests in your General Anton who worked for the King, and cousin Vorvoreanu who worked at the British Embassy. The last two even lived with you under the same roof in Armașului. You have an extremely difficult case going on here!"

Curiously enough, in the end his voice didn't seem so harsh any more. Though it sounded like a reproach, it seemed like he was worried too. My omissions about my background had now been brought to light. The fact that I couldn't keep them hidden anymore, instead of giving me a feeling of anxiety, stirred an interior rebellion which until then I had repressed in order to avoid annoying him. I kept reassuring myself that I wasn't personally guilty of anything. My anger grew as I remembered how I wanted to leave the country and the communists had repeatedly denied me the right to an exit visa. Or again, more recently, how I had repeatedly turned down the offer to take this position when they wouldn't listen!

I did not rush in giving an answer, because I intended to tell Comrade Gheorghe everything. Precautions were no longer necessary. I could now give my full and complete opinion, which I did with a firm voice, "Comrade Gheorghe, I think you remember how I was forced to accept this transfer. I did not want it in the first place, for reasons you are now aware of. I did not mention my 'sins' because I did not commit them in the first place. I had to earn an honest living. The alternative was to become a prostitute. What else could I have done, given such a background?"

Gheorghe looked at me for a long time, weighing what I was saying and what he would do. The silence was long, very long, but it came like the calm after a storm. He no longer seemed to dwell on my multiple "sins." It was almost as if he already knew he had decided. Eventually, he said, "I have heard what you had to say. In our ministry, all files are checked by a committee under Decree 282/1958, in order to eliminate dangerous elements. Your bourgeois landlord origin and your mother's conviction weigh extremely heavily. If this file stays here and gets checked by the committee, you will never be able to find another job for as long as you live."

Then he paused, reflecting on what he would say next. After another long pause, he added, "Tomorrow morning, come with your resignation written on a sheet of paper and hand it to me personally."

I replied in a pleasant tone, "I'll bring it tomorrow, Comrade Gheorghe and thank you."

"You don't have to thank me, just bring it," Gheorghe said.

I left without saying a word to Mr. Făgărăşanu. I suspected that Gheorghe would inform Tănase. There was only one thing that bugged me. How could St. Catherine's day, Maman Titi' name day, be so harmful to me.

While the in-laws were taking their siesta and after Cecil had left for the Institute, I sat down at his desk and wrote my resignation giving "family reasons." Then I picked up the phone and talked with Cristina, Mitzy, and Viorica and told them about the jobless situation I now found myself in.

The following day, with the resignation in hand, I went to Comrade Gheorghe. He read it, signed it, and added, "I didn't leave anything incriminating in your file. Otherwise I couldn't accept your resignation and I would have had to fill in the dismissal forms under the Decree. So you can look for a new job. Now leave the Ministry immediately."

"Thank you," I said, because I badly needed a job. As I was leaving, I mumbled to myself, "And may the Lord bless him with good health. There still are good people left in the world."

It was the twenty-seventh of November, the same day when—eleven years before in 1947—Stephen had left Romania. Now I had to quit a good job, and again, all because of the communists. The evil visited upon us in 1945 was about to roll over me again, ready to take me down. However, due to the resignation, my hope was that with a little help from above I would be able to make it.

I went to say good-bye to my colleagues. I told Mr. Făgărășanu what happened, because I appreciated his friendship and I considered him "one of us." He was shocked and saddened, and he seemed worried. I also went to my boss Tănase. When I entered, I understood by the way he looked at me that he knew and maybe realized why I had not wanted to take the job from the very beginning. Now he was feeling guilty for forcing the issue. He shook my hand and said, "I was just about to recommend you for a salary rise for the way you managed the French delegation. But now I want to see if I can find you another job."

We shook hands and parted. Before leaving the ministry, I went up to see Mitzy, to tell her what had happened. I stayed there a little longer, planning to arrive home at the same time with Cecil.

In the meantime, I pondered Gheorghe's lenient attitude. He had a certain responsibility as head of the Personnel Office, and the new Decree that forced him to take drastic actions—even though he also had to deal with the fact of knowing how much I had resisted accepting the position. Then, I realized why Gheorghe had decided to ask just for my resignation instead of forwarding my file to the Committee. The resignation was a solution not only for me but also for him. His Personnel Office was supposed to investigate and verify my file before I had been transferred. He should not have approved my hiring based on my statements alone. So my resignation was the solution for both of us, a way to save me from the Committee and Decree as well as a way to cover up his negligence.

It was time to leave the building. I regretted parting from my former colleagues with whom I had enjoyed a good time. With some I have continued to remain friends to the present day.

The unpleasant part was the burden of having to announce the "good news" at home. But I had no way out, because from now on I would be spending my mornings at home. I knew the news would cause panic with my in-laws. They were decent people, even if their entire *raison-d'etre* was their adored and pampered son. Walking home, I tried to figure out what words to use to break the news. But, curiously, at one point, instead of bitterness I felt relief. I started moving faster. One negative aspect was that I didn't have a salary anymore. But much of what I had earned, anyway, had gone into the household—except what I was sending to Manini and Tan Natalica. I was broke!

At home, while we were having lunch, I chose to remain silent until we had finished eating.

"I'm sorry, but I have news," I finally said.

All three raised their heads in astonishment. I was determined to say it all at once—speaking as fast as the water flowing downhill in the River Olt: "It is about my personnel file, which had been checked after the French delegation's departure. They went to Armasului first and then to Craiova. They found out not only that my mother is in prison, but also my whole past, about all the estates belonging to our family—the Vrăbiescu's at Genune, Vorvorenu's at Cilieni, Mirica's at

Bârca, Uncle Marinică's at Leu, Uncle Petrache's at Oieşti; Cionea's in Radomir, even about Radian's in Belcineanca. They knew about the detention of Uncle Anton and Ion as well."

As I was breaking this news, which was like a bombshell, I saw them turning green. Muţuleana and Cecil were downright stunned; a deep silence reigned, broken later by Uncle Gogu's remark, "I didn't know that your family had so many estates." I immediately added, "I have been asked to resign for family reasons, and my resignation has already been approved. So I won't get purged on the basis of the well-known Decree."

Cecil looked at me to make sure he could believe what I had said, then remarking in a more relaxed tone,

"This is a great relief."

I think he felt a little guilty because when he had heard about my new position with an increased salary he had encouraged me not to oppose the transfer.

Cecil left immediately for the Institute, and the in-laws retired to their room, but I don't think they could get any sleep. Rather, I suspect they stayed up late examining various actions to be taken. As I was alone in my room, it dawned on me that there was no place for me to go in the morning. That annoyed me very much. As I thought what to do and where to begin, I kept telling myself, "That's right, Monica, if you lacked the courage when you had the chance to leave with Stephen, don't whine now. You'll find a way to handle it."

A little later the phone rang. It was Cristina. In an authoritative voice, she told me, "Listen carefully to what I have to say!"

I could imagine her rolling big eyes, a gesture she did when there was something of importance.

"Today when I was coming home from the office, I accidentally met Sandu Missirliu in the street. I told him what happened to you, and he said tomorrow morning you should go immediately to see his friend, Săndulescu, who is head of the *normatori* at the Reparation Cooperative. Sandu is working at the cooperative headquarters. Săndulescu needs a 'normator' at one of the four sectors. What you have to do is to go to the cooperative headquarters. That's it, did you get it? As you can see, God is helping you and Sandu and I bring you luck." I replied, "You can be sure I'll be there; I need a job as much as I need to breathe. Your news is an absolute godsend! Do you realize how grateful I am to you for talking to Sandu about me? I'll speak with him there. Many hugs, I'll call and tell you what I did."

I could not have anticipated the whirlwind of events that were to follow a few days later.

I didn't mention anything about Cristina's call to my in-laws. Cecil, as usual, came home late and told me how worried he was about my situation. He asked me what my plans were going forward, while the in-laws were carefully listening. That was a good opportunity to justify my departure the next day.

"Tomorrow morning I'll be going to talk to Florica, ask her to prepare my father for the news that I am jobless. Maybe he can find a vacancy at his Ministry of Agriculture." Cecil broke in, "I don't think you have a chance, because the file you have right now is so tarnished."

I hadn't told him about Gheorghe and the file nor about the talk with Cristina, because I didn't want to give him any false hopes—not until I knew for sure what I might accomplish the next day. I couldn't sleep much that night, asking myself how I was going to justify, at the Cooperative the 'family reasons' for resigning from a prestigious and well-paid position.

It was the twenty-eighth of November when I went to see Săndulescu, head of department and my father's former student, who was expecting me thanks to Sandu's phone call. He told me he needed somebody for Sector No.1 and asked about whether there were any problems about my file. Relying on what Ghorghe had told me, I answered with confidence, "I have no special problems."

He seemed pleased, and smiled, knowing who my father was, and replied, "I must have a talk with the president, and if he approves you may start immediately."

I thanked him. I knew that after 1954 this cooperative had absorbed former Sovrom employees with file problems, but I was also counting on what Gheorghe had told me about cleaning up my file. With a sprightly step, I went to see Florica to inform her about what had happened. She was very kind and encouraged me, saying she was sure that I would get the job.

When I arrived home it was during mealtime, and I found Cecil having a conversation with Muțuleana. He immediately asked me if I had seen my father and if he knew about any vacancy. I told him I had only talked to Florica since my father was not home at the time of my call. That was it. When we sat down for lunch, Cecil was cheerful. By the time the soup arrived, he said he had good news. I looked at him surprised. I thought it was about his promotion. As I was lifting the spoon with soup toward my mouth, ready to swallow I heard him say, "Muțuleana gave me cash from the household money to file for divorce. How about that—isn't she understanding?"

The soup never reached my mouth. It landed right in my lap, burning as it spilled all over my skirt, as I frantically tried to clean it up with a napkin. I didn't say anything.

Cecil continued, obviously trying to mend his words.

"My dear, it's only a divorce 'on paper.' You will continue to live here. But I had to find a solution to the problems caused by your file."

All three of them were waiting for my reaction. I was so shocked that I turned my head away as if I hadn't heard a thing, silently repressing my feelings as I continued to wipe my skirt. I knew they would understand my silence. Muțuleana was looking at Cecil, encouraging him with her eyes, sort of indicating that he had done the right thing. Seeing I was quiet, he added, "If they offer me the director's position, I will say I didn't know about Mancy's arrest, your estates, and your family's arrests."

Cecil looked at Muțuleana with gratitude. I understood she, not him, had come up with the idea of the divorce as a solution to the problem. Seeing I didn't react in any way, he was kind of annoyed and firmly stated, "It would be a mistake for me not to take any action."

It was his way of trying to force me to react. The fact that I wasn't showing any emotion drove him nuts. Saying what I wanted to say would only have led to useless talks. Looking at him, all I could think was, "This man is a coward." But it was also apparent he wanted to show me what a good husband he was for not pushing me out of the house. In his view, he was just following practical steps to save his situation. He knew very well, before marrying me, all of my problems.

By the time we finished lunch, a wall had risen between us. There was an awkward silence. In a sour mood, I continued being silent to avoid a confrontation, though I knew he was trying to figure out what I was thinking. After a while he just left for the Institute, obviously to avoid further tensions.

I went to my room, shut the door behind me, and lay on the sofa. After cooling down, I concluded it was not surprising that Muțuleana was the one to find a way through divorce. She only wanted to protect her son. Her advice always had an effect on him. With a great power of conviction and a cold judgment that characterized her, she was his advisor and could make him act in any way that was to his advantage. As for her conversations with Cecil, which I had learned about through Leana, it seemed most probable that she had been weighing, all along, the danger posed by my mother's arrest. They had been trying to figure out a way to deal with that. My instinct told me that the decision was influenced by his parents. They were the ones to convince him to do what he himself had not considered doing. And I never doubted that my in-laws were fully aware that having him divorce me for political reasons was not fair; however, it would help him in case he was proposed for promotion.

It was clear that this solution would further damage our marriage. Cecil always did put his career above his marriage, regardless of the fact that he did not want me to leave the house. It was clear that our relationship had deteriorated ever since the incident that night at the Institute, and now I was even less inclined to win him back. The past was over. I was young and ambitious and never forgot my revenge against the communists who were at the root at all evil.

Right now, I had specific questions in my head regarding what I was supposed to do next. The only reasonable thing I could do was carefully weigh the facts. I was jobless and had no money saved, but at the same time I was sure I did not want to live here any longer, I wasn't "at home." This residence had become unbearable. I decided to gather all my strength to get through this storm.

As I was thinking about it, I finally got the idea to temporarily move in with Florica and my father. But I did not want to make any decision without being sure I could follow through with the plan. Suddenly full of enthusiasm, I got up, sat down at the desk, and wrote a letter to my father. If I had chosen to speak to him, I knew he would have told me to stay and wait because "things would get better, things would be okay." I wrote referring to my marriage, the "divorce solution," and the fundamental differences with Cecil. Since I had entered into this marriage with all seriousness, I had tried to be understanding, tolerant, and forgiving. But Cecil—apart from having many intellectual qualities—was a selfish, self-centered, violent, and stubborn man. He didn't even want children—though, thank God for that! And I added, that when Leana found out about the divorce issue, she immediately came to me and said she was leaving going to stay with her niece. Then I came to the point of the letter, asking Florica and my father whether I could temporarily come to live with them in the drawing room until I could find a place of my own. And I finished by asking them to call me and let me know if I could come.

After I finished writing, I went to my father's house on Miliţiei Street, slipped the envelope under their door, and left. I was expecting the answer by phone.

The following day, on the twenty-ninth of November, my father left home early and Florica called me to invite me to have lunch with them, also adding that my father was very impressed when he read the letter. As I walked through the door, both of them hugged me and encouraged me. They said I was welcome to come any time even if that meant there would be seven of us using one single bathroom. (Titi, Coca's husband had also moved in after being released from prison.) It didn't scare me anymore, because we had lived like that in the old house on Armaşului Lane. My father asked me when I would be moving in. I told him I would let him know, because Cecil didn't know anything yet—just as I had known nothing in advance about the divorce which he had already discussed with his parents.

Now my only concern was in regard to the answer I would receive from the Cooperative. I called Săndulescu from Florica's phone. He said, "It's a good thing you called. Come immediately and file an application; the director has basically agreed."

Understandably, I left the table immediately, kissed them both, and took off towards the Cooperative. There I handed in the application and also met with Sandu, thanking him for his help and telling him about the divorce.

Back in home, Muțuleana told me somebody from the Ministry had called to let me know I should go pick up the official approval of my resignation. I told her I was about to find a job at a Cooperative with the help from Sandu Missirliu.

Next day, on the thirtieth of November 1958, I went from the Ministry—where I got the approval of my resignation—to the Cooperative, where Săndulescu informed me the director had approved my application. I asked him about my personal file and the Personnel Office. Smiling, he said, "Do not worry, once the director approved your position, the personnel person will go to pick up your file from the ministry, period."

He added that the formal appointment would probably last two more days, probably occurring on December 2 when I would have to start working.

I was happy hearing that I would start to work, even with a lower salary of seven hundred lei. That did not matter; what was important was to be back "in the labor market." Like having an ID card, these seemed like a requirement for any other action, especially when—as in my case—I was looking to get a roof over my head.

On November 30 was the beginning of two-day whirlwind during which my life changed completely. Everything seemed precipitous. I realized I had only one day off before most probably I was to start the new job. Wanting to start a totally new life, I decided to move the following day. I called Florica to let her know about my intentions. She asked, "Who will bring you? Did you pack light?"

I replied that I had only suitcases, and that the Armașului furniture would remain in Scărlătescu Street. I said I would talk to Cecil about that.

Suddenly I heard Liky's voice at the other end. He was back from his job and just visiting them. He said, "Hey, Mona, I'm glad you took this decision; I'll come tomorrow with my truck and pick you up whenever you're ready."

When fate wants, everything works.

"Thank you so much, Liky," I said, "I could have handled it myself by taking a cab, but I'm glad to have you by my side at this unpleasant moment of my life."

I also phoned Cristina to let her know how it had gone at the Cooperative and to inform her about me moving out.

Cecil was not yet home. I decided to tell Muțuleana about my intention to leave. Truly, there was nothing left to hold me back after the decision was made to divorce me for political reasons. In a very relaxed way, like I was not announcing any special news, I said, "By the way I will be going to prepare my bags because tomorrow I am moving out. I will be staying at my father's house, and I start a new job the day after tomorrow."

She was more than surprised for both reasons—first, because I was getting a job so soon, and secondly, for giving such short notice about leaving my husband and the house. She appeared shocked, and confessed, "All morning, I wondered why my left eye was twitching! Too bad you're leaving. You were like a daughter to us. You know Cecil loves you, and the divorce is only a formality." To that I replied, "Well, my dear Muțuleana, I appreciated you and Uncle Gogu, and I know Cecil married me because he loved me, but his decision— together with the problem caused by my mother—has made me determined to set him free. I don't like to stand in the way of his promotion."

She nodded unhappily. When Uncle Gogu came in, she told him what I was about to do and informed him that I already had found a job. He did not react in any way. As far as he was concerned, that was just two less mouths to feed (given that Leana was going too).

When Cecil arrived home, he found me packing. Before he even reached my room, the in-laws told him what is about to happen. He had not imagined I would accept a divorce for real, and apparently it had not even occurred to him that I might have where to move. When he entered our room, he said in an imperative tone, "Mounette, please reconsider!"

Cecil wanted a divorce that was only on paper; he didn't like the thought of losing me. I suddenly understood the infinite despair he was facing—having to choose between his career and his wife. However, he didn't say that he would give up the divorce.

Then I told him, "My dear, you hurt me in the way you informed me about your decision of getting a divorce. You consulted with your parents about it, but never with me. I am aware that my presence hinders your future career. I must go away for our peace of mind—that way, my social origin will not be an issue again. The fact is, you knew exactly whom you had married."

For once, I put into words what I had never previously said. Cecil went silent. He had not expected that I would take radical measures, being convinced I had nowhere to go, and he couldn't even imagine I would be offered a job so soon. Now he seemed baffled. Seeing how determined I was, he said he couldn't watch me packing. He left the room and never returned. I continued, emptying Maman Titi's cupboard, together with the Law Diploma and all Stephen's letters, tucking everything into my luggage. I knew where I was going. I was not venturing into a no-man's-land. And I knew exactly what I was doing. I just hoped that my experience with such a complicated man as Cecil would help me in the future and that my eyes would be wide open before I jumped into another "problem."

In the morning, as I was packing my last things, the in-laws had already gone out to run some errands. Cecil was at home and—as he had never done before—he was lying in Muṭuleana's bed, looking tired. His face was drained of color. When we talked, he asked me to leave the large sideboard. In exchange he requested that I ask for something else instead. I told him I'd think about it after I had managed to find myself a place to live. For the moment, I decided to leave the sofa bed and Maman Titi's cupboard. Anyway, the side board was way too big to carry anywhere.

Cecil didn't say anything regarding my new job. I got dressed. All my bags packed and I was ready to go. I went to him to say good-

252

bye. Wiping his beautiful green eyes, he asked, "Will you ever think about me, even just a little?"

Ever since I had known him, I had never seen him so emotional. The explanation was, we were alone together without anyone else present. That was all the difference! I knew that if I had stayed, our lives would have gone back to where they were previously, with the four of us all living together. I didn't answer him; I just kissed him on the forehead. I turned, pulled the door shut behind me, and said good-bye to everything I had known for the last six years. Then I left the house.

Liky, together with Titi (Coca's husband)—who had come to help—both were waiting in front of the house. They carried my suitcases to the truck.

As I looked back through the window, in a strange way, deep down, I was convinced that from that point on nothing would ever hurt me, damage me, offend me, cause me injustice, and prejudice me. I was calm and felt peaceful. I was not afraid, any longer. I had my father, my Uncle Nicu, Florica (both of them), Viorica, Ziguța, Coca, and her husband Titi. I also had Mitzy with Liky, Viorica, Radu with Mieta, Helga, Cristina, Sandu Missirliu and Raia Nicolau. And within my memories I also carried Lulu and Stephen.

As we were driving down the street, I felt like a wave of freedom was lifting me. From now on, I could take my life into my own hands, and make it somewhat better than it had been. I had no clue, then, that this sudden break with the past was the beginning of a new hope. Definitely, I could never have foreseen how my mother's imprisonment would have contributed to my freedom. In an odd way I realized that I owed some of it to her.

Cecil filed the divorce papers. He called George Poppa, his father, and Virginia, his cousin, as witnesses. The stated motivations for the divorce were "fights caused in the middle of the night with insults, thus making the spouse's life a living hell." The application for divorce was granted.

I was officially hired starting December 2, 1958, without being asked the reasons for my previous resignation. I just shook hands with the Chief of the Personnel Office after Săndulescu has introduced me to the president. Praise the Lord! I had been assigned to Sector 1, managed by engineer Avram.

Looking back, in six years I had changed three jobs and three home addresses.

CHAPTER 8

10 Dr. Pasteur Lane 1958-1965

1958-1959

As we drove away from Cecil's house, Liky congratulated me for having had the guts to move out. When we reached my father's house on Miliţiei Street, I felt as if I had awakened from a deep slumber. Present to greet me on my arrival were my father, all four ladies of the house, Nicu and Nicuşor, Uncle Costinel, Mitzy, and of course Leana. They were all very emotional, and most had tears in their eyes when they hugged me. Only then did I feel relieved of the tension that had accumulated during the previous very eventful seven days—the period that started when comrade Gheorghe mentioned my "omitted sins" and forced me to resign, that continued with the unexpected good news of being hired by the Repair Service Cooperative, and that was followed by the stressful separation from my husband and my moving out to my father's house.

It gave me great pleasure to see again the oleander from our estate brought into the house during the winter; it was the only thing reminding me of Genune. I settled in the former drawing room, now a transit room where everybody passed through on their way toward the bathroom or kitchen. We were all forced to use the same bathroom, compliments of the communist regime. And in spite of all this, we were still privileged compared to others, because at least in our case the Housing Authority and Dwelling Space Administration did not force us to share our apartment with complete strangers who were often the dregs of society.

Next day, on December 2 engineer Avram—head of section 1 where I had been assigned to work—was expecting me. He stretched out his hand with a smile and introduced me to my new colleague, "Comrade" Artimon, who was glad I had come. Artimon was aware that my experience was in road building, not housing repairs, and told me, "I have to show you where our projects are and help you get a feel for the applicable norms in civil engineering. At the beginning we will coach you. You should also know that we have a lot of projects, and the end of the month is always hectic." That much I knew.

Being very sensitive to cold, I had a problem in that the building, a former street level shop, was unheated. Everyone worked with their coats and hats on. I thought, however, that I would survive this inconvenience, too, given that I had survived the hardships of my previous job as a " road normator" in the Bărăgan fields. After all, at least now I was in Bucharest. I got the official employment papers starting as of December 2, 1958.

In early February 1959, tired as usual after the month-end work, I was in Ziguţa's room talking with Titi about his prison experience. It was on a Sunday morning when winter was in full swing. Suddenly I went close to the window. I was in awe as I watched the enormous bright snowflakes falling from the sky. As I looked out, I saw a man across the neighbor's window waving to me. I called Titi, who recognized the man who waived. Titi said, "Ah, this is my childhood friend and classroom mate; I know what he wants to talk about."

He quickly put on a coat and ran downstairs.

When Titi returned upstairs, we found that the fellow's name was Graboveski and that he wanted to offer Titi a way to get a place of his own. He knew that, being recently released from prison, Titi was living with relatives. The Graboveski couple had just moved into a little apartment in the partially submerged basement of a townhouse in the Cotroceni residential area of Bucharest, but his wife did not like it and wanted to return to her mother's apartment across our window. Their problem was that they had already paid a four-thousand-lei retainer which they could only recoup if they could refer somebody else to take over the apartment. He assured Titi that he had the necessary connections at the local Housing Authority to get an official assignment to that apartment for anybody who was interested.

"So what did you tell him?" I asked, to which Titi replied, "Naturally, I thanked him but declined. I don't have the money."

As soon as I heard that Titi was not interested, I immediately realized that the apartment would be a great opportunity for me to settle in a place of my own, but I did not have the money either. Nevertheless, I thought it would have been a shame to miss such an opportunity, especially since I could move there legally on the basis of having an official dwelling assignment from the Housing Authority. So I immediately asked Titi to let his friend know that he did indeed know someone who wanted to see the apartment. Then I went to talk to my father and Florica about the prospect of getting the apartment for myself.

Of course, my father cautioned me that the man could be unreliable and that I could be throwing the money away. Florica disagreed and thought that Titi's friend was offering me a unique opportunity. When Titi returned he let us know that Grabo, as he called his friend, had agreed to show me the apartment as soon as he and his wife vacated it and removed their furniture. That fit me like a glove, giving me time to try to borrow the money.

Based on Titi's assurances that his friend was trustworthy, my dad gave me two thousand lei. Leana offered to lend me one thousand lei, but I was still short. Everything seemed up in the air until I got the idea to see Ms. Raia Nicolau and ask her to lend me the balance. I considered her a dear friend of mine, and I knew the feelings were mutual.

As usual, Raia Nicolau invited me over to her home. Long ago she had been my confidant regarding my mother's situation, and now I was telling her everything about my own dilemma, including the divorce. That impressed her:

"Monuca, you have been through a lot; too bad you couldn't have left the country in 1947."

Then she whispered in my ear, "Poor I. C. Parhon! He tried to help, but those in the Ministry of the Interior and the Securitate probably did not want to approve your exit visa."

Then she added in a normal, loud voice, "I will tell Fănică what happened to you, and rest assured that I shall try to find someone to replace Cecil. When do you need the money?"

I replied, "In two or three days," then thanked her and left.

On February 10 Grabo took me to see the apartment. Even before I saw it, I was confident I would take it regardless of the fact that it was in a partially submerged basement. One of the things that attracted me was the fact that it was in a three-floor building at the end of Dr. Pasteur Lane, a quiet cul-de-sac that reminded me of Armaşului Lane. To get to the apartment, we went down a few twisted steps. The first room was small, with a built-in closet on the right and, on left, an exhaust hood and space for a stove with a butane gas tank. A door led to a bigger room with a large window facing the street; a gas heating stove and a sink were on the right side of the room. There was a back door to a corridor leading to a large laundry, to other utility rooms, and to a toilet. Though the toilet was unheated, it had the advantage of being for the exclusive use of the apartment.

The place was small but functional, and most importantly I didn't have to share it with anybody anymore. It was bright, had central heating, and there was this laundry room down the corridor that could be used as a bathroom. It was spacious, with a large water boiler with gas that would heat up in a few minutes. All these advantages were more important to me than the fact that the windows were at the garden level. I agreed on the spot to have Grabo start the paperwork process to get me official approval to live in that dwelling. Besides the money, all I had to provide was proof from the Repair Service Cooperative that I was employed by them and therefore in the "labor field."

In the evening, I called Cecil. He was surprised to learn that I had already found a home. I told him that, in exchange for the large cupboard I left behind, I would like to have a gas stove with a butane tank. He agreed and kept the conversation very short. Two days later, Raia Nicolau called me to give me the money.

I gave Grabo the required proof of employment, and soon after in early March 1959, he handed me the official assignment to that apartment. In turn, I gave him the four thousand lei that he had paid as a retainer. Liky and Titi helped me move my things to Pasteur Lane. They brought me the sofa and the cooking stove from Cecil's house, and Maman Titi's Singer sewing machine and some furniture from Armașului that had been stored in Florica's basement. I also got a gorgeous Gallé table lamp, a gift received by my parents in 1925 at their wedding in Calafat. In the end, the big white snowflakes had served their fateful purpose as they helped put me in touch with Grabo and solve my housing problem!

After I moved in, I wanted to get to know my cotenants and of course I was curious to find out which of them was the Secret Police "informer." It was a known fact that the district People's Council made sure that there was an informer among the tenants in practically each house. Back in Armașului Lane Birișan living at the lower level, was the informer, and it was he who had told the authorities that we were former big landowners from Craiova, which is what precisely led to our eviction. The informer would monitor any movement of the cotenants to report to the street officers who in turn reported to Securitate. That system was part of what might be called "*Community organizing.*"

Grabo had told me that the Georgescu family living on the first floor with their son, Șerban, and a daughter, Irina, were the former owners of the house. They too had been turned from owners to tenants overnight. When I met Mr. Georgescu on the staircase and introduced myself, he was very distant, almost didn't want to talk to me. I realized right away what the problem was. I took the bull by the horns and said, "I know you're Mr. Georgescu, the former owner of the house. I'm the new tenant living downstairs. I was lucky to get this room after having been kicked out in only three hours from my father's own property."

Only then did he turn to me and ask, "Didn't the gentleman who moved out bring you here?"

"Yes, I came here with his help, since he knew my father George Vrabiescu, former professor at the Faculty of Law."

Mr. Georgescu seemed to light up at that. He reached out his hand and said, "Welcome! I thought the one who left brought in a girlfriend."

"No, Mr. Georgescu, he was only a well-appreciated intermediary, because following our eviction we were offered a dwelling in the Băneasa area on the outskirts of Bucharest, which we refused."

After my brief encounter with Mr. Georgescu, all the members of his family were very kind to me, and so was the Harnagea family, with whom the Georgescus were forced to share their apartment. Two other families shared the second-floor apartment. One of the husbands was a Securitate Major and most probably the building informer.

Finally alone in my new home, I was very happy and relieved. Using the *Singer* sewing machine, I began to tailor my own dresses with the help of patterns.

Raia Nicolau invited me quite often to meet people who, she thought, would make good prospective husbands for me. They were all a little old for me, but that was irrelevant because I wasn't tempted to marry again. I wasn't ready to make another commitment or ruin somebody's future because of my social background. I was one of those pariahs who ought to be marginalized or even annihilated through class struggle. So I had to stay in the world I was born in— the world that I appreciated and where I was appreciated in return. On the other hand, if I had started a relationship with someone of my own world, we would have run the risk of being doubly persecuted—which would have put the entire family in jeopardy.

At least now I was on my own feet. I had a job that did not require anyone to scrutinize too deeply into my past, I had a bright room with white walls (without the blue depressing wallpaper in Cecil's house), and above all nobody was intruding into my privacy.

Finally, I was able to eat whatever I wanted, whenever I wanted; to come and go whenever I decided and as many times as I wanted; and, to go to bed when I was sleepy. To sum up, now I could fly free and go as far as I could envision. I realized how much my prayers in Drăgășani had helped me to make the right decisions.

After the closing of the month of March, management called all employees with "normator" positions to informs us about a corporate decision; they would rotate us every few months from one sector to another. So in April together with my future colleague Andra Locusteanu, I was assigned to Sector 2, run by engineer Pavel. I hoped I would get along with him as well as I had with engineer Avram and my colleague Artimon.

Pavel was tall, thin, much younger than Avram, handsome, with blond curly hair, but less educated. He gave me a list of the projects that Sector 2 was responsible for, and together with Andra we started to visit them one by one. In one of the building yards, a young man caught my eye. He was tall, a little balding, with light brown hair, and was wearing a short coat with lapels that flapped in the wind. There was something elegant in the way he moved and spoke with the workers. One day, when I saw him again, I asked Andra, "Do you know the guy who's talking to Pavel?"

It turned out that Andra knew the guy very well as he was a friend of hers. His name was Rudi Kleckner and he used to be "normator" himself, but he had preferred to become a foreman. When Andra mentioned that the guy was very good at calculations, it occurred to her he could help us with the month-end work and save us the sleepless nights that were usually monthly the price we paid to finish our job on time.

One day when she came to visit me, I told her that I occasionally saw that foreman in the trolley bus on my way to work. She explained that he lived in the same residential neighborhood as I, and that we probably used the same trolley bus to get to work. Then it occurred to me that instead of doing the work at the Office, we might as well take the paperwork to my apartment and work in the comfort of my home where we could also have a cup of coffee or a snack. Andra assured me my idea was feasible, and proposed to call

Rudi as well to help us, not only because he lived in the same neighborhood but also because he had no family obligations since he was not married, had no kids, contemplating the possibility of leaving the country.

As decided Andra brought Rudi Kleckner over to my apartment to help us with the month-end for the month of April. We sat around the table, each of us taking a stack of forms, and started to work individually using our slide rulers to make calculations. Soon after we started, Rudi got hungry. So we set all papers aside and interrupted our work to feed him. The two of us wanted him to stay to finish the piles of unfinished forms.

When we were ready, Andra and I signed the papers and took them to our boss who randomly verified some before sending them to the Accounting Office.

Rudi was friendly, casual, cheerful, always had a good appetite, and wasn't picky about food. I invited him to come over and help us the following month-end, too. He ended up coming every time we needed him. I got to like him more and more. I had reached the point when I thought life without love is pointless. And his personality seemed the opposite to that of Cecil's. He was an optimist, always saw the future as bright, without factoring in thousands of potential unseen problems. He seemed to have a good character and most importantly, he wasn't and didn't want to be "a man of the regime." The big problem about him was that he was seeking an opportunity to leave the country, and I dreaded the prospect of another separation.

As they say "once bitten, twice shy," and that was the way I felt after the Iron Curtain cruelly separated me from Stephen, who was my first great love, and after I went through the humiliation of a divorce because of my "unhealthy" social origin. I decided I shouldn't get involved with this young man. That cautiousness kept me away from him.

At some point in June, he invited me to his place. He lived a few blocks away on Dr. Tomescu Street where he shared the apartment with Nelu Strass, his cousin's husband who was also waiting approval to join his wife abroad. Nelu was very curious to know me. They treated me to tea and ham sandwiches. When I left, Rudi escorted me to my house via a side street. The street being dark and deserted, suddenly he hugged me and kissed me in a way that I had not been kissed for years. Contrary to my previous reasoning not to get involved, I couldn't resist, especially after the years I had spent waiting for Stephen, or after my experience with Cecil.

Rudi's name was short for Rudolf, a name that reminded me of King Rudolf IV of Austria (the son of Charles IV of Bohemia). That seemed auspicious, as Austria was Haagi's homeland. What also seemed auspicious was the fact that he was living in my neighborhood, just like Lulu and Stephen, who both lived in Armaşului. He told me that his parents were divorced; he himself had been married to an older woman who had a sister in America. She had married him hoping it would give her the opportunity to leave the country and be with her sister. They had divorced ten years before and had no children. I also learned he had been drafted in the army and released after eighteen months.

After returning to Bucharest, Rudi worked in a cooperative while waiting for the approval of his application to leave for Israel. His mother, Silvia, was already there, and she had been waiting for Rudi and his brother Aristide to join her. But he told that after ten years he was tired of continuous waiting. I understood him perfectly after my own experience with Stephen.

Eventually Rudi asked me to marry him, but I declined because of his intention to leave and also because I wasn't yet officially divorced. Therefore, I refrained from introducing him to anyone yet, neither to my family nor to friends. Andra was the only one who knew about our relationship.

My divorce from Cecil went smoothly since there had been no children or property to share. I only appealed in writing to keep my married name Poppa, which was less compromising than my maiden name. Cecil had no objection, and the Civil Sentence of February 1960 declared the marriage null due to both spouses' fault.

One afternoon, in the middle of February, there was a discreet knock on the door. When I opened it, there was Cecil in flesh and blood. At first he was smiling, but then he seemed surprised by my indifference at his sudden appearance. I could see him trying to hide his disappointment at my reception. While arranging his tie, he said, "Mounette, I came to see if you are well installed here. Maybe we can spend some time together."

I didn't reply. Instead, I showed him in, and when he stepped into the room, I introduced him to Rudi in the most natural way. Cecil gave me a blank look. Knowing him well, I understood he was feeling miserable and confused. He tried to make up a reason for his visit, saying, "I came to make sure you are okay."

He shook hands with Rudi without asking who he was, and I did not offer any explanation. Given the circumstances, he decided it was judicious to leave. I knew he felt he had lost me forever. He certainly must have felt defeated, and I'm sure his manly pride was wounded. That was the last time I ever saw him.

The cycle of changes was in progress. In late February 1960, as I was going home I met Mario Navarra in the bus. He was a former colleague from Sovrom-IPSR. He told me he was working in an engineering institute called the Department of Systematization, Architecture and Building Design, known under the acronym DSAPC, where Cezar Niculiu, who also had worked at IPSR, was now director. I knew Niculiu since I had calculated his planning projects. Mario was glad to see me, and when I told him I was working in a cooperative he suggested I talk to Niculiu; perhaps he could get me a transfer. He gave me the address of the Institute and Niculiu's telephone number, adding that he would also talk to him and remind him about me. He promised to call and let me know if there was any chance. The address of the institute was convenient, as it was close to my home as well as my father's.

Niculiu received me right on my birthday, March 7. He was happy to see me and asked, "Simona, what is the status of your personnel file?"

I answered with confidence, based on what comrade Gheorghe had assured me, saying there were no issues that I knew of. Pleased with my answer, he said, "As soon as the Chief of Personnel has a chance to look at your file, we shall ask for your transfer."

I gave him the Cooperative address, thanked him, and went to Mario's office. He introduced me to a guy called Micu who was the

Head of the Employment and Wages Department and with whom I would be working if and when I was hired. Micu—a short and chubby young man with a friendly face—told me, "Mario mentioned to me about you, and I hope you'll be transferred soon, because I really need an assistant."

Next I went to see Florica and my father, being quite confident that I would get this job. As it was my birthday, everyone drank a glass of wine to my health. Then I confessed, but only to Florica, that I was going out that night for dinner with a young man whom I sort of liked. She was delighted.

During the dinner at the restaurant, I told Rudi about the possibility of changing my job for a better position in an engineering institute. When I finished talking, he announced emphatically, "The second surprise on your birthday is that here and right now I seriously propose to marry you."

He looked at me with questioning eyes. I felt the past repeating itself. On the one hand, I liked the prospect of marrying a man whom I liked—a man who was handsome, tall, with an athletic body, broad shoulders and narrow hips, blue-eyed cheerful, optimistic, full of enthusiasm, someone who did not care about my background. That gave me great joy. But I had to weigh all that against the fact that he was planning to emigrate, which might translate into another painful separation like the one I had experienced with Stephen.

Therefore, my reply was, "I would love to marry you, but I cannot accept it because of your plans to leave the country." He said, "I thought a lot about this lately, I do not want to lose you. So I have decided to give up the idea of leaving the country. Or better said, I don't want to leave without you."

What I heard moved me to tears as his and Stephen's approach stood in great contrast in my mind. I decided on the spot I would not lose a man who loved me so much and who was even ready to sacrifice his desire to live in a free country just for me. In short, I had no reason not to accept his marriage proposal. I told him, "Dear Rudi, if you promise not to leave, in any case not to leave without me, I will marry you, but I still have one request."

He was really curious to know what the request was. I told him about my drama with Stephen and the fact that for so many years that experience continued to haunt me. So I asked him to do me the favor of taking me to see Stephen if and when we were ever allowed to leave the country. That, for me, was like a closure for my unfinished business with Stephen and my revenge against the Iron Curtain.

With his optimistic nature, Rudi promised by saying, "First let's see if we succeed in leaving. And if we do, I promise I'll bring you to see him and you'll be able to have an explanation."

As we left the restaurant we were both happy and satisfied. I still had a problem, though, as now I had no choice but to introduce him to my family. Obviously Rudi was not exactly what they had in mind as an ideal husband for me: he was neither a descendent of former landowner family, nor did he have any roots in our beloved Oltenia region. I knew the problem I would be facing, as this was the third time I had to deal with the same situation. The difference between my previous similar experiences and this one was that, this time, I was quite determined not to give up. My further hope was that, this time, Florica's support would make a difference.

Always in the past I had gone to talk to her before Gică's arrival from work to test the waters and see how she would react any news I brought. On this occasion I cut straight to the chase, telling her when and how I had met Rudi, saying that he was Cecil's opposite in every respect, and insisting on the idea that he was ready and willing to sacrifice his emigration plans for me. After all the tryouts I had been through, I added that I was no longer willing to lose him in the way I had lost Stephen.

Florica suggested I bring Rudi over one evening to introduce him to the family. Until then, she intended to prepare my father bit by bit, knowing he would need some time to digest such news.

At the end of March, she told me I could bring Rudi over. She invited other family members as well. I thought that I would remain forever indebted to Florica for her help.

Rudi and I arrived at my father's house when all the others were already there. One thing that had given me some confidence was that Rudi looked really good and was very smartly dressed. But actually his charm was in his smile, and that was what won everyone over. After I introduced him to everybody, everything went well. Everybody behaved as if they had known him before. I left the place feeling satisfied with the results of the visit and also satisfied because I thought Rudi had a good time. He himself had no close family except for his brother Aristide. He had not had any relationship with his father after his parents' divorce.

Lady luck was smiling on me. Soon after that visit, Mario informed me that Director Niculiu had signed my appointment and expected me to start on April 18, 1960. I was delighted by the news, but mostly I felt relieved that my personnel file had not been an issue. I assumed it had been "cleaned up" as comrade Gheorghe had assured me it would be. Gică was also delighted by the news of my employment in a new job. After all the changes that took place and with Floricaţs help he seemed to be at peace with the idea of my marriage to Rudi. We set the date for April 23, which was his name day—St. George—for good luck.

After a brief civil marriage ceremony at the People's Council, which was the communist name for what was in face the district city hall, Florica's invited a few people for lunch at her home in Miliţiei Street.

On my last day with the cooperative I said good bye to engineer Pavel and all the other coworkers. Most of all, I thanked Sandu Missirliu because he had brought me luck. Not only did I owe him my job at the cooperative, but having a job I could get my own living quarters in Dr. Pasteur Lane and on top I found a husband. So one could say that at the Repairs Service Cooperative, my life too got "repaired." Of all my former colleagues, I remained friends with Andra, Mitzy, Viorica, Tănţica with whom we continued to visit each other quite frequently.

After April 18 and 23, my life changed for the better. The first day at DSAPC, the Chief of the Personnel Office handed me the official appointment without mentioning anything about my file. I was welcomed by director Niculiu and Micu, my future boss, who mentioned, "You are right on time—just before the end of April, when there is a lot of work!"

He, introduced me to the five other employees with whom I was to share the same office. Mario Navarra's desk was next to mine, reminding me of Radu at IPSR. When I visited the various Sections of architects and engineers, I had the pleasant surprise of seeing some of my former colleagues from IPSR, all brought there by Niculiu.

After a while, Niculiu was replaced by Octavian Țurcanu, also an architect, known as Tavi. At the end of the year, after doing some talking with Mario and my future friend Nelu Lungu, we managed to transfer Viorica Ruja-Stein who came to work with us.

After our marriage, Rudi and I often had meals at home because Rudi didn't like any longer the dishes served at the cooperative cafeteria. For the first time in my life I had to cook. Meat was hard to find; therefore when I looked out of my office's window and saw a truck supplying the butcher's shop on the other side of the street, I asked for permission to leave, then rushed out to be among the first in line to buy meat, fearing that the supply would be all gone before my turn came. The butcher would frequently throw in a heavy bone and only a meager quantity of meat so that the supply would feed as many people as possible. Not having proper wrapping paper, he would throw everything—bone and meat—in a newspaper. But I was happy to get some meat even though I knew I was paying for the heavy unwanted bone that was sold in the same package.

Maman Titi's *Singer* sewing machine caught Rudi's eye. He felt we had to sell it and buy a motorcycle instead. If my grandmother had still been alive, I wouldn't even have considered it. But as she was not, I agreed. Selling the sewing machine was quite easy, and soon we were the owners of an English-made Francis Lewis motorcycle. We parked it right in front of our window. "*Francis*" soon became indispensable; early in the mornings, before going to work, Rudi took the bike out for a ride to buy bare necessities such as ice for the fridge, milk, yogurt, and bread. In the evenings, we rode it to visit friends and family.

Luck had seemed to be on my side ever since I was kicked out of the Ministry of Transportation. I had a husband who loved me and my mind was refreshed, rejuvenated, reborn. Our relationship touched that sweet level when two souls can communicate in a relaxed way, free of tension. Together we managed to get out of debt; now we could afford to hire Aneta, the former cleaning woman who had worked for Rudi's mother. She came once a week, on Thursdays. Leana, who was our first choice, had turned down our offer, saying that she was too old.

After a while, we rode the bike to Craiova to introduce Rudi to Manini. When we arrived, Manini examined him briefly and, after exchanging a few words with us, brought us some coffee. Then she suggested we take a walk in the beautiful Bibescu Park while she fixed dinner. Rudi was really impressed by the beauty of the park. Then we stopped at Tante Lenuța Chiciu's house near the park entrance. She was the wife of my father's cousins. Very hospitable, as the Romanians are in general, she invited us over for a snack on our way home, Rudi said he could not eat anything more. I immediately panicked, "Do you want to destroy Manini?! I suggest you tell her you're starving, to make her happy."

As soon as we stepped in, Manini welcomed us, "My dears, you must be very hungry."

"Yes, Manini, I can't wait to eat!" Rudi answered, looking at me for approval.   She treated us to a huge meal. In the end Rudi turned pale when Manini came with a plate of strudel and put "just two pieces" on his plate. I started laughing, I couldn't help myself. Manini interpreted it differently, "Dear, I am so pleased to see you happy."

After dinner, we rode Francis to downtown Craiova where we had a long walk to help us with our digestion. By the time we returned in the evening, our appetites had returned, and we ate a lot, to Manini's great joy. The next day, before leaving, Rudi invited Manini to go for a ride with him on the bike, but he received a flat refusal from her: "Come on, Rudi, what would the neighbors think if they saw me?"

Back in Bucharest I had a big surprise. In my father's house was General Anton, whom I called Uncle Ionel. He had been released from jail after twelve long years (194–1959). He had been the Chief of Staff of the Gendarmerie on August 23, 1944, when the King had switched gears against the Germans. On the front, General Anton distinguished himself by capturing more than 7,200 German troops,

20 warehouses, and 300 German vehicles that were given back to the Romanian Army. Instead of rewarding him for his services to his country, the communists arrested him and sentenced him to a long prison term.

Rudi and I also invited Uncle Ionel to come over for dinner at our house on Dr. Pasteur Lane. Over dinner he told us about his two years of solitary confinement in concrete cells full of rats in which he was bound to stay without any light and completely alone. The food was mostly a kind of hot water, resembling a soup, and three times a week he'd get a slice of bread. The last ten years of his imprisonment, he was no longer in solitary confinement and was allowed to mingle with other inmates. They all had to sleep face up, with hands on top of the blankets and heads uncovered. He got beaten up and sworn at all the time. He had not seen a newspaper or a book for years. Poor Uncle Ionel! Considering how much he had endured, his mind was still sharp but he was extremely frail. Rudi drove him home.

Micu, my boss, departed for a four day vacation leaving me in charge—something that had never happened before. But why should things go smoothly when they can be complicated? After one day, on Wednesday November 16, I received a phone call from Craiova. It was Dănel who called to let me know that Manini had suffered a stroke and was in a local hospital. He advised me to come immediately. I told him that I couldn't, under any circumstances, leave the office at that time since my boss was on vacation, but that I would come as soon as possible.

Rudi bought me a plane ticket for Saturday at noon. That was when I flew on a plane for the first time in my life. From the airport I went straight to the hospital where I spoke with the doctor who took me to see Manini. She was in a room with about fifteen other patients. The doctor told me that her situation was serious, and he didn't know if she would make it, but if she did, she'd need two women to take care of her 24-7.

When I approached her, she recognized me, "My little one, I'm so sorry to have put you through such a trouble. How was your trip?"

After a normal conversation, during which I gave her all the details of my first flight, I heard her saying, "You see, you should be careful, I do not know why but a fire is burning there in the corner of the room," and she pointed in that direction with her hand. I realized she was delirious. Before I left, I promised to come again the next morning.

At home in Severinului Street, Mrs. Constantinescu, a tenant, told me how and when the stroke happened. I told her the doctor's prognosis and relayed my conversation with Manini. At that point Ms. Constantinescu confided to me that Manini had left her family's jewels with the Diamandopol family, my grandfather's relatives, Cionea Anastase. She suggested, "Go immediately to see and tell them that Manini wants you to pick up the jewelry, and bring them with you. If you don't go while she's alive, they could deny their existence. I'll give you their phone number."

I went there in the evening. They handed me the jewelry, for which I had to sign a receipt; I took it, put it in my bag, thanked them, and left.

Arriving home, I made an inventory of everything in the house, partly to know what I could sell in case I needed to pay two women to take care of Manini, but also to let the other people in the house be aware that I knew about all of Manini's belongings. I was dead tired when I went to bed at 3:00 a.m.

In the morning I went straight to the hospital together with Angelica, the seamstress, who offered to help me take care of Manini and change her shirt. I also took my suitcase with me because at three o'clock I had a flight back to Bucharest. Manini spoke normally, she was happy to see me. While I was talking to another woman next to her bed, Angelica began to wash her up. When I helped her to lift Manini to change her shirt, suddenly she turned all red. All the blood seemed to rush straight to her head in a matter of seconds.

The woman next to her said to me, "Ma'am, can't you see what is happening?"

She handed me a lit candle, which I tried to keep away from Manini as I didn't want her to see it. I did not realize that this was the end. When the blood slowly drained away from her face, she became increasingly pale, and her lips turned purple. Then I took the candle from the woman's hand and put it in Manini's hand, holding it with mine.[69] She took a last breath, sighed, and gasped out her life in front of my eyes. I said a prayer in my mind.

She died a painless death on November 20 at 11:30 a.m. with a candle in her hand, with her only remaining family member next to her.

Manini had many joyous moments in her life, but she also endured lots of pain. Now all was gone in a few moments. I was at peace because I had been next to her when I had to be. Nevertheless, I regretted the fact that she left this world without fulfilling her dream of becoming an opera singer. Instead she wasted her God-given beautiful voice to comply with a stupid provincial mentality. She could have brought fame to her country as —our Hariclea Darcle, Virginia Zeani or Angela Gheorghiu.

The doctor allowed me to make a phone call from the hospital. I asked Rudi to take the first train and bring with him some money and black clothes for me. I also asked him to announce Manini's death to Mitzy and Liky and ask them whether they could come to Craiova to attend her funeral. Also, I asked Rudi to call Micu at the office and let him know I'd come back after the funeral. At the hospital I made all necessary arrangements with the undertakers.

When I arrived home, I immediately called Tante Maya, my friend Tănţica's mother, asking her to make arrangements for the religious service. At home everyone was crying, including Ion and Coca Parhon and their children who were not family. They apologized for not being able to attend the funeral because of their social position, but they offered instead to give us all the food and drinks we needed for the memorial meal. Of course I understood the situation; people with official functions or connections in the communist regime had to avoid being seen at a church, let alone being seen at the funeral of a former big landowner.

The big trouble came when Mr. Diamandopol told me over the phone that there was no room for Manini's casket in my grandfather's crypt because the only available space was occupied by another

---

69.   In the Romanian folk tradition, it is believed that a candle fixed in the deceased's hands will light up his way to heaven

family member (someone who in my opinion had no reason to be there). I gave up any discussion, because I couldn't change the situation; however, I couldn't sleep all night, thinking, "What are you going to do now with Manini? Where are you going to bury her?"

In the morning Rudi arrived on the ten o'clock train. First we went to the hospital; I had everything I needed to get her ready, to comb her hair, powder her cheeks, and place her head on a small cushion with lace ruffles. Then we took the keys to the family crypt from Mr. Diamandopol and went to the cemetery administration. I found that Floricuța, my mother's little sister who had died when she was six years old, was also buried in the crypt. With one of the employees, I unlocked the vault's fence and we entered the crypt to identify Floricuța's coffin. We arranged for her remains to be placed in Manini's coffin at her feet, freeing up space for Manini. The administration agreed, but there was nobody available to do the job.

We went home and brought back a pillowcase and gloves. At the cemetery Rudi opened the lid of the girl's coffin and I put on the gloves, grabbed the dry bones and put them inside the pillowcase which would be placed in Manini's coffin in the crypt after the funeral service in the afternoon. Because of lack of services under communism I had to do even that.

For the funeral Dr. Parhon lent us his car. To my surprise, five priests attended the service in the cemetery's church, four of whom came on their own initiative to honor Manini's memory. The church was full of friends, acquaintances, and neighbors.

Back at home all preparations had been done for a memorial meal. After a few glasses of wine, those present remembered Manini and her personality, especially Dănel, who inherited Tata-Lae, his father's sense of humor, and Liky, who had known her she being his aunt. Both of them shared happy or funny moments with us, mentioning her singing, the way she acted, how she used to pray, and how much she suffered after the Herescus' departure, Tata-Lae's death, and Mancy's two arrests.

After the funeral, our problems were not over. We had to empty her room. Rudi went to the railway station to rent a freight wagon to carry some of the furniture to Bucharest, because we knew that within a day after the funeral the People's Council would come to take the keys to the empty room. I had to pack a lot of things—among them, two Turkish daggers with gold and silver filigree and semiprecious stones from the Calafat Palace.

Next morning before our departure a big truck picked up the furniture. Rudi, with some helpers, loaded the furniture in the freight wagon. I stayed behind to hand over the keys of the empty room to the clerk of the People's Council. That was the second time I had to go through that experience since our eviction from our Bucharest home. I left Manini's house with a heavy heart. I left Craiova, my beloved city, on a fast train to Bucharest, knowing that the period of my life I had spent with Tata-Lae and Manini was now over.

In Bucharest we had to absorb Manini's furniture. We had no other place to store it than our own room, which became so crammed that we had to jump from the door straight into the bed. All the floor space that remained was a narrow corridor to the sink. After a while I got an idea. Being on good terms with Mr. Georgescu, the former owner of the house, I asked if we could use the free space below his balcony to store our excess furniture. Mr. Georgescu agreed because he was not using the space anyway. Rudi made a fence in front of it, and into the space underneath we moved some of the furniture that we covered with blankets. The jewelry I put in an improvised pouch made of a piece of cloth, which I sewed around the edge. I gave the pouch to my father for safekeeping, because there was always someone at home in his house.

Little by little, we rearranged our room to accommodate the beautiful furniture that reminded me of Craiova and the Gallé lamp from Armaşului. We redid the wooden floor with parquet. Each Sunday, Rudi went to a flea market with "Francis" the motor bike to sell some of Manini's things, and with the money from the sale we bought a big Gründig radio. We used it to listened to foreign news stations, keeping the volume low and our ears glued to the radio, taking care not be heard by neighbors.

One evening after dark, we went to the Dâmboviţa River crossing the city, carrying the beautiful daggers from the Calfat Palace now in Minini's house and threw them into the water, all out of fear that we might be accused of possessing law-prohibited weapons. Letting them fall from my hand, I was overwhelmed with regret for the elegant past that was no more. The communist utopia had destroyed everything.

1961

One day Rudi's brother Aristide came over to announce he was marrying the landlady of the house where he lived, Mrs. Tanța Teodorescu. She was the mother of Cristinel Teodorescu—a future journalist and writer—who was then only four or five years old. Aristide was Rudi's opposite, both physically and personality-wise. He was shorter than Rudi, fat, with dark hair, with a difficult personality and a pessimistic nature. He was drawn to poetry. Tanța was the same age as he, slender, beautiful, with almond eyes, gorgeous teeth and a pleasant personality. After their marriage we visited them from time to time and liked to play with Cristinel, a lively little boy, cute, smart, who was happy whenever he saw us coming. A year later Dănuț, their son, was born.

In the spring, on March 21, Gheorghiu-Dej was appointed president of the State Council and First Secretary of the Romanian Workers' Party. He continued to promote foreign trade with the West. Obviously, the foreign policy circumstances were not going to allow for internal domestic improvement.

In the spring, Rudi and I agreed to sell our Francis Lewis motorcycle for a newer and more powerful CZ. Our first trip with the CZ was to Craiova. We stopped in front of Mitică's house, he had moved there with his wife Silvia. It was an emotional reunion because I had not seen them for fourteen years, since August 1947 when I had left Genune with Stephen.

After we parted, we went straight to Genune. Although I knew that expropriated owners were not supposed to get fifty kilometer. close to their former property, I could not resist seeing Genune again. I hoped that nobody would recognize me; I was wearing trousers, with a scarf over my head, and dark sunglasses. My heart was pounding with excitement; after fourteen years I was again climbing the

Bucovăţ hill, passing through the oak forest, following Lazu's abrupt coast and the country road to the left that led to the former mansion. The fountain looked like it was waiting for me. Since some planks were missing from the fence, we could see the bustle of activity around the house, which had been turned into a crop depository. Workers were rolling down full bags of grain down from the top of the main staircase, an operation that must have been repeated many times since the edges of the stairs seemed very worn down.

We began walking toward the pool which, in former days, had been filled with water that we used to irrigate the vegetables. This was the place where I used to swim and cool down during the hot summer days. Next to the pool was a marble slab on which our names were carved: Ecaterina, George, Nicolas and Mona Vrăbiescu. On top was a white marble cross, donated by Uncle Iancu Hagi-Preda. The pool was now dried up and untidy, but the marble slab and the cross still stood untouched. I was overwhelmed with emotion. I wiped my tears, and told Rudi, "Come on, let's go!"

I had satisfied my curiosity, but at the same time, had a broken heart. Here were the roots of my family; here I had spent many happy childhood days and where later Lulu and Stephen came to visit.

* * *

On August 15, 1961, there was bad news from Paris. Nicolae Herescu, Uncle Nuca, had died in Zurich during a conference. A former professor of Latin studies and former president of the Romanian Writers' Union, he had been awarded the order of Knight in the second degree by King Carol II. Uncle Nuca was buried in the presence of his daughter Ioana and a friend, the writer Horia Vintilă.

In the fall evictions continued when, my father, was removed from his position as Legal Counselor at the Department of Agriculture, leaving him with nothing more than a meager pension. And we did not hope in the Parliamentary elections in November, which did not bring any changes for the better. Life continued in misery, poverty and terror.

1962

At DSAPC I found the same pleasant climate I had formerly in IPSR, and I made a few new friendships, among them Mario and Nelu Lungu, as well as his wife Maria (Cici), also an engineer. We were taking turns hosting bridge on Saturday evenings. Having my home nicely furnished now, I started to invite people over.

Ever since I had left the ministry, now at DSAPC and previously at the Repair Service Cooperative, my personnel file had ceased to be an issue. Or at least I thought so. But that proved to be a wrong assumption. One day, Micu being part in a special meeting with the director, opened the door to our office and, with a pale face, called me out to the hallway and confided in a low voice,

"Well, Simona, I thought your file was an acceptable one. However, I didn't suspect it is so bad."

His words made my head reel. Who could expect something like this to happen after two years?

"Micu, what is it about?" I asked.

Then it hit me: it must be the information which Comrade Gheorghe got from Craiova. My blood burned in my veins again while Micu, in an annoyed voice, told me, "The institute is now working to oust dangerous elements, especially those from key departments like ours. Director Țurcanu asked for the files, and when yours came from our Personnel Department, he saw what was in it—information that had not previously come to his attention. Perhaps when director Niculiu said he wanted to hire you, the Personnel Office bringing your file from the cooperative didn't look too closely. It must be, they put your file on the shelf and never touched it until now."

While Micu was talking, I made a quick count in my mind: it was obvious that comrade Gheorghe certainly had left inside the file all information about our estates and my mother's prisons. Most probably, he put them in the bottom of the file, which was indeed quite thick because the same file had been carried over from my first job in Alexeni to the current one.

I braced myself to tell Micu everything: "What is in there is the truth, which I have been hiding for years. There's nothing I can do about that; this is the family I was born into. Yes, I have lived on estates, and had family members in prison."

Micu was staring at me. I had no idea what he was thinking. Eventually, he replied, "Let me see what the director will say and decide."

That whole day he didn't return to my office. By the time I left for home, I still did not know what he had done or what had been the reaction of Director Țurcanu. And when I got home I felt devastated and my rage against the communist regime grew again and my revenge with it. Rudi comforted me, telling me he earned enough to provide for both of us and pay the rent. Then he added, laughing, "If you stay home, you'll cook more!"

It was just another reminder of the great difference between him and Cecil.

The following day, I fully expected to be called in and dismissed. But nothing happened, either that day or during the following days. For a while I had some sleepless nights and was in a bad mood, because again I had the feeling of being one of the "class enemies," and I was fed up with it. Finally, after a number of days, Micu told me in a whisper that the director had decided I would be transferred from the Personnel Department and assigned to a different office with a lower salary. But physically I was to remain in place and continue to work with him.

I was very happy and thankful to all the members of the committee who had reviewed my file without finding it in their heart to fire me. Thank God for that.

On the evening of seventeenth of February, I heard about John Glenn being launched into space, the first American astronaut after the Russian Yuri Gagarin's flight the year before. This gave us great satisfaction.

Another surprise took place in late April. One evening when I was already in bed, Rudi was just taking off his pants—the right leg was out and the other was still in the trousers—when the phone rang.

Holding his pants in one hand, Rudi picked up the receiver/

"Hello?…I don't think I know who you are…Oh? Wait a moment, please."

Then Rudi turned to me.

"There is someone who claims to be my uncle from America. He says he is staying at the Athenée Palace Hotel, but I really think it must be a joke."

"Ask him the room number," I said, "and also ask him to give you his name, and you can call back."

He did so. When he called the hotel and gave the room number, the "uncle" answered the phone. I heard Rudi, saying, "Wait for me in front of the hotel; I'm coming in ten minutes."

With that, he put his other foot back in the trousers, fastened the belt, kissed me quickly and left, giving me the following details, "His name is Henry Bloom, which is in fact my mother's maiden name, so he might be for real. I'll be back soon."

I heard the CZ zoom away. I was really scared, as well as concerned about Rudi, since it was dangerous to have any relationship with foreigners—especially those staying at the Athenée Palace which was guarded by numerous plainclothes secret agents. After a long while, when I heard the engine of a motorcycle in the distance, I hoped it was Rudi returning. Indeed it was. He told me he had talked with the guy in the street, so that no one could bug their conversation. As it turned out, the mysterious uncle was a cousin of Rudi's mother who got our phone number from his mother's sister who lived in Canada.

"I had no idea I had relatives in New York," Rudi said. He then related to me what happened:

"He was speaking freely and asked me whether the situation in Romania was as bad as everyone was saying. I asked him to talk only about family matters, to be careful whom he saw or whom he talked to. He said he wasn't afraid, and he had come to Romania in part to see for himself whether the horror stories that his sister Aida told him about Romania were true. But that was only part of it. He also wanted to visit his father's grave. I invited him to come over and join us for a meal."

We could barely sleep that night. I was worried because it was dangerous to have contacts with foreigners in general and especially with people from outside the Iron Curtain. Rudi was already talking and making plans to go to New York, a dream he'd had for a long time. From that moment on, he wouldn't stop talking about going to New York.

Three days later his uncle came to visit us. As he walked through the door, he looked scared. Closing the door carefully, he asked if we could talk without anyone hearing us. He was even more fearful than we were, not being accustomed to living in constant terror. He said he had met with some people who were all too intimidated to talk to him. Then he promised to kiss the ground upon his return to America and apologize to his sister Aida Fass, born Bloom. He also promised to ask her not to spare any effort to get us out from that inferno, ASAP. I saw how he had been transformed in those three days; his courage had turned into fear. I was moved by his good intentions for us, but privately thought nothing could be done. I'd had some experience in that area.

On the day Uncle Henry left, Rudi went with him to the airport. I felt relieved just knowing that this Uncle Henry—who had given me insomnia—was finally out of country.

In September the big news was that the Government had decided to lower the prices on household goods. However, concomitantly, food prices were increased. One afternoon Rudi and I were looking at electrical supplies displayed in a shop-window. When I saw the old price crossed with a red line and the new price written in red underneath, I stated quite loudly, "You see, the lower prices are only for electrical appliances, but no one says anything about the prices going up for meat, bread, oil, and sugar. It's all an obvious…"

I couldn't finish my sentence. Rudi grabbed me by my elbow and pulled me away from the window. Urging me forward quickly, he said quite angrily, "What are you doing? Didn't you see the guy next to us? After all your experience, haven't you yet learned to be cautious?"

We hurried to the safety of our home, fearing that someone might be following us. That was the life of ordinary citizens who lived in constant fear of speaking out or saying what they believed.

Ever since Uncle Henry had come in the picture, Rudi remained obsessed with the idea of getting out of Romania. He wanted to file the necessary applications for an exit visa. I tried to calm him down, reminding him we might lose our jobs in the process and that there was no guarantee that we would ever succeed in leaving the country.

* * *

Over the year, Romania's supreme leader G. G. Dej continued to arrange commercial deals with the West in order to maintain a certain independence from the Soviets. In 1962 he signed a decree for the gradual release of certain political prisoners. Many of our acquaintances who had been serving different jail terms for political "crimes" were released on the basis of that decree.

One evening in the fall, someone knocked at the door; it was my cousin Ion Vorvoreanu, who had just been released from prison. He was thin and weak, with a pale but smiling face. It was a really pleasant surprise to see him out of prison after eight years. He had been convicted for having worked as an English translator at the British Embassy. Rudi immediately welcomed him with a glass of wine. Ion had come by to ask me about Aimée's situation. As it happened, my cousin Ioana Mirica, Liky's daughter) had told me about Aimée's divorce from Ion, which had come as a total surprise to me.

After being released from prison, Ion went first to his parents' house as a precaution. Uncle Costinel, his father, advised him not to return to Aimée because he had heard about some of her affairs while he was away. Now, Ion wanted to know what I knew and what my opinion was about his returning to Aimée. I understood his dilemma and told him, "It is not unheard of for the spouse of a political prisoner to seek a fake divorce in order to distance themselves from an 'enemy of the people' in the hope that somehow that might help them to avoid repercussions from the communist regime."

Next day, Ion called to tell us that he had gone to Aimée; he had decided to stay and give their marriage another chance. We were happy for them, but later on, when we saw Uncle Costinel in my father's house, he was really furious about Ion's decision. He was fuming!

When Ştefan Potârcă (Ioana Mirica's cousin) was released from the Piteşti prison, known as one of the worst during the communist era I had been impressed the way he looked. Later I read about the Pitești prison in Virgil Ierunca's book: he described it as "a place of absolute horror, of Marxist reeducation," like none other in the entire geography of communist prisons. "Reeducation" meant the prisoner was forced to acknowledge imaginary crimes, destroying one's personality. (Ierunca, Virgil, op. cit. page 107)

1963

Spring found me planning our next trips. On Sundays we went to the monasteries around Bucharest. In early May we decided to visit Curtea de Arges.[70] It was an unfortunate trip because, on the way back the rear tire of the motorcycle blew up when we were going at full speed. I found myself tossed high in the air and landed in the middle of the road. Rudi, too, ended up lying in the middle of the road alongside the CZ. Luckily, there was no traffic on that road at that very moment. My only injury was a broken finger on my right hand. That was all. Rudi too was okay, but we were terrified.

Soon after the accident, we were invited for dinner by Dr. Ecaterina Rădulescu, my gynecologist. The conversation naturally revolved around our accident, and everybody pointed out how lucky we had been, not to be killed. One of the guests, actor Puiu Codrescu said loudly, "Well, Rudi, I think it is time for you to buy a car."

He added that he was selling his German DKW car, which was in very good condition in order to get a bigger car. That had been all Rudi needed to hear.

Without further delay, next day Rudi met with Puiu, saw the DKW, and told him he wanted to buy it. But to pay for the car, Rudi had to sell his bike first. When he came home, he had my head spinning as he described how "gorgeous" the DKW was. It was a convertible painted in two shades of gray, in perfect condition. Rudi sold the CZ for a good price, and we borrowed the money to pay the balance.

---

70. The church of the Curtea de Arges is a historical monument that houses a cypt with the tombs of the members of Romania's royal family.

We were deep in debt, but the DKW car was now ours. We parked in front of the house, and I nicknamed it "Diky." There were no other cars in the area, which is how we became a noticeable presence on the street. Occasionally, Rudi gave neighborhood kids a ride in the car, which of course made them love him. Whenever they saw me alone, they would ask, "Aunt Rudi, when is uncle Rudi coming home?"

*　*　*

One day I was surprised to pick up the phone call and hear an English-speaking voice. It was again Uncle Henry, this time calling from New York, wanting to let us know that his sister Aida was arriving with her husband Sam Fass. He said they would be staying at the Athenee Palace Hotel. I immediately notified Aristide. Again I was frightened, but nonetheless, on the day of their arrival we went to the hotel and I met them.

Aunt Aida was a bit plumpish, blonde with green-brown eyes, rosy complexion, with an open, good-natured attitude. She was elegant looking and very friendly. Speaking perfect Romanian, she declared how happy she was to meet us. Her husband, Uncle Sam, was of Polish origin; the only way to communicate with him was in English. They had brought lots of gifts for everybody in the family. After a while, I realized that Aida was quite an energetic woman. She was constantly telling stories, organizing, and making decisions.

Aunt Aida and Uncle Sam stayed in Bucharest for a week, during which they went with Rudi and Aristide to the Filantropia Jewish cemetery to visit her parents' graves. They came for dinner to our small studio, where I introduced them to Florica and my father, who talked in Romanian with her and in German with her husband. Rudi drove them around on lots of sightseeing trips in and around Bucharest. I could not leave my office.

Before they left, Aida invited all their acquaintances and relatives for stylish dinner at their hotel restaurant. She told us in a whisper,

"Try to leave. I will talk to my son Norman about paying for your trip if you succeed in coming to America rather than going to Israel."

We thanked her, but I remained skeptical about our prospects of leaving the country.

After their departure in early June, Rudi was restless, wanting to go and apply for an emigration visa again. I was afraid that if he submitted the emigration applications, the Passport Office would inform our workplaces and we might be kicked out of our jobs. We had no way to be sure we would ever get the approval to leave. So for a while, Rudi gave up the idea.

* * *

The unusual situations continued. Around June I wasn't feeling well. I had a strange feeling of light heads, a kind of dizziness accompanied by swelling of my ankles. Dr. Missirliu, Sandu's father, advised me to avoid salty food including even bread. I began cooking double portions, one with salt and one without, and was very concerned that I had become a burden on the family. As soon as I tasted salt, the symptoms began again, though their severity depended on the amount of salt ingested.

I met with Dr. Şerban Georgescu—or Banu, as we used to call him—our neighbor upstairs, who was to become in the future, a famous radiologist from Fundeni Hospital. When I told him about my unpleasant symptoms, he suggested I should be examined at the hospital. With his help I got a room with two beds. First I had to follow a salt-free diet. After two or three days, the doctors prescribed food with salt and checked my weight. The doctors observed that I gained pounds, and I went back on the salt-free diet. Meanwhile, all I did was sleep and sleep, then sleep some more. I couldn't get enough sleep. They ran all kinds of tests, all of which showed me in good health. After about ten days of sleep, I felt better, although I had not taken any medication, not even an aspirin. The disconnection from everyone and everything and, most importantly, the ten days of sleep healed me.

After I left the hospital, the doctor gave me a certificate recommending sick leave for a month. When I returned to daily life, my only concern was to pay back Diky's debt, which was decreasing slightly with each passing month.

* * *

I was barely out of the hospital when, early on a Sunday morning, I heard a knocking at the window. I raised my head and saw Leana. I headed to the door, where she met me with a solemn expression on her face, saying, "Miss, yesterday, as I was standing in line to buy eggs, a lady asked me whether I had worked for the Vrăbiescu family."

When I nodded, she said, "Tell them I was in jail with Mancy Radian, and I think she is dead, because she was very sick. They took her to the infirmary and she never returned."

Leana's news gave me the creeps. I had no way to be sure what she said was accurate. Rudi advised me to write to the Penitentiary Department. So I did, asking if my mother Clemenţa Radian was alive and, if so, if I could send her a package or could talk to her. I also mentioned that Lucreţia Defleury, her mother, had died on November 20, 1960, and I gave my new address and phone number.

Shortly thereafter, I received a postcard with the following text: "The person in question is alive; your requests are denied." Just like that!

At least I knew that Mancy was alive, but the wording angered me. It was as if she wasn't even a human being. I was not even allowed to help her by sending a package.

* * *

I spent my sick leave at the Black Sea. I started to feel better and better, even when I began eating bread with salt. Later, I found I could eat any kind of food with salt without having any negative reactions. At the office, Micu and Nelu, two admirable souls, got me a union subsidized ticket, the first I had ever received. They wanted me to continue on, after two weeks, from the seaside to Sinaia in the mountains—all so I could get better.

In Sinaia I got another surprise, which I could have imagined happening there, of all places. Arriving by train, I was accommodated in one of the Union's villas, where I was put in a room with a room-mate whose name I can't remember. During meals and strolls, I spent a lot of time with her. She was younger than me, friendly, and single. Actually, as I discovered, she had been engaged for a long time, but she couldn't make up her mind whether to get married or not. She liked to talk about everything—office, family, fiancé, and friends. I never said anything about myself, neither about my past nor my present, except to say I was happy with my job, I had been married for three years, and that I had no children. That was about all!

One evening when the sun went down in the mountains and the snow was shimmering up there on mountain tops, the young woman and I went for a walk and she started to talk. Again she returned to her favorite subject: she couldn't make up her mind to get married because she was not the type to make advances to men who, she said, for the most part were not trustworthy anyway. To reinforce her argument, she started to tell me a story about the experience that one of her girlfriends did in her endeavor to find someone to marry. I was politely listening to her story although I had no particular interest.

Finally, she said, "I have this girlfriend who wanted to marry her boss. The man was married at the time, but meanwhile he has been divorced, which encouraged my friend to escalate their relationship in hopes that the guy will marry her."

After a pause, seeing I didn't react, my roommate continued, "What do you think, Simona? Men are no saints, but some women are even worse. So my friend managed to seduce her boss. He was a medical researcher, and she was his assistant. You can't possibly know them, her name is Florica Ciuntu, and she works at the Institute of Hematology. He was the deputy chief doctor, a certain Poppa, who eventually divorced his wife. But to this day he had not married my friend."

I was stunned. Trying hard not to show my reaction, I replied casually, "I haven't heard of either of them."

But inside I felt myself overwhelmed by such a far-fetched coincidence, being assigned to a room with a stranger who had confirmed to me what I had already suspected but didn't want to know. We continued our walk back to our villa. Just for the sake of the conversation, I encouraged her not to waste her youth, to follow her heart and get married. I said in my opinion there were many nice people out there, and people like those in her story were not the rule.

"Do you think not?" she asked.

"Yes," I answered.

At night, alone in my bed, I began wondering if Muțuleana had known about Cecil's affair and whether she had actually encouraged it, seeing Florica as a potential replacement with healthier social origins. However, all those questions without an answer pertained to my past. Eventually, I turned on my side and fell asleep.

In time I found out that Cecil didn't get the position as the Institute's director. After the death of my former in-laws, Cecil married a doctor, a decent woman, who was taking care of him.

*　*　*

Surprises were not yet over. One day, Ion Vorvoreanu came alone to see us, telling us a less common story. He had been summoned to the Militia Office, which worried him. Once there, he was asked which place he would like to emigrate to. Perplexed, he answered he didn't want to go anywhere, being scared they wanted to send him in an "obligatory domicile," but then added, "If I have to leave the capital, I prefer Craiova."

The clerk, astonished and annoyed, said, "This is about that you can leave the country and take with you anybody who wants to join you—relatives or friends." Ion said he couldn't believe it. After some further questions he found out that, indeed, the British Embassy had offered to help people who had worked for them, and been jailed for it, get out of the country.

Then Ion added that he had remarried Aimée and decided to leave for London and he went on, "In view of this opportunity, I came to ask you and Rudi if I should include your names on my list, and to ask what country and city would you prefer to emigrate to."

Rudi was about to accept, but I refused. I thanked Ion for thinking of us, but explained that my mother was alive, and if she got out of prison and we managed to get out of the country, she would not have anywhere to go, especially now that her mother was dead.

Shortly after, in the month of November, Ioana Mirica invited us to a big party she was giving to celebrate Aimée and Ion's departure. Ioana had been married, in the meantime, to engineer Sică Costescu, and together they had settled into the apartment of her in-laws in downtown Bucharest. When I arrived there, I recognized Uncle Marinică's gorgeous furniture, which I admired so much. It had been hidden in the basement of his beautiful house in Craiova for fear that the Russians would steal it. Now, having enough space, Ioana had brought that furniture to her Bucharest apartment. Now, on this occasion the apartment was full of friends, all excited to see some human beings who were being allowed to leave the communist "heaven" behind and cross beyond the Iron Curtain. That was something completely unusual, unbelievable!

Ion came and hugged us. To my surprise Aimée didn't greet us, although I noticed she had seen us. Ignoring us, she started talking purposefully to others in a lively way. She continued to behave like this until we left. I was taken aback and infuriated beyond belief. I actually knew her ways, and this was how she acted when she didn't like someone. I did not know what her problem was, especially since I had advised Ion to go back to her when his father was against it. Now she was doing to me what I had seen her doing to others. But why behave like this with me now? Was it because of Cecil who disliked her? I couldn't understand what was happening. I didn't understand Ion's attitude either, since he could see what was happening.

After we left, Rudi tried comforting me, but without success. Aimée had hurt me profoundly! Years were to pass before I finally got an explanation (but that I shall deal with later.)

* * *

After about two days, something strange happened again, which took my mind off Aimée. On our new Gründig radio we heard that on November 22, 1963, the American president, John F. Kennedy was shot and killed by a certain Lee Oswald. Kennedy was replaced by President Johnson

However, incredible as it may sound, in order to maintain the lucrative cooperation with the USA, Dej had been compelled to make more internal concessions, not the least of which was suspending political arrests and releasing political prisoners.

1964

Due to the lack of freedom at home—and, in general, due to the whole situation in the country—it was everybody's wish to leave. My friend Dinu Missirliu, with his mother Aunt Cellica, had left earlier for Paris. Now it was Sandu's turn to join them. We went to see him a few more times before he succeeded in leaving.

The most important news was when we received a letter from Silvia, Rudi's mother, saying that she would be visiting Bucharest for a month to see her sons, both of whom had jeopardized their chances of emigrating to Israel by marrying Christian Romanian women. Silvia arrived at the Băneasa airport of Bucharest on July 29. We arranged with Aristide for her to stay two weeks with each of us. Obviously, she was going to be more comfortable at Aristide's apartment where there were a bathroom, a kitchen, a hallway and two rooms, rather than in our place where a slightly modified laundry room also served as our bathroom. (Rudi had built a big wooden grill on which we stood, pouring hot water over our head with a big mug when we wanted to take showers. It was an unusual, but very functional system, allowing us to use as much hot water we needed.)

Silvia was going to sleep in our bed. Rudi and I borrowed a mattress from the Georgescu family, which we planned to unroll on the floor at night and bundle away in a corner during the day. Before Silvia's arrival, I cooked various Romanian dishes and put them in the fridge. By making room for the fridge outside the entrance on the staircase, we gained a little more living space.

We went to the airport with "Diky." I saw Rudi was excited, which was when I realized how much he loved his mother. Later I could see the resemblance between them; she was blonde, of medium height, neither skinny nor fat. An elegant woman, she appeared wearing a white summer dress, nice shoes, and earrings. Her two big suitcases were made of aluminum, covered with a thick plaid fabric colored black, red and white. The moment she saw us coming from afar, she said, "You're a beautiful couple." Then the hugs came. She immediately called me "Simona," and I called her "Silvia," since I wasn't used saying "mother." Tanța called her "mother," and she still refers to Silvia as mother even now when she talks about her.

When Silvia saw Diky, she was pleased to find out we had a car and how good a driver Rudi was. But when we got home and went down the stairs to our tiny apartment, she asked shyly, "How do you manage to live in only one room? How are we going to sleep?"

"You'll see, don't worry, we've arranged everything," said Rudi, bringing in the suitcases.

Silvia didn't say anything else. She took out the presents she brought for us, unpacked some pretty summer dresses for herself. The presents that were for Tanţa, Aristide and Cristinel she left in the suitcases.

Then, she asked if she could take a shower. Rudi immediately said, "Mother, take your necessary things," and grabbing by her arm, led her toward the door and up the stairs.

We had arranged with our Georgescu neighbors that she could use their bathroom, at least for her first shower. The first impression counts, and we did not want her to find out right away about our laundry turned into improvised bathroom.

"But why do I have to go up the stairs to go to the bathroom?" she asked, with a hint of astonishment.

"Because we don't have a bathroom, you can shower at the neighbors' place," Rudi answered flatly.

"At the neighbors'?"

She looked even more puzzled, and all the while Rudi was leading her up the stairs.

At lunch all of the discussion was about the bathroom. Silvia rendered her opinion with indignation and persuasion in her voice: "You can't live without a bathroom. You have to think about departure!"

I considered ourselves privileged because, in five minutes, we could get as much hot water as we wanted, and valued the fact that the improvised bathroom was in the evening for our exclusive use. This had not been the case in any of my previous dwellings where I had to use hot water sparingly in order to leave enough for the others. I even had heard cases where people were forced to bathe in someone else's leftover water. Everything is relative; it depends on experiences and viewpoints.

In the afternoon we drove to Aristide's, where we left the pretty suitcases, since there wasn't enough room in our place. At home in the evening we prepared the bed for Silvia and we rolled out our mattress, thinking it wouldn't be the end of the world if we slept on the floor for two weeks when others had been cramped in prisons for years. And indeed we slept quite well.

* * *

The morning of July 30, 1964, a Thursday, Rudi and I went to work as usual. Aneta, whom Silvia knew even before her departure back on 1948, had come to help with the household chores. It was our plan that Aneta would serve Silvia breakfast and then chat with her until we came back, after three o'clock. At least that was the plan.

That morning, I couldn't have imagined how the day would turn out to be. When I arrived at the office, Mario and Micu were curious to know how my mother-in-law's visit was going. I told them cheerfully about Silvia's adventure with the bathroom at the neighbors', and they had a lot of fun remarking on it. I had just sat down to start my work when the phone rang and I heard Mario say, "Monica, it's for you."

Aneta was muttering nervously, "Miss Mona, I don't know how to tell you. A woman phoned and said she is your mother and that she's waiting for you at the North Rail Station."

I sank into the nearest chair and whispered, so that others couldn't hear me.

"What did you say, Aneta? Are you sure she said she was my mother?"

"That's what she said, go there and see."

Another lightning strike!

I quickly added, "Aneta, if she calls again, tell her I'm on my way. What about my mother-in-law, how is she doing?"

"She is upset and doesn't know what to believe. Why would you call your mother today when your mother-in-law has just arrived?"

There was no time for explanation. Because of the communists, now I also had family problems!

I knew Rudi had not written to Silvia about my mother's situation because he didn't want to ruin his mother's hopes that he would be able to join her.

I put the receiver down and went back to my desk. I have no doubt there was a very troubled look on my face, because I was in a shock at the news that I would be seeing my mother after nine years, just at the time when my mother-in-law had come to visit.

Observing me, Mario asked if something happened. I whispered, "I found myself with two mothers in less than twenty-four hours."

Staring at me incredulously, he asked, "How come?" Then, with deep concern in his voice: "What are you going to do now?"

"First I have to come to my senses, and then get some money for a cab, in case I find her at the train station. I have to go there anyway to convince myself whether this for real or just a bad joke. Then I'll have to explain to Micu why I have to leave exactly at the month's end when we are busier than ever."

Mario immediately offered his help.

"You can count on me. I'll go to get you the money."

I don't know what he did or said, but when he returned he brought back twenty-five lei, while I talked to Micu. Since they saw how confused I was, they gave me careful instructions on how to get to the train station...

On my way, I was thinking how lucky I was that all this happened on a Thursday. It was the only day Aneta was in our home, and she had been there to spend the first day with Sylvia. On top of that, it was fortunate that she knew how to call me at the office to give me this incredible news.

But if it really was Mancy on the phone, I was wondering, how I would manage with two mothers arriving one after the other? As I was getting closer to the station, I felt excited to think I would see my mother, but I was really nervous at the thought that the phone call might have been a hoax. If so, it had forced me to leave the office in one of the worst days at the end of the month.

What followed were the series of events that I have described in the Prologue.

* * *

On our way home in the taxi, Mancy was eager to get information about what had happened while she was gone. The police had given her only my phone and address, but hadn't informed about Manini's death, and I had to break the news to her. She calmly said.

"I thought so, because they gave me your address, not hers."

She didn't cry; perhaps the emotion of getting out of prison had annihilated any other feelings. Then she asked about Gică and Nicu, and inquired about who was this Kleckner guy. I could see that even though my mother was physically weakened, her mind was sharp, and she had clear opinions.

Before we got home, I told her that my mother-in-law had arrived from Israel the day before, and she was staying with us. My mother looked at me and listened, but she didn't really register what I was saying. Her only concern was that I not forget and leave her bundles in the taxi.

The taxi stopped in front of our house. We went down the steps and entered the room where the two mothers now met. Silvia was all dressed up and elegant. She had found out from Aneta where my mother was coming from. Silvia became very emotional, especially when she saw Mancy's appearance. It was her first experience seeing somebody just released from prison—and not just any kind of prison but one with especially harsh conditions reserved for political prisoners. My mother was in a miserable state, having not slept, washed, or eaten for many hours.

Two worlds were meeting—-one of civilization and one of terror! There was no need for introductions or explanations. The two of them started talking to each other and my mother indignantly explained to Silvia that she was the last one to be released from prison. Looking at them, I couldn't believe my eyes: I suddenly had two mothers in my house, a picture I could not have imagined a day earlier. And at the same time, I was mentally comparing the cloth bundles at my mother's feet with Silvia's new, beautifully colored suitcases. Again, two contrasting worlds!

I phoned Micu at the office and told him briefly, "I found her, I will be in tomorrow."

In a way, it had been to my advantage that Comrade Gheorghe left information in my file, because Mancy's situation did not come as a surprise now. Faith always helped me!

When Rudi entered with Diky in the alley, the children were screaming, "Uncle Rudi, uncle Rudi, can you give us a ride?"

But this time, Rudi ignored the children and hurried to see how Silvia had spent her morning. I went to the door, took his hand and loudly announced, "Here are our mothers!"

My mother's appearance Rudi understood immediately, since he had already heard, in the city, a rumor about a massive release of political convicts. He hugged each mother, told them they were welcome in our house and that he was happy they could meet each other.

Out of curiosity, Aneta lingered after her work was done. I thought again how fortunate it was my mother had come on a Thursday when Aneta was home and able to connect the dots. God was helping me!

Like Silvia, Mancy asked for a shower. I took her straight to the laundry room. I heated the water, brought her one of my robes, a pair of Rudi's slippers, and everything else she needed, and explained her how to use the mug to pour the water overhead—explaining how the water flowed away under the grill towards the drain. In the meantime, Silvia was arranging the dishes. Rudi opened a bottle of wine while waiting for Mancy.

When I brought her back in, wearing my pink robe, she was looking better. I gave her the watch I had found at Manini's, and she seemed livelier with a glass of wine in front of her. But she still continued to ask me what I had done with her bundles. Then, she happily said how wonderful it was to be able to shower alone, without guards watching, without being hurried, and being able to use as much water she wanted. She added, laughing, "I even wasted too much water."

Rudi and I burst into laughter, while Silvia was slowly digesting what she had heard. Still, Silvia insisted, "It's better for the children to leave the country and have an apartment with a proper bathroom and kitchen, like normal people have."

My mother agreed, but she also stressed that for the time being our improvised shower was divine! Again I thought that everything is relative in this world; it depends on what reference marks you have.

Forced by the new circumstances, Rudi told Aristide we would be bringing Silvia over to sleep at their apartment. I also called my father's house.

When Florica answered the phone, I said, "Now we have two mothers, not one."

Florica, knowing what was happening in town, replied with a note of humor, "I'll invite all of you, including my husband's ex-wife, to our house to celebrate." She always was wonderful!

And Silvia did something I will never forget: she gave my mother three of her dresses, which would fit Mancy if she belted them at the waist. As for us, as it turned out we would sleep far longer than two weeks on Georgescu's mattress.

When things get complicated, they also get untangled. As a foreman, Rudi had free time between commuting to different construction sites, so he was able to take Mancy to the beauty parlor, to the Militia Office to get an identity card with our address, to the dentist, and other places. I was thinking that CZ's accident was really fortunate, because it made us buy a car (and the debts for it were now paid off). We were able to transport the two mothers much easily, taking them here and there on small trips through Bucharest.

At the end of August, Silvia left, and we promised her we would start the emigration procedures, and she replied by promising to send us some money in case we needed it. And we would ask Aunt Ida to sponsor our coming to America.

Physically, my mother was still very weak, but getting better and better by the day. She even started walking alone in the neighborhood. Her behavior hadn't been affected and she hadn't lost her humanity, even though she had been through extreme suffering and endured barbaric treatment.

Mancy had never been much of a mother to me, but she was a great lady, a patriot who survived the hell of humiliating and agonizing situations without breaking down. The way she was raised and educated played an important role. *"Elle est restée fidèle à soi-même!"*[71]

She was obsessed with the idea that Bobo, Dan Defleury's wife, was the one who had informed the Securitate about the spiritualism. And indeed, it was the very next day the Securitate had come, found the notebooks, and arrested my mother. Mancy was sure she wasn't wrong. I didn't want to believe it, but I didn't dispute her claims since both of us were only making assumptions.

Getting accustomed to a free lifestyle wasn't exactly easy for Mancy. Now she was sixty-one years old. She still hoped Romania would escape the communist system which had crushed thousands of souls—basically turning the whole country into an immense prison. Naturally, the anticommunist feelings were very strong. After so many years of imprisonment, she was eager to see places. So encouraged by the good weather, we left for a few days, taking her and Tănţica to the shores of the Black Sea to visit and see all that was worth seeing.

As our room had a street-level window, I couldn't help but see what was going on outside. One time, as I was talking to my mother, I saw something unusual—a big, grey Mercedes parking in front of the house. I wondered who it may be. Out of the car stepped a tall man who appeared to be looking for a house number and then headed towards our entrance. Immediately I heard the door bell ringing. I hurried to answer. And from the top of the stairs, whom did I see? It was Johann Schobel, my mother's former administrator from Radomir. In a burst of joy, knowing he had been arrested years ago, I asked him, "Where are you coming from, Johann, and where have you been until now?"

He kissed my hand and answered, "From Germany, actually from Craiova. I had to find out from Mister Dan where to find you. I heard about the death of the old lady. I'm sorry."

I invited him in, saying, "Wait, you'll be surprised!"

---

71.   French for "she remained truthful to herself."

It was like a bomb exploding! Mancy and Johann hadn't seen each other since they were both arrested on April 2, 1948. The reunion was the biggest event for both of them.

"How do you do, ma'am?" he asked while kissing both her hands. He was very excited to suddenly rediscover "people of his past" after all these years.

Mancy started questioning him to find out how long he had been imprisoned, in what prisons, where he was now living and what happened to his brother, Hansi. Before he could answer, I heard Diky and went to warn Rudi, who was quite annoyed that his parking spot had been taken up by this Mercedes. I told him who the Mercedes belonged to. Though Rudi hadn't met Johann, he knew who he was.

After introductions, Johann told us he had been sentenced to seven years and released in 1955. Hansi had been deported to URSS, where he died. He told us that he was married to a woman named Dorle who was also an ethnic Saxon[72] and together they had emigrated to Germany, where they were now living in Amberg, not far from Frankfurt and had two sons. They had come to visit Romania and were staying at a hotel for a few days. Johann first went to Craiova to find out about my mother's fate and where she could be found.

Johann looked really well. His blond hair had turned somehow whitish, but he was very energetic and asked us if he could send us anything from Germany. We promised that we are going to see each other again—next time with Dorle, too.

After Johann left, Rudi immediately thought that his offer was an extraordinary opportunity to replace Diky, which was requiring all sorts of expensive repairs. He suggested that we ask Johann to send a second-hand car, which we would pay for by asking Silvia to send Johann the money she had promised us.

I had another idea, also connected to the unique opportunity offered by the appearance of Johann—namely, that we could ask him to take Manini's jewelry to Tancy, in Paris. I knew the jewelry had no

---

72.   The label "Saxons" (in Romanian "'Saşi'") was applied to German settlers who migrated during the thirteenth century to southeastern Transylvania.

value in Romania since it couldn't be sold or worn, and we couldn't take it with us if we were able to leave. It was a valuable without value.

When Johann came the second time with Dorle, Rudi asked him about the possibility of sending a car. I asked him if he could take the jewelry package to Tancy, adding that he could sell a small brooch that had been intended for me by Manini, in case Silvia's money wasn't enough. After thinking it through, Johann said, "I can, and I want to help you. I'll first take care of the car to see how much it costs, and then I'll go to Paris to deliver the jewelry to Mrs. Tancy."

I had told my mother about the jewelry that Diamandopol gave me, and she agreed with my proposal, trusting Johann. Then I gave him the cotton canvas package that I had taken back from my father. Thus, I had one less thing to worry about—the feeling that Manini's jewelry, as I have mentioned, was exposing us to all kinds of dangers.

During our last meeting with Dorle and Johann, Tănțica came to join us. She had been forced to divorce Gică Busuiocescu—who had been found and arrested—to get a job for herself. Now she was staying in a studio on the top floor of a building in the center of Bucharest. Then my mother recounted the story of her arrest in Craiova and told us a great deal about what happened afterwards. (Much later, when she was in New York, she would write about these events in more detail in her memoirs.)

After Johann and Dorle left, I was eager to find out whether they arrived safely in Amberg, whether Sylvia sent them the money she promised us, and whether the new car was on its way.

After a few days, I got a call from Johann and I was relieved to find out they had arrived safely in Amberg. Shortly after, I got a letter from Silvia letting us know that she had sent the money to Johann; and by the end of October, we got word from Johann that he had sent us a grey, second-hand Ford Taunus. Right about that time, a gentleman came from Paris with Nicu Herescu's fur-lined leather coat, a gift sent by Tancy for Rudi. The same gentleman conveyed to us the information that Johann had come to visit Tancy in Paris and she thanked us for the package he had delivered to her. Everything worked out as planned!

Mostly, I was glad that I could save something from underneath the communist claw and that I had fulfilled Manini's wish.

The only concern now was finding my mother a place to live. I put out the word, and shortly thereafter, Tănţica gave me an address where two sisters living in an apartment were renting out a room. We went to see it. Mancy liked it because it was next to the Cişmigiu Park and had access to a kitchen and bathroom. The problem was to get the official approval from the local Housing Authority and Dwelling Space Administration. I had to show proof that I was employed, since I was the one who was going to pay her rent. Again, DSAPC's director Tavi Ţurcanu, showed a lot of sympathy and signed the certificate knowing well why I was asking, and for whom. Looking back, I'm glad he had found out from my file about my mother's situation; thus it was no longer a surprise for him, nor was it an embarrassing or difficult situation for me.

After getting official approval from the Housing Office, we had to actually move my mother over there. That's where Rudi stepped in. He took out the furniture from underneath the Georgescu family balcony, and we bought a bed. After Mancy settled in, we finally got to sleep in our own bed—after three months of sleeping on a mattress on the floor.

Now that Mancy was better, she started seeing her friends. She was always welcome, along with us, in my father's house. Fortunately my father's wife Florica and my mother, his ex-wife, were getting along very well. Bottom line, Mancy ended up socializing mostly with the Vrăbiescus —the same people she had been running away from after she divorced my father.

Ever since we had gotten married, Rudi used to tell me about New York. "I close my eyes and just see myself there," he would say, without even knowing he had family there. Now, ever since the visit from Rudi's New York family members, he had dreamt even more frequently of going there. And after Silvia's arrival he became more insistent about filing emigration application papers.

Once when we were visiting Mrs. Raia Nicolau, who just came back from her brother in New York, she told us with a sad smile, "I'm afraid you're going to be unhappy there; people are different from

Europeans and from us." Looking at Rudi, she added, "Maybe you are better off staying here."

Of course, she could not convince him because his mind was already made up. He was set upon leaving for the West and escaping the communist dictatorship that still ruled the country with an iron fist. The idea of immigrating to a normal democratic country also started to appeal to me since I was a pariah and a "class enemy' in my own country. So with every passing day, I was more and more convinced the time had come for us to break free from this system that poisoned our existence. Luckily, I was still at an age when my imagination was seeking to explore the unknown, of which I was not afraid compared to where we were coming from. I was certain nothing could possibly be worse.

I often thought about the changes that came after 1945—all modeled after the Russian system—which finally brought me to the point where I was now ready to leave my own country—a country where I had grown up and had my roots.

In retrospect the evil started during the WWII, when Roosevelt trusting Stalin was seeking his friendship, naming him "Uncle Joe." Dr. H. Kissinger gave a clear picture of what happened: "Roosevelt rejected the idea that a total defeat of Germany might create a vacuum, which a victorious Soviet Union might then try to fill. Churchill had wanted to reconstruct the traditional balance of power in Europe. This meant rebuilding Great Britain, France, and even defeated Germany so that, along with the United States, these countries could counterbalance the Soviet colossus to the east. Stalin…strove to extend Russian influence into Central and Eastern Europe…to turn them into buffer zones to protect Russia against any future German aggression."

And "Roosevelt envisioned a postwar order in which the three victors (the USA, England, and Russia) along with China would act as a board of directors of the world, enforcing the peace against any potential miscreant, which he thought would most likely be Germany—a vision that was to become known as the Four Policeman. He refused to countenance safeguards against possible postwar rivalry among the victors, because these implied the reestablishment of the balance of power, which he in fact wanted to destroy. Peace would be preserved by a system of collective security maintained by the wartime Allies acting in concert and sustained by mutual goodwill and vigilance…an international harmony." (Kissinger, Henry, *Diplomacy*, pages 395–398).

As a result, after the Yalta Conference, Eastern European countries were swallowed up by a system where people were treated as mere objects, as described by Mark R. Levin in his book *Ameritopia*.

Just around that time, though, the Ford Taunus arrived from Germany. It was a brand new toy for Rudy, and drew his full attention. As soon as the weather got warmer, he wanted to test the car by taking a longer trip. Thus, starting the paperwork for our exit visa application got postponed for a while. We sold Dicky, the DKW car, easily but I had a hard time letting it go, since I had pleasant memories related to it.

1965

We were usually invited by Sandu Missirliu, but this time his girlfriend Graţiela was the one to invite us, and we found out that he already was gone to Paris to his brother Dinu and mother. Graţiela told us she was going to stay in Sandu's apartment with her mother until he would be able to get her out as well.

During this time, there were elections for the Romania's unicameral communist Parliament called the Grand National Assembly, when Romania's leader G. G. Dej initiated an even more autonomous direction away from Moscow. We were taken aback, when we heard the news of Dej's death on March 19. His death aroused suspicions, some believing it to have been caused by an aggressive cancer that was the result of an assassination (using a form of high-intensity radiation) that had been ordered by Khrushchev. Dej's successor was Nicolae Ceauşescu.

Following these events, Rudi and I waited to see what would be Ceauşescu's position on emigration. We had to choose Israel as our destination if we stood any chance at all of leaving. In Dej's time, between 1958 and 1965, Romania opened its doors and allowed over one hundred thousand people to emigrate each year. (Ioanid, Radu, *The ransom of the Jews*, page 93). In June 1965 Ceausescu finally stated his views on Romania's international policy. He proclaimed an internal liberalization of sorts and a kind of active neutrality in international engagements. What he wanted to show the Occident was Romania's external emancipation, a sort of declaration of independence from Moscow. He strove to create an image of someone who, just like Dej, was in opposition to the COMECOM Treaty.

In fact, just like Dej, Ceaușescu clung to Stalinist internal policy, favoring the system of strict planning and censorship. A Communist Party Congress nominated Ceaușescu to succeed Dej, and on August 21, a new Constitution was adopted when the country was renamed plainly "Romania" (replacing the pompous "People's Republic of Romania"). Private initiative was encouraged, and small private businesses were allowed.

The subject of emigration was never brought up during the Congress. We were afraid that Ceaușescu would reduce the number of emigrant Jews (The number of emigrant Jews was 10,949, and in 1966 they fell as low as 3,647 (Ioanid, Radu, op. cit., page 93) Therefore, Rudi and I decided to submit our applications, fearing that if we waited any longer they might suppress emigration altogether. At the time, the flight from Bucharest to Israel passed through Rome, where we hoped to be able to switch our route toward the USA.

We went at the Passport Office at three in the morning and waited in a very long line for the office to open, hoping the office would not close its doors before our turn came. I was actually very skeptical that we would ever get the approval because I was not Jewish.

Knowing the answer to our request was going to take a while, immediately after submitting the papers, we left with the new car and drove Mancy to the Black Sea. After all these years that she had spent in prison, we were happy to be able to give her the pleasure of spending time outdoors.

After we returned, Mancy joined some of her former cellmate friends on a trip to the mountain resort of Vatra Dornei. Nothing

happens without a reason. Over there they met by chance a gentleman who had just gotten out of prison himself and was waiting
for approval to go to Paris. When mother heard the word *Paris*, she
told the gentlemen about her sister Tancy who also lived there. The
gentleman, whose name was Penescu, turned out to be the Minister
of Internal Affairs in the last "bourgeois" government. He had managed to leave for Paris in September 1968, and there he had met
Tancy, who was Herescu's widow, living there since 1958. Penescu
proposed and they got married. This was Mancy's indirect doing for
her sister. In Paris Penescu kept in touch with the Romanian Royal
House in Versoix Switzerland, and worked against Ceaușescu's communist government.

* * *

One morning, I was in the office when a coworker told me that Rudi
was waiting for me downstairs and wouldn't come up. I wondered
why he didn't want to come upstairs, as he had done so many other
times. This time, we met on the stairs where he told me in a whisper,
"I read the list of emigration approvals at the Israeli Consulate, but
only my name was on it, not yours. I asked where I could find out
more on the matter, and I was told my best bet would be to set up an
appointment to see the Consul. The Consul agreed to see me, and I
told him about my problem. He calmed me down, saying that if in
two weeks your name does not appear on the list, I should go to see
him again."

We were both extremely excited. I was reliving the hard
moments with Stephen and was glad I hadn't said anything to Gică
yet. Of course Rudi assured me that he would not leave without me;
he headed to the exit door while I returned to my office, trying not to
look nervous or upset. I only shared Rudi's words with Mario. Later,
back at home, the conversation revolved about a single subject.

After two weeks, my name came up on the list as well, and in
the middle of September, we received a postcard in the mail from the
Ministry of Internal Affairs with approval for both of us. The postcard indicated what documents we were supposed to submit and told
us where to go. To most people a post card is just a piece of paper,

nothing special—but I felt as if I was looking at something beyond this world, the message I had been waiting for so many long years, ever since I had tried to join Stephen. And now that I had it in hand, my feelings, strangely, were, as always, of great joy and sadness at the same time. I called Florica to let her know what had happened, asking her not to tell my father. What I wanted her was to prepare him with her own thoughts—that, abroad, I would have a more fulfilled professional life free of the menace of a dangerous "file." In speaking to Florica, it was with the knowledge that Gică had to be prepared beforehand of the news that would be like a blow to him. Florica just was my good luck!

When Rudi came home, he jumped with joy. He thought everything had been solved. But nothing was actually certain. Even after having their passports approved and issued, some people found that the Passport Office revoked them on the basis of some error that was a "technicality." If you were allowed to leave the country—only with a very limited number of personal belongings, and supposed to give up your dwelling and register it with the Housing Authority—sometimes some passports were revoked, living people on the streets, without homes and without any income. In any case we had to prove we had no properties at the Revenue Office, no debts at work, no unpaid telephone bills—and so on and so forth.

The ownership of the car was the big problem, because we had to find a buyer to pay customs. When the Taunus was brought into the country, we paid half of the custom tax with money from selling Diky. If we sold it in less than ten years from the day we received it, the law said we had to pay the rest of the tax, meaning another twenty thousand lei, which we didn't have. So we were in a hurry to leave, but we were stuck because of the car. There were no buyers, and Rudi was nervous and anxious.

One night, I dreamed about a pink elephant, as huge as the surrounding houses, sitting on his back legs like a dog, at the head of the alley. When I woke up, I told Rudi that the elephant was good luck and maybe represented a buyer. He didn't believe in dreams, so he laughed. Around lunch time he called me at the office to tell me that in the morning after I had left, a guy called and then came to see the Taunus, liked it and agreed to pay forty thousand lei. Rudi added, "From now on, I'll believe in your dreams!"

A weight had been lifted from my chest! Two days later, we were no longer registered as owners at the Revenue Office.

We still had to obtain a certificate from work to prove we didn't owe anything to the State. I got mine from DSAPC, on November 5ᵗʰ 1965. I will never forget when I went to say good-bye to Director Tavi Ţurcanu. He gave me a hug and whispered in my ear, "I'm happy for you, Simona and I wish you a good trip!"

I was really moved by his gesture. Even though I went through a lot of trouble because of my personal file that was traveling with me to all jobs I had, I met a lot of nice people in the process I owed my thanks to people like Octavian Ţurcanu, Nelu Lungu, and Micu who got me out of trouble; thanks to them I was able to hold on to my work until my departure from the country. What is indeed moving is the fact that the Lungu's, their daughter and her husband Bebe Popovici, have remained our friends until today.

Regarding Rudi, he met a bump in the road at the Cooperative before getting his approvals, being under suspicion for doing illicit business with the State's money. The leading people in his Cooperative were probably wondering where he got the money for a fur-lined leather coat and how he was able to afford the Taunus car. Since he knew he wanted to leave the country, he was totally clean. He had avoided any kind of wrongdoing such as taking or giving bribes for favors, which was almost a common habit among his coworkers.

Rudi got all the required signatures from the lower-level managers, stating that he didn't owe anything to the State. But now, when it was time for the president to sign the approval document, he dragged his feet and did not sign. Rudi immediately suspected that he probably expected a tip, but it was impossible to know whether he wanted the money for himself or whether he was laying a trap to offer the Securitate people proof of Rudi's corruption.

This is how Rudi described the scene, "The president was looking at me, not signing, and I was looking at him, waiting. There were tense moments with neither of us backing off. If I had given him money, I would have taken a great risk, so I decided not to.

He wasn't signing, and he wasn't saying anything. Finally, without a valid argument against signing, and seeing all the other signatures, he finally signed the paper and gave it back to me, in a rude way. I could have given him the money, because I had it, but I didn't want to take the risk."

At the beginning of November, we went to submit the required documents to the authorities to get our passports with "exit visas." We were told that we would be informed where to go to get the travel documents. We thought that was the right time to tell Gică and Nicu, because I wanted to give them some time to get used to the idea. However, as usual, I only informed Florica first.

I went to see Ileana Crătunescu, Ioana's first cousin, who promised me that as soon as she knew my departure date, she would call Ioana in Rome so she could meet us at the airport.

Also, one of my office colleagues, Irina Luca, asked me if I would take a letter for one of her dear friends in the USA. I answered that I did not know whether I would end up there, and besides I was not allowed to carry any kind of written document with me, not even an address. She insisted and showed me what she had written to her friend, Edith Răileanu from New York, with her address and phone number on the envelope, adding, "If the customs people take it, don't worry. But if you can get it to her, she will be very happy."

What was I to say? I took with good will the envelope, which was a simple courtesy gesture on her behalf, and didn't appear to be compromising me in any way. But little did I know then that God was really taking care of me already—and so far in advance?

I finally saw Mario, who offered us a money-exchange deal. Based on what we would give him—some money for his former girlfriend's mother in Romania—we were to receive the equivalent of money in any currency we preferred from her daughter in Switzerland. I was grateful, as we were not allowed to take any money with us and that seemed to be the only way for us to get some pocket money abroad. Mario gave me the address indicating where I should go to request the foreign currency. Obviously, I had to memorize it.

Having had no answer from the authorities by Thursday, November 11, I came up with the idea of visiting Tănțica, since she was really good at fortune telling. We went in the evening. I told her that we had submitted the emigration papers and we were waiting for a reply. She was happy for us, immediately prepared some coffee, started to shuffle the cards, and looked for the corn kernels which she then let fall on the table. She examined the shape in which they fell, and after looking at the palm of my left hand, she started to tell my fortune. It lasted nearly an hour.

I will only provide a summary of the main ideas, but her words are ones that I have not forgotten to this day. She said, "You're leaving. But there will be a big commotion. You're getting out like a camel through the eye of a needle. I can't say when—two weeks or two months, but not two years. To be fair, I'll just say in two points."

After a moment of silence, she added, while twisting the coffee cup, "You're going somewhere but you won't stay there, you'll settle somewhere else."

With a darkened face, and while exposing the cards, she looked at me with her blue eyes—eyes which I had known well, ever since I had been a child in Bârca. Then she added, "After another two points, be it months or years from the time you settled, you will be between life and death. But, Monile, you'll make it!"

Seeing that she was sure of what she was telling me, I asked, "How did you learn to tell people's fortunes?"

"My dear," she answered, "before 1949 when I still was in Bârca, a gipsy woman passing by our estate entrance told me, 'Missis, come, let me give you the power of the ghioc.'"[73]

The gypsy did not lie. I could attest to that myself, later in life. Tănţica got this gift from the gypsy woman in Bârca and was able to foresee her own future (a story which I will tell in full detail later).

Next day, Friday November 12, we received a postcard letting us know that we should report at the Bucharest Passport Office on Saturday November 13 at 9:00 a.m. That was all.

We had no idea what was in store for us, whether we would get the passports or if we were being asked to bring other documents. Meanwhile, we hadn't done much except preparing Manini's

---

73.   A concha sea shell

coliva.[74] This was a commemoration at Saint Elefterie Church to honor her passing—which had occurred one week before November 20, when she had closed her eyes forever under my watch in the Craiova hospital.

On, Saturday November 13, arriving at the Passport Office, we were wondering whether the thirtieth day would be a good omen or not. Having heard our names, the clerk told us to wait for a moment. He left. My heart was racing. He came back quickly holding some papers and saying, "These are your travel papers released by the Ministry of Interior of the Romanian Popular Republic, for a trip from Romania to Israel."

I couldn't believe my ears. We figured that no passport or additional documents were needed! After being handed these documents, we were asked to sign the Romanian citizenship renunciation forms. This was the most difficult signature I had written in my whole life. In short, we entered this Office as Romanians and came out being stateless!

Back in the street, we looked at the travel documents. Rudi's was approved on July 24, 1965, and mine on August 14, 1965. They were both valid for one year, the entry in Israel being limited to August 30, 1966. The documents had transit visas through Austria and Italy, also valid for one year. So there was no reason to rush, we had plenty of time. But Rudi was keen to get out as fast as possible.

We went to the Romanian air transport company TAROM to buy our plane tickets. After standing in line for a long time, we found out that the planes to Israel via Rome were fully booked and were told to try again in two weeks. Rudi was unhappy about the delay; I felt more at ease since that gave me more time to speak to my dad, to schedule the requiem for Manini, to get my things from the tailor, to pack the luggage for customs, and to give away everything I had in my house (which had to be done because our room would be handed over empty to the People's Council). As we were advised, we bought

---

74. Boiled wheat pie with raisins, chopped walnuts, and honey, which is used liturgically in the Eastern Orthodox and Greek-Catholic Churches to commemorate the dead

a few links of Romanian Sibiu hard salami and Kent cigarettes. Both were on the list of items that we were allowed to take with us and that could be easily sold upon arrival for Italian liras. We had plenty to do, but I thought two weeks would be sufficient for that. At least that's what I thought.

It was too early in the morning to go to my father after we had left the TAROM offices, so I suggested to Rudi that, instead, we should go to the Ministry of Foreign Affairs to find out about the possibility of having my Law Degree translated. All of a sudden, while on our way, Rudi had to use the toilet. We were close to Sandu and Graţiela's house, and we thought that even if she had already left for work her mother would let us in. When we approached we saw her car first, and then she herself opened the door. I asked her why she wasn't at work that day.

She replied, "I didn't feel like going. But what are you doing here so early in the morning, and without telling me beforehand that you were coming?"

While Rudi was in the bathroom, I gave her all the necessary details, relating what TAROM had told us. Gratiela looked at me wide-eyed and seemingly alarmed, almost shouting, "There is no way you can wait for two weeks. These guys can always take your travel documents back and leave you jobless and on the streets."

Of course, she was right, we had heard of such cases, but what were we to do? Then I saw her walking towards the phone. S h e dialed a number and asked, "Is that you, Carmen? Look…they got their travel documents today, but you told them that all flights to Rome were fully booked."

There was silence, during which the one named Carmen was obviously speaking.

Rudi was just coming out of the bathroom when Graţiela, holding the phone and speaking loudly, asked him, "Could you leave on Monday, fifteenth, in the morning. Carmen has just received two returned tickets to Israel via Rome?"

Without even glancing at me, Rudi answered, "Yes. We can. We'll go to get the tickets straight away."

I froze; all my plans were shattered. What would I do about Gică and Nicu?

On our way back to TAROM, I thought about what had happened. We had gone to Grațiela's only because of Rudy's needs; she happened to have skipped work that day; she happened to know this TAROM employee Carmen who just got back two tickets after we had just left TAROM. There had been one coincidence after the other, all meant to expedite the "two points" departure predicted by Tănțica.

Then we gave Grațiela Tante Ida's New York address, so that Sandu could inform her that we had received authorization to leave the country, and Ida could proceed accordingly. Back home, I wrote Silvia a few words to let her know what happened.

We were in a terrible rush, becoming "the camel going through the needle's eye." We got the tickets, called Florica to let her know we were going to visit them in the afternoon, spoke to Aristide, called Aneta to come and finish the slow boiling coliva. We asked my mother to attend the religious service without us and asked the tailor and shoemaker to have everything finished by the evening since all our belongings had to reach customs the next morning. (Each of us was allowed to bring only one suitcase.)

We rang Tănțica and Ileana Poenaru and asked them to help mother with Manini's service.

Rudi ran to the People's Council to see Mister Andreescu, Nelu Strass's acquaintance, asking him to send someone over the next day, a Sunday, at four in the afternoon, to get the keys and give us a note saying we freed our "dwelling space." Our departure depended on that note since we could not leave the country without it.

In the meantime, I packed our bags with unwashed laundry and hid Irina's letter in the lining of my bag. When Rudi came back, we both went to Miliției Street. I was overwhelmed and tired. Who would have imagined in the morning the avalanche of things that had come upon us?

Tănțica later said to me, "Have you noticed the two points I predicted?"

Obviously the span of time had been from the thirteenth to the fifteenth of November 1965, dates I'll never forget.

My father had found out from Florica that we had the tickets for the day after tomorrow, early in the morning. In hindsight, this great haste was welcomed. It was like an emergency surgery, when no one has any time left to consider the risks and to wonder whether you should have it or not. So arriving at Miliției Street after the hugs, what came next were not tears of sorrow, instead, we proceeded to organize for emptying our room. From there we went to the tailor and the shoemaker to pick up our orders and to pack them our shoes and clothing in our luggage. We were all in full alert, it was pure madness!

The two of us had a long wait at the Customs' until we got through, but the inspection went quickly, and there were no issues. We had packed nothing but clothes, fifty kilograms per person. Irina's letter passed inspection, unseen in the lining. As I previously said, I had thought it was nothing more than a goodwill gesture for two friends. However it was much, much more!

When we got back home, our room was empty. Nothing was left. I was pleased that part of Manini's furniture was now with Tănţica and that the big Galle lamp was now with my father. We didn't care about the rest.

It was critical for our departure to get the note from the People's Council man. He had to give official confirmation that we had handed him the keys to our vacated apartment that could now be assigned to somebody else.

It was well past four o'clock, and no one came. Physically and mentally tired, we both sat on the floor looking out the window. In the afternoon silence I left the house for a while, then returned, impatiently checking my wrist watch. As I peered out the window again, I could feel something like a block of ice forming slowly in my stomach, sending continuous shivers up and down my veins. I felt like I wanted to shout aloud, just to let it all out. We were waiting for a man we didn't even know personally. We had no idea what he looked like; we had no name; nor did we know where he was coming from on this Sunday afternoon! Our entire future depended on him.

He was now the one person who could ruin not only our departure, but we would get stuck in the country with no place to go to, no clothes, no income, nothing. A disaster which happened to others in our situation.

In those difficult moments I tried my best to remain rational and keep my sanity. As the tension grew, I started saying prayers. It was almost five now, and started getting dark outside. I knew that mother had invited people over to her house to share Manini's coliva, and we should have been there as well. I left Rudi in the apartment and went over to Mancy, thinking that my presence couldn't bring that man anyway. Actually, even as I left the house and the Dr. Pasteur Lane, it was without even realizing that it was the last time in my life I would leave that place. I had said good-bye to my neighbors the day before.

I was really tense. When I arrived at my mother's, she was star-tled to see how I looked. There I was, sitting on a bed of nails, with a knotted stomach. Around six o'clock, Rudi rang and told me, "The guy came slowly down the street around a quarter to six, after his lunch and an afternoon nap; he didn't even look into the room to see if it was empty or furnished. He handed me the proof that the apartment had been vacated and, after I rewarded him for taking the trouble to come on a Sunday, he left. I'll be over soon."

Only then did my stomach settle down, and I could finally have a taste of Manini's coliva. May God rest her soul!

When Rudi arrived, we took the rest of coliva. Then Mancy, Tănţica, and Ileana, we all crammed into a taxi going to Miliţiei Street.

There were almost sixty friends gathered to see us for the last time. Luckily, some people were just arriving while others were leav-ing. Cristina promised she'd come to see Gică often and take care of him, and so did Liky. An unexpected guest was Bacal, the lawyer, who was supposed to help me join Stephen. What comes round goes round! It was now Bacal's turn to ask me favors, since a friend over-seas had promised to help him somehow. Bacal gave me the friend's address, which I again I had to memorize. My head was about to explode!

All those present promised they would visit Mancy frequently, so that she wouldn't feel alone.

Out of all my friends who were saying good-bye, the parting from Nicu was the most difficult. He asked me not to forget my country, my roots, and the Romanian land. He was the only one in whose arms I cried. It was like we both felt we wouldn't see each other again.

Nelu and Cici were to come in the morning and drive us to the airport in their car. Others said they would be at the airport in the morning, coming by car and motorbike.

I couldn't sleep a wink during the short night that followed. Early on the morning of Monday November 15, 1965, I jumped out of bed, standing on my toes with my hands straight up in the air. This was the day that was going to take me to freedom. I was glowing with joy, but it was most usual, happiness mixed with sadness and grief as I always had to experience.

My sole comfort was that I was leaving Gică surrounded by three ladies—Florica, Viorica and Ziguța. Coca and Titi had managed to move out, but they were coming daily to visit. Saying good-bye to all of them was very difficult. With Florica in particular, I found it very hard to say good-bye; she was an extraordinary person who had offered me a tremendous amount of support. We promised Gică and Florica they could come visit us as soon as we got everything organized—and we were making this promise with certainty in our voice and hearts. This separation broke my heart in two, because I was leaving the country I loved with no prospect of coming back.

Nelu came over early, at half past five in the morning. The tragic moment had come. I asked my father not to come with us to the airport; Gică and I had tears in our eyes but we were trying to hold them back, although unsuccessfully. I hugged him and the others, then quickly turned my head, going down the three flights of stairs with Rudi behind me. In the car, Cici comforted me while I looked out the window, registering the last remaining images that I would keep in my mind.

Our friends who had come by car or motorcycle met us at the airport: there were Pupi and Costin, Grațiela, Mitzy and Liky, little Ioana, and others. All of us were together, chatting, when suddenly someone shouted that all travelers to Rome should proceed to another room. In great haste, with no time for hugs, Rudi and I headed for that room. It had been a rapid rupture.

Rudi was still apprehensive, wondering if the authorities could still hold him back because of some error or some misrepresentation in the emigration papers. Every time the door opened and a clerk scrutinized us, Rudi's blood pressure shot up. When the door closed, he calmed down again. This happened several times, until we were taken to the exit and led towards the airplane.

We climbed the airplane's stairs, got in, and took our seats— me at the window, Rudi next to me. Yet he remained tense because he had heard stories about people being called back, even from the airplane. Every two minutes he would ask me to look out the window and check to see if the stairs were still there. He held my hand, squeezing it until it hurt, especially when I answered that the stairs were still in their place. I kept my eyes on the stairs until finally, they were taken away. With the engines running, the airplane began slowly moving as we headed towards the runway.

We could still see the group of friends we were leaving behind. They waved good-bye while we were crying. During the lift-off, we watched that group became smaller and smaller until it disappeared. Soon we were flying over Romania's plains, which were quickly scrolling under our eyes. Then we were in the clouds, and the earth below disappeared as well.

I couldn't believe we were flying away from the communist hell, even though it was all happening seventeen years later than I had hoped. The difference was that back on 1948 I had only wanted to see Stephen. But now, with Rudi next to me, the twenty years of communist experience became pregnant and precisely more important. They had become an indelible part of my consciousness, and will remain so, fact that I will have the opportunity to deal at the right time. But for now, I was calm in that airplane and my soul empty. All I had left was Rudi.

CHAPTER 9

Italy and France
(November 15, 1965-
April 27, 1966)

Rudi and I were now on board the plane, our destination Rome. Rudi continued to be very nervous at the thought that a simple phone call from authorities might be enough to force the pilot to bring us back to Bucharest. I, on the contrary, was quite sure that in another three hours we would finally be in the free world—after twenty years of anticipation and repeated disappointments. I was more concerned about how we would manage to make our way from Rome to America instead of going on to Israel. But I was convinced that this was in the hands of the Lord.

Although I was distancing myself every second from Romania, in my mind I was still there. With eyes shut, I saw myself again in Genune, sitting next to Nicu, who would tell me about my ancestors while he passed some of the rich soil from hand to hand, saying, "When you grow up take care of this land of ours, it is the cradle of our family."

My eyes filled with tears, knowing that I would be far away from the land I loved so much, not because I wanted to leave but because I had been pushed in this direction by impossible circumstances.

I recalled the big tongues of fire rising in Genune's backyard on August 23, 1944, like an omen of danger and bad fortune; or the Russian tanks biting up the pavement with their engines spitting black smoke when they passed me by with deafening sound on Severin Street in Craiova. I remembered March 23, 1945, great expropriation when we'd lost almost all of Genune's agricultural land; or the November 19, 1946, so-called free elections when the communists faked ballots and stole votes and remained in office; or the August 15 monetary stabilization when the government took away all our savings. Still vivid in my mind was the date August 16, 1947, when Stephen made his marriage proposal and when I left Genune forever; or the December 30, 1947, when our Monarchy was abolished, crushing the last obstacle before the communists were able to take over complete control and impose their criminal policies. I went back to the big 1949 agricultural collectivization, resulting in the complete destruction of landowners, the kulaks, and peasants; or the April 19, 1950, nationalization of private houses when we ceased to become owners and were turned into tenants to the State; or the date August 7, 1952, when, in three hours, we were ruthless evicted from our house in Armașului Lane. And finally, I recalled my married life which started and ended caused by political reasons.

With all these memories overwhelming me, I could only relax when I recalled the courage I had to move in with my father and then, finally, when I got my own place in Dr. Pasteur Lane.

While the old engines of a DC 7 jet were whirling, my mind was fighting my soul. The former had to convince the latter that I did the right thing leaving the country. The real and only cause was the totalitarian-communist system, which works against human nature.

Finding myself up in the air, between two worlds, I had the opportunity to weigh what I had done and was confident that I had been right to leave. Moreover to demonstrate that I could ignore the Iron Curtain, freedom that was denied to me three times. However, I felt the pain of separation from the people I loved and regretted leaving Romania in Ceaușescu's grip of power; he was a shoemaker apprentice with Marxist-communist ideas who had now turned into supreme leader.

While deep in my thoughts, all of a sudden I was brought back to reality by a thunderstorm, the plane jolting very hard as it fell into an air pocket. We had to fasten our seat belts. Since this was Rudi's first experience flying and I had travelled on a plane just once before, we were really scared. And besides, I was curious about who would take care of us and what would happen next. As time passed, my nervous tension got bigger and bigger.

Then, the storm calmed down, we were flying smoothly, and at last I could see the airport in the distance, like a shining square. I breathlessly awaited the landing and felt great relief as the wheels made first contact with the ground, turning our plane into a gigantic taxi. When we got permission to leave Rudi was still hoping that our name would not be mentioned before descending.

When we had safely arrived on Italian soil, Rudi looked more relaxed. Nonetheless he urged me to move ahead as quickly as possible to the customs desk, beyond which the Romanian government had no more authority.

Arriving in front of the customs, the officer stamped our travel certificates without asking any question, and we stepped into the Fiumicino airport's premises. Then only, we finally shook off that feeling of uncertainty or danger which I had been feeling for the past twenty years, ever since communism had swallowed Romania, and even during this flight. What an unspeakable relief that was!

Rudi mentioned, as well, having the same feeling.

"It's just now that I no longer feel tension and fear! I will keep in mind this day of November 15, 1965, as one of liberation."

In no time I got back the energy I needed to face other kind of worries, namely the problem of avoiding Israel in order to reach America. Indeed, it wasn't long before a gentleman approached us and introduced himself as Mr. Sommer. He told us in Romanian that he was the representative of Israel's SOHNUT organization and informed us that he would accompany us to Napoli. At the same time, he asked us to hand him over our travel certificates. I was looking for Ioana. When I raised my eyes and looked beyond the glass doors, I saw her tall silhouette. It was obvious that she was looking for me. And also then Rudi saw Hugo who was there, too. (Hugo had left Bucharest two months before us, and Rudi wanted to find out from him all the details about changing our path from Israel to the USA.) We told Mr. Sommer that before we did anything else, we wanted to see the friends who were waiting for us.

Seeing Ioana after twenty one years, I found her nearly unchanged. We embraced, crying and laughing with joy. When I introduced Rudi to her, Mr. Sommer intruded to take us with him. Then Ioana, full of life and initiative, as I had always known her to be, intervened in Italian and persuaded him to let us go to the rail station in her car. She said we needed to have a brief chat and catch up with things after so many years. Mr. Sommer, being polite, didn't object, secure in the knowledge that our travel certificates and suit-cases were with him.

As we were crossing Rome, Ioana tried to give us details about various tourist attractions—statues, fountains, the Coliseum or Roman amphitheater built by Emperor Vespasian back in the '69-'79s. At the same time, she was insisting, "You have to do whatever you can to go to America. Look me up at this address and telephone me if you need me."

I tucked her address and phone number into my purse.

Also I was listening to what Hugo had to say, to Rudi in the back seats. Knowing that we were tired, he had written everything down on a piece of paper, which Rudi handed to me saying, "Keep it, I will read it later since right now I cannot retain anything!"

He was right, our heads were spinning and we couldn't retain anything! There had been too many events since our wake-up early that morning, with separations which tore our souls, a stormy flight, and seeing again dear friends. And now we were finding ourselves at Mr. Sommer's mercy—an unknown man bent on sending us to Israel via Napoli.

When we reached the railway station, following farewell hugs, Hugo returned downtown with Ioana while Mr. Sommer installed us in the train. Being late, the only empty seats he found were in first class, but he said that wasn't any problem, since controllers were used to accommodating refugees travelling from Rome to Napoli. We were in a compartment with an Italian middle-aged couple, sitting by the window. The lady was wearing a mink coat and had in her lap a small Pekinese wearing a topknot of hair tied with a little red bow, which she was cuddling and scratching with long fingers whose red polish nails matching the dog's bow. The gentlemen had grey hair and a tiny mustache resembling Don Ameche's; he was wearing a grey blazer with a handkerchief in the upper left pocket. After the train's departure, I fell asleep. Later I was awakened by the controller who punched the two passengers' tickets first and then, seeing that we didn't hand him our tickets and were not speaking Italian, the elder gentlemen said in French, "Lady, if you were late and hadn't time to buy tickets, you can buy them now from the controller." I answered, "I thank you, but we don't have money." Looking stunned, he continued, "If you don't have cash, perhaps you have a card and an ID." I said, annoyed, "We don't have a card, we don't have money, we don't have ID, and we are part of a group!"

A little out of temper, he said, "*Ecoutez, madame, on ne part pas sans argent ou sans un passeport!*" (Look lady, you don't take a trip without money, or a passport!)

The controller was waiting for the translation of our conversation.

The gentlemen turned to the controller and said with disgust, "These passengers have no money, no card and have no ID, saying they are part of a group."

Only then did the controller realize that we were part of the group of refugees and said that we could stay in place. Our companions looked quite astonished, so I then felt bound to explain our situation. They listened; however the man wondered why the Romanian authorities would allow people to leave their country without at least a minimum amount of money. How could I explain? All I could think was that I immediately became aware how ignorant the Italians were with regard to what was going on in the communist East, not too far away from their border. I was thinking how naïve these uninformed Italians were.

In Napoli, we were lodged at the Naples Hotel, where we had lunch and dinner. The hotel functioned like a guesthouse; that's where we were supposed to stay until we were assigned a town of residence in Israel. In the meantime, Mr. Sommer kept our travel certificates and gave us a small amount of Italian pocket money so we could travel around the city.

Once installed in our room, we read Hugo's letter. He was advising us to go to the JOINT's office, the Jewish organization of social assistance. He gave us the address and instructed us how we should explain our reason for wanting to go to America rather than Israel. Hugo underlined the fact that we should insist a lot, because their rules were very strict, the problem being that Israel was paying the Romanian state a certain amount of currency for each emigrant; therefore, it was expecting that emigrants should reach their destination in Israel rather than Europe or the USA. At that time, we were not yet informed about the fact those Romanian authorities had a preferred means of payment: instead of taking money, they preferred to receive livestock or agricultural products supplied through the diligence of Mr. Jacober, a London businessman who was acting a liaison with the Romanian government. I would come to wonder how many cows I represented!

In the evening in the dining room, we met other emigrants, but being dog-tired, we went to bed early with open windows. We also woke early, due to the noise in the street—a hustle and bustle of merchants with small square carts on two wheels that were pulled along by small donkeys.

After breakfast we inquired about the location of the JOINT organization and left. Leaving the hotel, we were surrounded by young Italians who knew that a new group of emigrants had arrived and were looking to buy cheap Romanian-made "Snagov" cigarettes and Sibiu salami. And we were stunned when we turned to the right and saw a big window display with weapons—guns and rifles of all sorts and sizes—that any man who had money could go in and buy. It was hard to believe the contrast with communist Romania where I had been so afraid to keep the two exquisite daggers that I had thrown them into the Dâmboviţa River. Here and now, I realized that I reentered the world I had experienced once before in my past.

Arriving at JOINT's office, we had the unpleasant surprise of seeing Mr. Sommer sitting at his desk in the same room opposite the JOINT representative, a Canadian gentleman, whose name I forgot. After I approached him, Mr. Summer understood right away our reason for seeking his colleague. I explained to the Canadian representative in French that we are a mixed marriage, me being of Christian-Orthodox religion; therefore, I would prefer to go to America to avoid religious discrimination in Israel. He listened patiently, and in the end told me politely that he could only take over our case if the SOHNUT representative—pointing to Mr. Sommer—approved the change of our itinerary.

Hearing that, Rudi turned around his chair toward Mr. Sommer and resumed his discussion in Romanian, repeating the reason why our preference was to go to America. The discussion got unpleasant because we knew that we were in debt toward Israel which had paid to the Romanian government to get us out of the country. Mr. Sommer strongly upheld his position, using all possible arguments to persuade us to change our minds. From his viewpoint, he was right. Having no other choice, we said we would think it over and then return. We left, heading toward the hotel without having any clear idea what will happen after this discussion and wondering what new arguments we could invoke next time. We were keenly aware of Hugo's advice that we must continue to insist.

Having recently escaped from the communist camp where citizens' rights were denied, we were a little worried that we might expose ourselves to unpleasant consequences here. We had a problem, and I knew that problems are among the few things in life you can count on. I had to pray for help.

To pass the time, we visited the town, stopping at a lot of churches where I prayed to the Holy Lord to help us. We also visited central markets, like del Plebiscito, del Municipio, de la Borsa, San Martino Garden, Villa Floridiana, as well as the historical fishing quarter of the Santa Lucia harbor, dating from the ninth century.

After a few days we thought we would again go see Mr. Sommer in the afternoon and try to bargain again over our situation. I decided to be firm, to point out loud and clear that I had not changed my position. I knew how to act, but apart from whatever influence came from my daily prayers, I felt there was no guarantee of a successful outcome.

Before seeing Mr. Sommer, as usual we took a morning walk and then went to the hotel for lunch. During the meal I suddenly heard my name being called. There was a phone call for me. I was astonished! Who could know where I was, and who wanted to talk to me here? When I picked up the phone, I heard, "Hallo, Mona?" with the accent on last syllable, the French style. It was a familiar man's voice.

I said "Oui?" and I heard in Romanian, but with a French accent, "It's me, Lulu. Sandu Missirliu had told me you are on your way to Israel, and we have to do something to help you. Anyway, I had to search a lot to find out where you are—right here in Napoli. I want to send you money; tell me the address."

Very touched by the interest he was showing me, I replied, "Lulu, I thank you a lot for caring about the situation I find myself in, but I have no ID to pick-up the money. So please call my girl-friend Ioana Raush, former Crătunescu, in Rome, and send her the money. Tell her to call me here as well when she gets it."

While I was digging into my purse to find Ioana's number, I thanked him for helping me in a very critical moment.

When I told Rudi who it was and the purpose of the call, we decided to postpone our visit to Sommer and wait for Ioana's phone call informing us she had the money which would allow us to reach Rome. The date was November 22, seven days after we checked into the Naples Hotel.

While we were still in the dining room, a second event took us by surprise. Mr. Sommer made his appearance calling a few names—among them, ours. He told us that we would have to move from the hotel to Pensione Contini, without giving any special reason, adding that we would be transported there in two hours. Henceforth, that's where we were installed; the room was acceptable but the menu did not include hot meals, only hard-boiled eggs and sardines. It was explained to us that the Pensione could not possibly give us "kosher" dishes, even though they could had offered some pasta. Later on, we found out that this regime was for those who intended to avoid going to Israel. My main concern, however, was that Ioana would no longer be able to find us. Luckily, I had her phone number.

Rudi and I tried to figure out how Lulu had succeeded in finding me. Probably Graţiela had written Sandu in Paris giving our departure date; he in turn informed Lulu, and together they decided we would need some help if we were to avoid Israel. Lulu through the Israeli Embassy, must have found out about the location of certain hotels assigned for emigrants in Napoli. Making many more phone calls, Lulu found out the place where I was located. As a result of his concerned effort to find us, I felt much more confidence about speaking to Mr. Sommer again. Lulu had always offered me pleasant moments, but now his intention was more than that; his actions proved that his friendship was still very strong, even though we had parted ways nineteen years before, in 1946.

So we decided to see Mr. Sommer again. When we did, I repeated my position that I did not want to go to Israel. In turn I listened to him trying to persuade me to the contrary, but I was fully aware that his arguments were part of his job description. I replied that now I belonged to the free world and nobody could force me to do what I didn't want to do. I continued with my explanations until I felt myself tired by my own arguments—without, however, having succeeded in persuading him to change his opinion. He became very irritated. But due to Lulu's monetary intervention I felt that we would be able to fulfill our goal once we reached Rome. With Mr. Sommer I didn't reach any conclusion; we were on opposite sides, our arguments frozen one against the other.

One week after Lulu's phone call, I called Ioana. Yes! She had received the money and I asked if I could stay with her for a while, and Rudi would stay with Hugo. Having her positive answer, I mentioned that we would let her know when we would arrive. Immediately, Rudi sold the cigarettes and the salami to get money for the train tickets to Rome.

On December 7, without saying anything to anybody, we left the suitcases with all our belongings in the Pensione Contini and departed. Ioana was waiting for us at the Railway Station. She gave us Lulu's money, we dropped off Rudi at Hugo's house, then Ioana and I drove to her apartment.

We talked through the night about all that happened to us since our separation in the summer of 1944. She had been married to a Swiss guy, had a little girl, Elisabeth, who is in Paris taken care by her grandmother, Zizella. Ioana kept her married name Raush after her divorce, then settled alone in Rome. Here she was seeing a certain gentleman with whom she was in "very friendly terms," and she had many friends. Obviously, my experiences had been totally different from hers. Notwithstanding our differences, I felt we were now as we used to be, due to our past profound friendship.

In keeping with Hugo's advice, in the morning we went to IRC, International Rescue Committee, which was an international salvation organization for Christians. Again I explained that we were a mixed couple, and without any difficulty they understood the situation and told us that IRC would accept us. The IRC representative immediately called Napoli and succeeded in speaking to Mr. Sommer. He told him that we had applied to IRC, which had accepted us for immigrating in the USA instead of Israel, due to my Eastern-Orthodox religion.

I couldn't hear what Mr. Sommer said, but then the representative gave the phone to Rudi. I noted Rudi's expression as he held the receiver, listening and nodding in response to what Sommer was saying. In the end I heard Rudi say, "Yes, Mr. Sommer, thank you, I'll do so. Good-bye." And he handed the receiver back to the IRC official.

Rudi told me that Mr. Sommer had changed his attitude and became friendlier when he found out that we approached the IRC. He told Rudi he was no longer opposing our departure from SOHNUT, but added, "Please change the IRC with HIAS, the JOINT, and HADASA for help, especially because HIAS has already received a letter from Norman Fass (Ida's son) who declared that he is sponsoring you to come to the USA. And he would send his agreement to

HIAS and we should come to Napoli to pick up the travel certificates and our luggage without any unpleasant consequences."

I was stunned! My ears were not sure they heard what Rudi was saying, and neither could I believe Mr. Sommer's extraordinary change. That was also a surprise about Norman's sponsorship letter. It meant Mr. Sommer had already known about the existence of Norman's letter and hadn't said anything while he was still trying to force us to go to Israel!

I must specify here that HIAS was a Jewish organization approved under chapter 203 (a) (7) of the USA Law for the Immigration and Naturalization, of February 1966.

Furthermore, Sandu, having had our address from Graţiela, also wrote Ida a letter, who in turn asked Norman to sponsor us. And when Sandu got in touch with Lulu, hearing about my situation decided to send us money and encouraged us to come to Rome. Moreover, Hugo's advice to go to IRC, had contributed to this unexpected turn of events. Lord fulfilled my prayers, making all of them act in a certain way to change our destiny!

From the IRC building, we headed directly for HIAS where they already knew about us from Mr. Sommer's phone call and Norman's letter. We told HIAS we would return when we had our travel certificates. From there Rudi took the train for Napoli, while I went to Ioana's, who had given me the keys to her apartment.

Next day, Rudi came with the certificates and suitcases, which we left with Ioana, then went directly to HIAS to fill in the forms requesting an entrance visa to America. My personal data showed, first and foremost, that the "reason for leaving Romania was to escape the communist regime and to emigrate into the USA with my husband, to be able to work and leave into a free democratic country." I also provided a lot of other information about my past, my education, my former working positions, and the present refugee situation in Italy.

HIAS left the travel certificates with us so we could use them as IDs during our stay in Italy. From there we went to the Pensione Diana where we stayed for a week, during which time we were expected to find a place where we could stay for a few months until our visa applications were approved.

When I arrived at Ioana's, she was delighted to hear that we had succeeded in our plans to go to America. She cooked Alfredo fettuccini, which we never had eaten before, and we drank a wonderful Chianti red wine to celebrate the victory of that memorable day of December 9, 1965. And she offered to make a phone call to Gică in Bucharest to let him know the good news.

Talking on the phone, I experienced an extraordinary burst of joy, not only because Gică could hear my voice for the first time since our departure but mainly for all the big news I had to relay. I started with the money forwarded by Lulu to encourage our trip to Rome; then Norman's sponsorship letter; and now, most importantly, our successful attempt to circumvent Israel and apply for an American visa. I also told him that we would stay through the winter enjoying the warm Italian climate in Rome; and. moreover, I was now with my friend Ioana. Then my father asked to spike to Ioana, to thank her for taking care and helping us.

After that call, we had to drink another glass of wine since everything went so well and left with the suitcases to Pensione Diana. Exhausted by so many emotions we did not even open the suitcases, knowing that we would soon be moving again.

Now we were concerned about finding a furnished room with a rent within our allowance of $100 per month. We went to a new neighborhood north of the city, hoping that we would find apartments with kitchens that had refrigerators. On Via Somalia nr. 289, in a new building with an elevator, we found an apartment on the fourth floor with a sunny room for rental that had access to a bathroom and to a kitchen with a refrigerator. The owner was a widow from Yugoslavia who had previously lived in Egypt but had left because of Gamal Abdel Nasser's leftist policies, backed-up by the Soviet Union. (Nasser had replaced King Farouk in 1956, when the Suez Cannal crisis took place.)

We liked Madam Ilaria and her daughter Hilda, and they liked us. We bonded as soon as we discovered that all of us had left communist countries. Right away, we decided to rent the room for fifty dollars per month, even though we would enjoy hot water in the bathroom just once a week. That's when I remembered the advantage of our laundry room in Dr. Pasteur Lane, where we used as much water we needed or wanted!

We returned to HIAS to tell them that we found what we needed. The JOINT gave us two blankets, winter garments, some edibles (sugar, oil, and pasta), monthly tickets for buses and tramways for our daily trips to ORT. The JOINT also offered to pay for an English language school or a professional school, if necessary.

We moved to via Somalia on December 16 where we then spent a few very agreeable months. Madame Ilaria was very kind; she told us where to do our shopping cheaper and how to cook Italian-style pasta. In the evenings she invited us to her drawing room so we could watch movies together on her TV.

One morning, my cousin Ioana Herescu called from London to tell me that although she would like to come to see me in Rome, she could not. The following day, she said, she was undergoing a breast surgery that had been indicated after a biopsy. This was bad news! I was sorry I wouldn't be seeing her in Rome, but of course her surgery was the most important thing. She was so young to have anything like that!

Our schedule was quite busy. In the morning we did our shopping and cooking or we would take walking trips recommended by a tourist-guide book of Rome. In the afternoon we went to English language classes or wrote letters to Gică, Mancy, Tănţica or Mario in Bucharest, Aunt Ida in New York, Silvia in Israel, Ioana Herescu in London. or Tancy in Paris. Evenings, we were either with Ioana or with Madam Ilaria.

Visiting Rome, we saw churches, statues, fountains, and main-square markets. Among the sights I vividly recall were the Pantheon, St. Ignatius of Loyola, San Petro in Vincoli, with the statue of Moses by Michelangelo; Santa Maria Maggiore; San Giovanni; San Paolo; Emperor Trajan's Column with sculptures representing the fights of roman army with the Dacians; the Catacombs, the shelter of Christians from persecutions, and the gardens and the palace of Medici family.

We went to the Vatican each Saturday of the month, in total four times, since visits to the Library were free. Also there we visited Bernini's San Pietro square, church, the Sistine Chapel whose ceiling is painted by the renowned Michelangelo.

Once a month, on Sunday mornings, we went to Porta Portese, Rome's bazaar, a big flea market with stands, stalls, small tables, even tents. We were looking for clothes or fabrics for Mancy, because she had no pension and was making a living selling what Tancy and Ioana sent her in occasional parcels, or by giving French lessons to persons found by Tănţica.

With the fifty dollars left over every month from the rent allowance, we were able to eat well, buy cigarettes, and yet still send packages to Romania. To me this was incredible as I was used to Romania where, every other week I had to borrow money from my father's savings to tide us over until the next salary.

During weekends, we were seeing Ioana with her friends or Hugo, who was awaiting the American visas for him and his family. We were amused when he told us that when he once met Mr. Sommer, he asked, "Please, tell me honestly, what is the Kleckner's situation, because Mrs. Kleckner's loud and insistent arguments, defending her position as a Christian Eastern-Orthodox made me think that in fact she is Jewish, not her husband?"

Hugo, laughing, said that he assured him I was a Christian, and moreover from a really old Oltenian family.

During the spring we took weekend day trips with Ioana's car either to Villa d' Este, to see the superb artesian fountains, to Orvieto, where I bought some painted ceramic cups, or to Siena, where it seemed to me we were driving in a scenery painted by the Venetian Vittorio Carpaccio.

Another time we went to Florence, the town dominated by the Medici family, with Lorenzo the Magnificent, the XV century famous arts' protector. There we stayed for two days, absorbing a climate of spiritual antiquity, the creations of the greatest painters and sculptors of the Renaissance era, including the celebrated Leonardo da Vinci (1452–1519), son of a countryside housemaid. But Florence also remains in my memory for another reason. Here I had my first

Bloody Mary, the name of which came from Scotland's Queen Mary Tudor, a fervent Catholic, who was called bloody because she killed many Protestants, who had been introduced in England by her father Henry the VIII.

During our stay in Rome, an outstanding event was Lulu's arrival during the Catholic Easter. He drove a Maserati from Paris together with his Italian wife Nicole. They invited us to a fancy restaurant, called Da Meo Patacca, located in a basement with brick walls. The restaurant was overcrowded, but Lulu, as usual, had taken care to book a table beforehand. Nicole was quite beautiful, dark haired, skinny, rather quiet, but friendly. I spoke with her in French. Since I had last seen him, Lulu had changed a bit, putting on a few too many kilograms, but he certainly remained the same good friend.

Before his departure, Lulu took me aside and said, "I want you to see Paris before you go to America, since you don't know when you'll be able to come back to Europe. I also want you to see your aunt Tancy Herescu, after all these years."

He gave me an envelope, adding, "Here is some money for travel and hotel, for a few days." We both thanked him warmly.

Another surprise was the coming of Johann and Dorle from Frankfurt, with their big Mercedes, the one that carried Manini's jewelry from Buharst through Germany to Paris. We enjoyed seeing them and the car. Now I could personally thank him for the Taunus he had sent us and for bringing the jewelry to Tancy. After a few adorable days spent with them in Rome, we left together in their car, passing through Florence, Padova, and Venice. In Venice we searched and found the Danielli Hotel where my parents had stayed during their honeymoon back in 1925. Johann, with Dorle, continued their way northward while Rudi and I took the train back to Rome.

Having returned from this beautiful tour, we were preparing for Paris, but we had to make sure we had Italian approval to be able to return to Italy. That required a certification from HIAS regarding our emigrants' situation.

We left for Paris at the beginning of April by train. Sandu was waiting for us, and Tante Cellica had rented an inexpensive room not far from her.

Cellica did accompany us everywhere, even to visit Tancy, who was located in the middle of the city near Place de la Concorde. Tancy was living alone—having been widowed since 1961. (Ioana had settled in London.) I recall with pleasure that after twenty-six years I found her just as tall and thin as I remembered her, with a beautiful silhouette. She was wearing flats, had the same blonde hair and great sense of style.

She took me in her arms, kissing me and saying, "Monile, how happy I am to see you again, to know you left Romania, and on your way to America!"

Then she looked at Rudi, obviously taking the measure of him. I think she liked him, admiring how tall and slim he was. And she knew from Mancy how nicely Rudi had treated my mother when she came out from prison.

Somebody rang at the door. To my surprise, it was Lulu. I did not know he would show up here. Tancy thanked him for offering us this trip, allowing her to enjoy my unexpected presence after so many years. I don't remember what she offered us, but I recall she wanted to know what had happened to Manini after my mother's arrest, and how we took care of her funeral, as well as details about my mother.

Knowing we were in Paris, Ioana Herescu also came from London after her medical intervention (about which her mother knew nothing). I felt compelled to tell them both about how I knew where Manini's jewelry was and how she had decided which piece should belong to whom among the four of us.

Seeing Ioana again, it was very emotional for the two of us. She was as slim as Tancy and Uncle Nuca, spoke perfect Romanian without English accent and perfect English without a Romanian accent. We recalled the moment when I had come with Haagi in Eforie Nord at Hotel Belona, which was our last chance of being together before the total unexpected separation occurred. We both relived now a few scenes from our happy childhood, memories which the communism couldn't take away from us. For all this, we were grateful to Lulu!

Ioana took the plane back to England after sending a lot of greetings to Ioana Crătunescu, whom she had met in school and in Armașului Lane, and added she was expecting us to visit her in London.

As I had expected, Lulu had become a successful engineer and prospered in his career—being serious, intelligent, persevering, with skills in foreign languages. He acquired the diplomas of *"Ingénieur Civil Diplômé de l'École Polytechnique de Zürich," "Ingénieur de l'École Polytechnique de Zürich ET de Lausanne" and "Ingénieur Conseil CICF."* Among his achievements, he designed the first tubular steel used in high-rise buildings, playing a part in building the Air France administrative building and others. When he managed to open his own office, he employed Romanian emigrants, to help them start a new life. Lulu always kept his friendly personality; he remained warm and sentimental. Whenever he spoke about his past in Romania, it was with great emotion.

He invited us home to his mansion in a chic Paris suburb where he lived together with his wife, two kids (who had their own babysitter), a cook and valet, two housekeepers, and two big greyhounds (that always stuck by his side). In his parking lot he had a number of different cars, among which I recognized the Maserati that he had driven to see us in Rome. After we arrived, immediately he led us to his kids, when I saw how much he loved them. After dinner, Lulu told me that George Kandel, Stephen's brother, had settled in New York and advised me to contact him as soon as I arrived. He gave me his telephone number and underlined the fact that George could give me good advice. The clue about our friendship had been Armașului Lane.

One evening, Lulu and Nicole took us to Montmartre, where, besides the superb Sacré Coeur basilica, we also saw the famous Moulin Rouge Theater. Here the painter Henri de Toulouse-Lautrec had come to find inspiration for his drawings. Another time we had lunch on a cruise on a bateau-mouche on the Seine.

With Sandu we visited Versailles, where we saw the superb palaces, the Big Trianon, built by Louis the XIV and the Small Trianon, by Louis the XV, where in June 1919 the Peace Treaty of the First World War had been signed, as well as the park designed by architect Le Nôtre.

Besides our car rides, we walked a lot visiting the city—Place de la Concorde, rue de Rivoli with nice shops under archways, rue St. Honoré; Place de L'Étoile, the Arch of Triumph; Place de la République; Place de la Bastille; Place Vandôme (mostly with jewelry shops), Palace de la Justice and Louvre Palace, the Tuileries and Luxembourg Gardens, Blvd. des Champs Elysées, and finally, the elegant masterpiece of gothic architecture, the Notre Dame de Paris church, bringing back memories of the years spent at Notre Dame de Sion in Bucharest. Paris seemed to us to be divine (as Mancy used to say), a town which gave an impression of happiness. Or maybe I was just seeing it so, because I really was happy, freed from the feeling of terror. Also, I understood why Gică and Nicu loved Paris and so much and why they were so upset when it had been occupied by the Germans back on 1940. I was grateful to Lulu that he helped us see this city before leaving for America.

Lulu and Nicole drove us to the railway station, Gare de Lyon. Before we boarded the train car, Lulu gave me some dollars, the first in my life, for pocket money for New York. I put the envelope in my new beautiful black crocodile leather purse, a gift from Ioana Herescu, which hung from my left elbow. Together Rudi and I were at the open window while Lulu and Nicole were on the platform in front of us, giving final advice and promising to visit us in New York. When the train started to move, we waved good-bye, watching the figures on the platform become smaller and smaller until finally they disappeared from sight.

When we returned to our seats, I opened the purse to see how many dollars I had. The envelope was gone! I was dumbfounded! Of course, while we were concerned to talk to Lulu, somebody had opened my purse and pickpocketed the money so smoothly I hadn't felt anything. (The result was that we would arrive penniless in America.) All the way from Paris to Rome, I felt sick, thinking that I had been a victim of a robbery. I couldn't forgive myself for having been so stupid as to let my purse hang from my elbow instead of clutching it under my arm.

Back in Rome, we enjoyed returning to our usual routine. But the interlude didn't last long. HIAS informed us that our USA's entry visas had arrived, the departure date was scheduled for April 27, 1966, and that HIAS also contacted our sponsor who would be meeting us at the airport that day.

Contrary to our departure from Romania, all we had to do was pack the luggage and say our good-byes to Madame Ilaria and Hilda—both very nice people—and then say farewell to Ioana Raush and her friends.

We spent our last evening with Ioana. She had recommended that I should contact the "Golescu sisters," namely Despina Hodoş and Ştefana Cantacuzino (the latter being Dan's mother, who used to come to our Bucharest parties back in the 1940s). Ioana gave me their phone numbers and then called them on the spot, telling Despina that "[m]y girlfriend Mona Vrăbiescu, a classmate at the Central School in Bucharest, is coming to New York with her husband Rudi, as immigrants. I gave her your phone number. Maybe you can give them some useful advice."

So far, in New York, we had three other contacts. There was Rudi's family, George Kandel's phone number in New York, and Irina Luca's letter to her friend Edith Răileanu.

Our overall stay in Italy was five and a half months. That made me remember Tănţica's forecast that I would leave Romania for somewhere, but that I would not stay there; I would settle somewhere else. She was right again! So far, she hadn't misrepresented anything.

On April 27, 1966, Ioana drove us to the Fiumicino airport, hoping that when we saw each other again, it would be sooner than last time, now that I was a free person, able to come and go. Or she could visit us.

At last, Rudi couldn't believe that in a few short hours he would be seeing New York, the long awaited dream. Our mood was quite different from what it had been when we arrived in the Fiumicino Airport in November 15, 1965, when I was very anxious about our future. Now Rudi and I were both relaxed, knowing that we would arrive in a city in the "new world" where his family would take care of us as long as necessary.

It is true that during the flight I became concerned thinking about my career. The problem was that my law diploma in civil law was not compatible with American common law, and therefore I wondered what I would be able to do. On the bright side, I knew I would no longer have to worry—as I did in Romania, so many years in a row—about my compromising family records.

And I had another thought that occupied my mind during this smooth flight of less than eight hours. It was a thought about Romania. I regretted leaving her in Ceaușescu's grip of power. I wanted to do something against this utopian communist ideology, with its totalitarian government, lack of freedom, and crushing of initiative. I wanted to take revenge, but how?

These thoughts were twisting around in my mind almost until the moment the landing was announced. Then, both Rudi and I looked through the window. We believed we would see tall buildings, but at first we saw nothing like that—just a lot of low houses, some with swimming pools, and vehicles that looked like tiny ants.

We arrived at JFK airport at 14:30 New York time. Rudi took me by the hand, and we left the aircraft. When I stepped on American soil, I felt a surge of confidence and I said to myself: "You regained liberty, from now on you will be able to manage your life to the best of your abilities with the only asset you have, your education. At last, you will no longer fear being stopped by a compromising file regarding your family background!"

ANNEX

Historical Note on Romania

The Romanian population originates from the Dacians, people who suffered greatly during centuries of countless barbarian invasions. The land originally called Dacia had been a buffer zone between East and West during the Middle Ages. When the Dacians fell under Roman influence, the local population adopted a new romance language, culture and identity, all of which tied it to the West. However, because of their geographical location and the adoption of the Eastern Orthodox Church, the Dacians remained connected to the East.

Only after 1866 was the country able to liberate itself from the influence of various, multiple intrusions. It adopted, for the first time, a modern Belgian-inspired Constitution with a system of checks and balances, with freely elected representatives in a bi-cameral parliament, and an independent judiciary. In 1877 it declared its independence from Turkish invasion, and in 1881, Romania decided to become a constitutional monarchy under the reign of King Carol I, from the German Hohenzollern Sigmaringen Family.

During World War I, Romania fought against the Central Powers. Under King Ferdinand and Queen Mary (a descendant of Queen Victoria of Great Britain), it became a modern nation called

"Great Romania" which included the provinces of Transylvania, Bessarabia, and Bukovina. Again a new *Constitution* was adopted in 1923, reflecting Romania's new status, and there was distribution of land to the peasantry. The interwar years were a time when the Romanians built democracy and modernized the economy. Romania became one of the richest countries in Europe.

In 1939, Romania was subjected to fascism against her will. Romania came to the help of the Allies in August 1944, but the country was left defenseless. Her effort was not recognized after World War II ended; *nor* when a communist government had been installed in 1945; *nor* when King Michael I was forced by the Soviet-dominated government to leave the country (on December 30, 1947). By that time, democracy and economic development had ended. Moreover, although Romania had fewer native communists than other Central and East European countries, the nation suffered more than any other from Soviet communism.

Soviet domination finally ended after forty-five years, thanks to the intervention of the American president Ronald Reagan and Pope John Paul II. The worst of the communist era ended in December 1989. The soft ending of the Cold War did not weed out former communists. Those having worked in foreign trade became entrepreneurs—most of them became corrupt, big-time entrepreneurs—while those in the second echelon of the previous regime remained in internal or external secret services. Other executives called themselves "overnight democrats." The West's strategy of "neutrality" caused long-term problems by preventing swift reforms and keeping neo-communists and their descendants in power—with a four-year exception between 1996 and 2000. Notwithstanding this, due to favorable external circumstances, Romania was admitted to NATO in 2004 and to the EU in 2007. However, the lack of managerial skills, incompetence, and enormous corruption have hindered proper economic development.

On November 16, 2014, Mr. Klaus Iohannis, the former mayor of the city of Sibiu in Southern Transylvania, was elected the new president of Romania. As I write, he seems to be a different breed of politician, striving for anticorruption and for bringing Romania's precommunist market economy and mentality back on track.

However, as I am writing, he faces a difficult task, having to work with a prime minister and a Parliament from the opposition. And in foreign affairs, he has to consider the Russian aggression provoked in Eastern Ukraine in 2014, which worsened in 2015.

Photos

My father, George (Gică) Vrăbieseu, Penal Law
Professor at Bucharest Law School

My uncle, Nicolae (Nicu) Vrăbieseu, Lawyer

My grandmother, Ecaterina (Maman TiTi) Vrăbieseu

My governess, Betty (Haagi) Haager

My mother, Clemenţa (Mancy) Radian

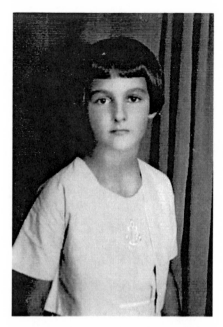

My cousin, Ioana Herescu, 1938

My grandmother, Lucrece (Manini) Mirică-Defleury, 1949

Ioana Herescu and Simone M. Vrăbieseu, 1938

Simone M. Vrăbieseu and Vlaicu Maltezeanu,
1942, in Romanian national costumes

My Friend, John (Lulu) Şarf, 1946

Simone M. Vrăbieseu and her fiancée, Dr.
Stephen Kandel, November 26, 1947

Simone M. Poppa and her husband, Dr. Cecil Poppa, 1955

Mrs. Raia St. Nicolau, August 1952

Rudolf Kleckner, my husband, 1966

Silvia Kleckner, my mother-in-law, 1966

Myself, Simone M. Kleckner, 1965 passport photo

Bibliography

"*A Romanian charity event to raise funds for the victims of the Romanian army during the First World War.*" *Feuille d'Avis de Lausanne.* Lausanne, June 5, 1918.

Churchill, Winston. *The Second World War.* London, Cassell. 1948–1954. 6 v.

Filderman, Willy. (Romanian Jews) *The Romanian Morning Star,* Mai 1993, 17p.

Ierunca, Virgil. *Pitești.* Paris, Limite, 1981, 107p.

Ioanid, Radu. *The Ransom of the Jews,* Chicago, Ivan R. Dee, 2005, 217p.

Kissinger, Henry. *Diplomacy,* New York, Simon & Schuster, 1994, 912p.

Levin, Mark R. *Ameritopia; the Unmaking of America.* New York, Threshold ed. 2012, 270p.

Manuilă Sabin și Willy Filderman, *Dezvoltarea regională a populației everiești romăne.* Iași, Fundația Culturală Romănă din Iași, 1957, 34p.

Meacham, Jon. *Franklin and Winston: an intimate portrait of an epic friendship*. NY Random House, 2003, 490p.

Micescu, Istrate. *Curs de drept civil.* Bucureşti, ALL BECK (Juridica), 2000, 414p.

Porter, Ivor. *Operţiuna Autonomus*. Bucureşti, Humanitas, 1991, 336p.

Romalo, Mihnea. *România în al doilea război mondial, 1941–1945.* Bucureşti, Vestala, 2001, 223p.

Şafran, Alexandru. *Un tison arraché aux flames, La communauté juive de Roumanie, 1940–1947.* Paris, Ed. Stock, 1989, 277p.

Şerbănescu, Alexandru. *Generalul N. Rădescu, prizonierul istoriei* nr. 14, *Caietele INMER,* martie 2009, 11p.

Vulpe Ilie şi Nicolae Mihai. *Un craiovean pe meridianele globului (Vrăbiescu, Nicolae, 1868-1944)*. Craiova, Alma, 2007, 270p.

Vrăbiescu, Nicolae. *Bune şi rele, în război cu reg. 9 Artilerie : 1916–1918.* Bucureşti, Tip. Penitenciarului "Văcăreşti," 1937, 110p.

Wiesel, Elie. *The Night.* New York, Hill & Wang, 1985, 116p.

About the Author

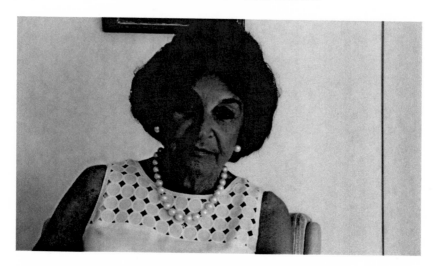

Simone Marie Kleckner was born in Bucharest, Romania where she grew up. In Romania, she graduated from Bucharest Notre Dame de Sion Lyceum and the Central School for Girls in 1944. Simone earned a Juris Diploma at the University of Bucharest School of Law in 1949. She left for the United States of America in 1966. She has a Master's degree in Library Science from Columbia University and a Master's degree in International Public Law from, New York University. Simone Marie has always been interested in politics. She was the co-president and president of the Ad Hoc Committee for the Organization of Democracy in Romania (ACORD), the Personal Advisor of the Romanian President, E. Constantinescu, Bucharest, 1999-2000; and a member of the *Republican National Committee*. Simone has written two Romanian documentaries, *O mărturie provo-cată* (*A Provoked Confession*) Bucharest, Themis, 2004 and *Din exil: lobby în SUA pentru România, 1990-1998* (*From Exile: Lobbying for Romania in the U.S.A.*) Bucharest, Ziua, 2006, and her memoirs entitled *Pe urmele mele în două lumi, România-SUA* (*Retracing My Steps in Two Worlds—Romania U.S.A*) Bucharest, Curtea Veche, 2013-2014 in two volumes. In the United States, she has published various library and legal articles. Simone currently leaves in South Palm Beach, Florida with her husband, Rudolf.

CPSIA information can be obtained at www.ICGtesting.com
Printed in the USA
LVOW06s1546081115

461593LV00001B/20/P

9 781682 133934